CODE NAME CAESAR

THE SECRET HUNT FOR U-BOAT 864
DURING WORLD WAR II

Jerome Preisler and Kenneth Sewell

BERKLEY CALIBER, NEW YORK

THE BERKLEY PUBLISHING GROUP
Published by the Penguin Group
Penguin Group (USA) Inc.
375 Hudson Street, New York, New York 10014, USA

USA I Canada I UK I Ireland I Australia I New Zealand I India I South Africa I China

Penguin Books Ltd., Registered Offices: 80 Strand, London WC2R 0RL, England
For more information about the Penguin Group, visit penguin.com.

ISBN: 978-0-425-25362-5

The Library of Congress has catalogued the Berkley Caliber hardcover edition as follows:

Preisler, Jerome.
Code Name Caesar / Jerome Preisler and Kenneth Sewell.
p. cm.
ISBN 978-0-425-24525-5
1. U-864 (Submarine)   2. Venturer (Submarine : P68)   3. World War, 1939–1945—Naval
operations—Submarine.   4. World War, 1939–1945—Naval operations, German.
5. World War, 1939–1945—Naval operations, British.   6. Submarine disasters—Environmental
aspects—Norwegian Sea.   I. Sewell, Kenneth (Kenneth R.)   II. Title.
D782.U195P75 2012
940.54'293—dc23   2011039130

PUBLISHING HISTORY
Berkley Caliber hardcover edition: July 2012
Berkley Caliber trade paperback edition: July 2013

PRINTED IN THE UNITED STATES OF AMERICA

10 9 8 7 6 5 4 3 2 1

Cover design by George Long
Cover photos: submarine by AKGImages; British and Japanese flags by Shutterstock; German flag by Getty
Book design by Tiffany Estreicher

For Suzanne and Beatrice

Memento mori

—ANCIENT ROMAN MOTTO

AUTHORS' NOTE

Submarines are designed to steal upon surface targets, their submerged, unseen presence giving them a distinct advantage over their unsuspecting prey. While underwater, subs are blind to each other. Their purpose is not to hunt enemy submarines.

The interception of the German U-864 by the British Navy's HMS *Venturer* is the only recorded instance of one submarine stalking and killing another while both were submerged.

This operation's success is credited in newspaper articles, magazine features, television documentaries, and Internet sources as one of the more dramatic accomplishments of Project ULTRA, the British effort to crack the Nazi Enigma code—but those accounts are inaccurate, or just partly accurate, as are other details of U-864's mission that have been presented in popular media.

What is particularly unfortunate amid the blurring of fact has been history's complete omission of the crucial role of the Norwegian underground in the events that occurred in a remote stretch of the North Sea on February 9, 1945. The errors committed in previous accounts of U-864's mission—and destruction—might present a tidy and linear narrative, but war is messy, and the actions of many who fought it can be obscured when squeezed into the time line of an hour-long television script or five-hundred-word newspaper article relying on that script for its information.

This book tells the story of U-864's mission as it really happened, and in doing so gives overdue credit to the forgotten heroes of Norway who helped end it.

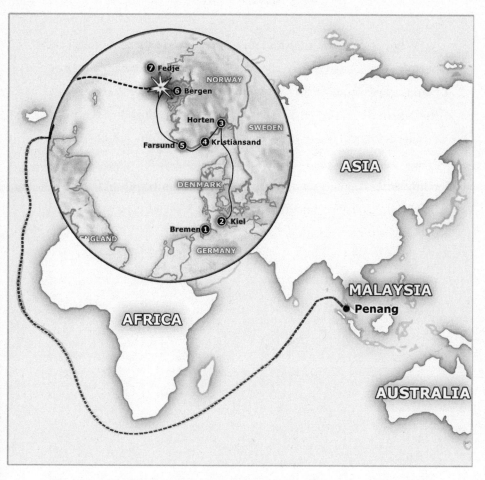

The broader map represents the course U-864 intended to take from Germany to the Far East, the circled area within it the portion of that route the submarine traversed before her interception and destruction by the British HMS *Venturer*.

Numbered waypoints are:

1. Bremen, where U-864 underwent refits in preparation for her journey.
2. Kiel, her point of embarkation.
3. Horten, the site of her snorkel and dive training and certification.
4. Kristiansand, where she stopped for refueling and resupply in anticipation of the months-long trip to Asia.
5. Farsund, the fishing village where U-864 made an emergency stop after detecting snorkel problems and grounding in a near-shore fjord.
6. Bergen, the Norwegian port city and Nazi submarine base where she was sent for repairs.
7. The waters near Fedje island's Hellisoy lighthouse, where the *Venturer* attacked and eventually sank her after a cat-and-mouse pursuit lasting several hours.

I KNEW IT WAS A SUBMARINE

1.

February 9, 1945

Kristoffer Karlsen had climbed the rocks in time to see the blast hurl a tall, white spout of water into the air about two miles from shore. The cold wind slicing through him, he watched it rise more than sixty-five feet above the chop in a vertical column, and then saw a thick jet of smoke follow it skyward.

Though only twelve years old, Kristoffer knew at once what he was witnessing as a long, dark shape broached the surface, rearing briefly into sight before it settled back into the depths. Decades would pass before his belief was officially confirmed, but he could not have been any surer than he was when it happened.

A windswept little island of less than five square miles, Fedje sat off the western coast of Norway in the North Sea, inhabited by several hundred fishermen, whalers, and their families, along with the scattered sheep and cattle in the modest pastures outside their cottages. The coastline was boulders and gravel; the interior, swamps, moors, and peat bogs; the surrounding ocean dotted with an archipelago of over a hundred bare, stony islets and humpbacked reefs. With timber for heating and cooking a scarcity, the islanders had discovered the value of harvesting the abundant peat as fuel; high in carbon, the spongy turf burned more efficiently than firewood. Beneath the sward, or outer layer, was the tarry black material that islanders would dig up with a hand spade, cut into strips or squares, and then dry for later use.

Kristoffer had been out gathering peat with his grandmother when he went up atop the bluff on the west side of the island, wanting to enjoy the view of the sea. He was not surprised to learn afterward that his fellow islanders had failed to notice the explosion; it was wartime, and they were under occupation, and things of that sort had in a sense become commonplace. The Germans had invaded the country when Kristoffer was just a boy of seven, garrisoning over three hundred soldiers here on an island whose population barely doubled their number. The occupiers had blown concrete bunkers and gun emplacements into the hillsides; they had thrown up barracks and target ranges on private land, fenced them off with barbed wire, and planted mines around them to keep out the families that had lived there; they even created a railway to haul granite blocks blasted from their quarries to the site where they had erected a radar tower in Vinappen—the island's highest point, 140 feet above sea level.

The smoke and noise, then, were nothing extraordinary or startling to the members of Fedje's tiny fishing community. But if they remained unaware of the event Kristoffer had observed, the garrisoned German soldiers had a very clear and immediate reaction. The boy noticed them break into hurried activity, sounding a general alarm and rushing to their bunkers and gun emplacements. With a sweeping view of the ocean from north to south, and their men on the alert for British naval and merchant convoys, they could not possibly have missed the explosion from their overlooks on the western shore.

Kristoffer Karlsen would never know what further action, if any, the incident prompted from the Germans. But in the weeks, months, and years afterward, the offshore submarine wreckage became widely known to the islanders—whether through Karlsen telling the story, or German soldiers interacting with the locals in the village pub, or local fishermen who'd glimpsed pieces of the wreckage from their boats. There were persistent rumors of it carrying Nazi gold, atomic bomb components, even Hitler's last will and testament in its stowage areas. The stories long outlasted the war, as did the submarine's secrets.

It was only in 2003 that the vessel's presence and exact location was officially charted by the Royal Norwegian Navy, thanks again, in large part, to a Fedje inhabitant's chance discovery.

2.

At first Karstein Kongestol was baffled and frustrated by the situation. Cast from his small fishing boat to a depth of five hundred feet, his net had gotten snagged on something large and heavy, caught so stubbornly that it thwarted his repeated attempts to pull it free. A strapping islander and professional fisherman, Karstein had good strength in his arms. But he'd been about to give up and detach the lines.

As fate would have it, the net jerked loose on what would have been his last crack at recovering it. His exertions had left it in tatters, although he found his curiosity piqued while hauling it in over the keel. Tangled in its ragged strands was what appeared to be a tarnished, lichen-encrusted "lump of brass" about the size of a man's fist. But on closer inspection, Karstein realized the object was some sort of valve. Imprinted on the bottom of the fitting were measurements, serial numbers, and a German swastika.

When he'd steered his cutter back to shore, Karstein brought the fitting into his small wooden boathouse, storing it away there with his line, gear, buckets, and tools.

This was 1993.

The object would remain in the shed for years before an unexpected visitor from Germany arrived to ask about it.

3.

A lifelong resident of Ludwigshafen on the Rhine, Wolfgang Lauenstein was a well-respected politician, engineer, and amateur historian with a special interest in submarines that was driven in part by the loss of a family member on aboard a U-boat. In the spring of 1997, he and a couple of elderly friends, Gretel and Reinhold Mantay, were poring through a shoe box crammed with photographs at their home in town when they came across a black-and-white photograph of a lean, strong-featured young man in the uniform worn by U-boat sailors during the Second World War.

Wistfulness overspread Gretel's face as they studied it. "Ah, yes, Willi," she said. "He was so young, so naive."

Willi Transier, the Mantays explained, was their great-nephew. He'd died in the war . . . toward the end of the war. Something had happened to his submarine. The details were fuzzy, or maybe they'd never been revealed. Memories faded after half a century. But they did recall that his commander's surname was Wolfram. And there was something else. Willi had gotten hurriedly engaged before he'd left Germany for the final time. His Edith had always loved him.

Lauenstein had been intrigued. Edith?

Edith Wetzler, the Mantays said. She and Willi had grown up across the street from each other. In fact, she still lived in their old neighborhood . . . just a couple of miles away.

That same day, Lauenstein had rushed to see what information could be found in his extensive home library of submarine history. His best lead was the name of the submarine's commander, and he went through the official listings. Soon he found it: Ralf-Reimer Wolfram. He'd commanded a submarine known as U-864 that had been lost while on a secret mission in 1945 . . . torpedoed by the British submarine HMS *Venturer* near the Norwegian port city of Bergen.

But that was it. There was little or nothing beyond these basics. The answers he'd gotten only spawned more questions about the nature of the boat's mission, its mysterious and unattained destination, and the precise location of its sunken remains.

His interest aroused, Lauenstein dashed off letters of inquiry to the national archives in Berlin and Washington, D.C., the military archives in Freiburg, Germany, and the U-boat archives in Cuxhaven, Germany. Without waiting for their responses, he began talking to submarine veterans—driving to their homes to speak with them in person if necessary—to seek out additional literature about the boat. His thoughts often turned to the young sailor whose photograph he'd discovered in the shoe box; like Lauenstein himself, Willi Transier had been a Rheingönheimer—a native of the Rhein area. "One of us," Lauenstein would write later on. He hoped someday to visit the sailor's watery grave and pay his respects. His fascination with wartime submarines, coupled with his unusual sense of connection to Transier, had turned solving the mystery of U-864's last mission into a kind of obsession.

Over the next two years another reason would find its way into the mix. Since nearly all of Germany's wartime submarine records had been intentionally destroyed at the end of the war, Lauenstein's richest sources of information would be declassified military records he found in the United States and England. These revealed the details of the violent encounter with *Venturer* that sent the submarine and crew to the ocean floor, and also told Lauenstein the wreck was somewhere near the tiny Norwegian island of Fedje in the North Sea. But the most gripping documents proved to be a series of decoded and translated radio intercepts—known as transepts—

that related to Project ULTRA, the Allied intelligence effort that broke the Nazi Enigma code by which all high-level German messages were transmitted during the war. According to the decrypts, U-864 had been loaded with a top-secret cargo that not only cast a remarkable new light on the past, but could have a dangerous ripple effect on the present. Finally, a link to another submarine, U-235, which had been captured by U.S. naval forces within days of Germany's surrender, persuaded Lauenstein that sub's remains had to be found and closely inspected—and that every delay was potentially catastrophic.

In September 1999, Lauenstein traveled to Fedje in hopes of learning more about the wreck's location. There he heard firsthand many local rumors about the submarine, and was soon introduced to a fisherman named Karstein Kongestol, who invited him to his jumbled boathouse for a look at the find he'd stashed away inside it.

Lauenstein knew what the object was the instant Kongestol fetched it for him, pulling it from where it had lain in a barrel of tackle. Even without its telltale serial numbers, his expert eyes would have recognized it as an antiquated air pressure filter manufactured by the German company Draeger, which had pioneered compressed air and diving technology in the late nineteenth century, and been enlisted into the Third Reich's military-industrial effort during the Second World War. Most likely, Lauenstein thought, "it came from a submarine."

And Kongestol had an added bonus waiting for his inquisitive guest: the GPS coordinates recorded from the spot two miles out to sea where he'd accidentally captured the pump in his fishing net.

Lauenstein had been shown the approximate position of U-864's sunken resting place. That much was accomplished. Now he had to convince the Norwegian government to dive on the sixty-year-old wreck—and head off the awakening of its deadly ghosts.

PART ONE

WHERE THE CHERRY BLOSSOMS BLOOM

KIEL

December 5, 1944

The submarine known as U-864 would set out on her perilous journey from Schleswig-Holstein, Germany's extreme northern province on the Baltic Sea, just a hundred and twenty nautical miles west of the Scandinavian peninsula. Viking raiders had once built their longhouses here along the shores of Kiel Fjord, their ships making their way up the strategic inlet's icy waters, their red-striped sails inflated in the wind and casting broad shadows over the land they came to invade and conquer.

But that had been in ages past. Now black banners emblazoned with swastikas snapped in the wintry gusts as the IX D2-class U-boat's crew and passengers—seventy-five men in all, a dozen over her maximum listed personnel capacity—climbed aboard for her maiden voyage. Their commander was thirty-three-year-old Kor-vettenkapitän Ralf-Reimar Wolfram, whose only previous commission had been the U-108, an older version of the sub that had seen limited action in the Atlantic. Having been fast-tracked through the ranks, Wolfram may not have been entirely prepared for the dangers of his passage, but few officers of greater experience were available, or even alive, to undertake it. The period German submariners had called the "happy time," when their wolf packs had prowled the oceans to target Allied shipping with impunity, was over. Their fleet had taken heavy losses. Now the hunters had become the hunted.

The U-boat force was far from alone in its desperation; Allied advances had Hitler's Reich feeling hemmed in and threatened on all sides. Days earlier, armored cavalry units with the U.S. 3rd Army had breached the Siegfried line on the western frontier. In the east, the Red Army had crossed the Danube and was roaring toward Buda-pest, capital of the Hungarian satellite state. In Southern Europe, the Axis dominoes had been falling since Italy's surrender over a year before. As the situation worsened for the Fatherland, some of its military leaders—particularly Grand Admiral Karl Dönitz—had begun accelerating plans hatched earlier in the war with Japan, its wartime partner in the Far East. Neither he nor his imperial-navy counterparts intended to see their implementation delayed.

Built at the DeSchiMAG—AG Weser shipyard in Bremen, and launched in 1942, U-864 had been attached to the 33rd Untersee-bootsflottille of the German Kriegsmarine after a year of sea trials. With almost forty submarine berths at Kiel, the 33rd Flotilla maintained its headquarters in the nearby village of Flensburg and had operational authority over little-known U-boat bases in distant Penang and Jakarta, as well as a repair facility in Kobe, Japan. Almost three hundred feet long and twenty-four feet wide, the latest IX submarine to enter service with the flotilla was roomier and more capable of long-distance travel than previous models—and in fact was the largest sub in the German navy. This made her perfectly suited for her mission in the eyes of Admiral Hans-Georg von Friedeburg, the deputy commander of the Kriegsmarine's submarine fleet and chief of the Ubootwaffe's Organisationsabteilung, which oversaw distribution of supplies and personnel to the U-boats. Friedeburg, in turn, had been tasked to oversee U-864's mission to Japanese waters by the Marinesonderdienst Auslands—Naval Special Service/Foreign—a clandestine department of the Wehrmacht tucked away within its elaborate bureaucratic maze. Managed by Dönitz and his high command, the department's function was to coordinate and direct blockade-running operations.

The nonregulars, or guests, sailing with the boat included two Japanese scientists: rocket-fuel expert Toshio Nakai and acoustic homing torpedo specialist Tadao Yamato. The Japanese naval attaché to Germany, Rear Admiral Hideo Kojima, had been trying to secure their passage home for months, finally arranging for them to leave aboard a Japanese transport submarine on the return leg of its planned round trip between Asia and Germany. But the scientists' departure had been delayed by the pressing chaos of recent Allied war victories—among them the sinking of the transport en route to Europe. Almost at once, Admiral Kojima had resumed intense negotiations with the Kriegsmarine to hasten them onto another outbound vessel.

His impatience was understandable; Yamato had been in Germany four long years, and Nakai, a graduate of the prestigious Tokyo Imperial University, was one of the Imperial Japanese Navy's top civilian researchers. The knowledge they had gained abroad was vital to Japan's war goals against the United States—and the island nation's reproduction of the technological wonders carried aboard the U-boat.

Yamato and Nakai weren't the only experts getting onto the submarine in the bitter Prussian cold. In the same secret cables asking for their return, Kojima had requested that eight German specialists be sent to his country. The attaché had chosen these men for much the same reasons as Yamato and Nakai had been selected— they had unrivaled expertise relating to U-864's secret freight.

The request led to feelings of resigned acceptance in Dönitz, who'd been skeptical of using U-boats as personnel or cargo transports for any reason. But in the end he'd had no choice except to put aside his reservations and give Kojima the specialists he wanted in the order they were listed.

Leaving with U-864, then, were a pair of high-level civilian Messerschmitt employees, including deputy head of engineering Rolf von Chlingensperg and Riclef Schomerus, the top aerodynamics expert for the company's cutting-edge jet aircraft department.

In charge of several covert projects for Messerschmitt, Chlingensperg was a folk hero of sorts in the Third Reich for reasons few people attached to his position with the aviation firm. Seven years before, he had been with the first expeditionary team ever to scale and return from the Himalayan slopes of Nanga Parbat, Germany's storied mountain of destiny, the world's eighth loftiest peak—and perhaps its deadliest. Backed by the Nazi Party, the ascents had been publicized as symbolic of Aryan cultural and physical suprem-acy. Instead, the massif's craggy white flanks had dealt out tragedy and death on an operatic scale. Chlingensperg's group, in fact, had discovered the frozen, preserved bodies of two previous expedition-ers on a ridge near the summit, an image he would never forget. Nor could he have failed to appreciate that his current mission aboard the submarine had its own grimly epic qualities. While it lacked the spiritual dimension his countrymen attached to moun-taineering, and was necessarily veiled from the public, it was no less dangerous or romantic, taking him into the silent depths of the ocean rather than windswept alpine heights. He had once helped write a book about his exploits at the top of the world, and may have wondered if the voyage he was about to undertake for the good of the Fatherland might be offered to readers hungry for inspira-tional tales of daring and triumph.

Like the Japanese passengers, Chlingensperg and Schomerus had received officers' commissions prior to the trip, donning the uniforms and aluminum breast eagles of Luftwaffe lieutenants. The step was taken for their protection; if captured behind enemy lines as civilians, the men stood a greater chance of facing espionage charges according to the protocols of the Hague and Geneva Con-ventions. A third German, Franz Türk, appeared on the crew list as a regular seaman, although a number of questions would eventually come to surround him and suggest that he, too, may have been a nominal guest aboard the sub.

Later, when U-864 made an unplanned stopover at Bergen, Norway, shortly before her final embarkation, there would be two more supplementary crewmen coming on. One of them was Lieutenant Jobst Hahndorff, who had commanded a torpedo boat in the Mediterranean and served on the Deutschland-class battleships *Admiral Scheer* and *Admiral Graf Spee.* The other man, also a lieutenant, was Sven Plass, a handsome, blond, twenty-six-year-old ordnance specialist, loving husband, doting new father—and, notably, the son of a Frankfurt business executive whose employer had close, longtime connections to Japan's military-industrial complex.

But in early December their assignment to the submarine was still several weeks off, and Bergen was not even a scheduled destination. After leaving base, she was slated to make two stops before embarking for distant Asia: a lengthy stay at Karljohansvern naval base in the tiny Norwegian village of Horten, near Oslo, and then a one-day stop for taking on added provisions and refueling up the coast at Kristiansand.

From there she was to travel across the equator into the South Atlantic, around the Cape of Good Hope into the Indian Ocean, and then south of Madagascar to Penang in Malaysia—a distance of almost twelve thousand nautical miles.

The stint at Horten was for underwater testing and certification of a snorkel mast installed in October 1944, while the submarine had been attached to the 4th Ausbildungsflottille, or training flotilla, for tactical exercises off Stettin to the east. The snorkel would allow her to take in fresh air for the crew and diesel engines while submerged at periscope depth, and thereby travel great distances undetected by the enemy.

The Germans had first become aware of this apparatus in 1940 after finding one on a captured Dutch submarine. But it was only late in the war, when advances in Allied radar technology had increased their proficiency at long-range detection of submarines' conning towers, that Dönitz ordered snorkels built into all new boats coming off the assembly line. Commissioned before Dönitz's order, U-864 had required modifications for conversion into a snorkel boat; thus the work done at Stettin. Prone to snags, these retrofits had made the exhaustive submerged drills at Horten vital to her certification.

In preparation for her voyage, U-864 was packed full of standard operating equipment, armaments, spare parts, fuel, and six to nine months' worth of food—fresh, canned, and powdered—at the busy submarine piers. The provision loading was done by gang, one man passing a box to another from trucks and trailers lined up along the dock, the crates and barrels lowered through hatches into the boat's interior compartments and then moved back into the storage holds. There was also a lot of ammunition; a big boat designed to stalk and kill bigger surface vessels, U-864 carried a number of formidable weapons. Her conning tower had an M-42 heavy cannon on its lower wintergarten platform, and a smaller Flak 37 AA gun on the upper platform. Belowdecks were as many as twenty-seven 7.16mm torpedoes, six loaded into her four bow and two stern tubes, the rest stowed for reloads. Before departure, torpedoes were slid down the chute into the fore and aft torpedo rooms, where the crew used hoists to move them to their racks.

The sub's advanced war machinery and blueprints were brought on without need for special camouflage; packed into nondescript wooden crates, they would have been indistinguishable from the ordinary freight coming off the submarine pier and lowered into hatches by mobile cranes.* But the weightiest and most space-consuming commodity was mercury—sixty-seven tons of it valued at over $5 million—and it had been loaded aboard at an earlier point.

The night before she set sail, many of U-864's sailors had done their prepatrol carousing in the bars and brothels of Kiel, with only the skeleton crew assigned to the duty watch required to stay aboard. Earlier in the war, when it seemed nothing could go wrong for the German submarine force, the carrying-on had been loud and uproarious, spilling over onto the streets in the late hours. But in recent years Allied bombings had pummeled and gutted the city, dampening the revels and chasing away a large segment of the population.

The contents of the loading containers remained secret from all but Wolfram and his closest aides . . . officially at any rate. There had been a surfeit of rumors fed by sightings of high-ranking naval officials on the boat. Their inspections had led her hands to believe she was being prepared for something out of the ordinary.

Twenty-year-old machinist first class William Transier was one of the young petty officers leaving with the submarine. Although he'd been raised far from the ocean in the Rhineland-Pfalz area, Willi had been enthralled by stories of undersea adventure and long dreamed of joining the Kriegsmarine's elite U-boat force. The U-boat commanders were portrayed as heroic figures to adolescent German boys, with photographs of famed real-life commanders like the Great War's Otto Weddigen appearing in popular maga-

---

* See chapter notes for the fullest available cargo list.

zines and postcards, and the noble, selfless fictional character Kapitänleutnant Hoffmeister from the Reich-produced movie hit *U-Boat Westward!*—played with steely-eyed forcefulness by the actor Herbert Wilk—hooking into their teenage yearnings for travel and adventure.

After his mandatory registration for the draft in 1942, Willi chose to join the navy rather than chance a call-up by the manpower-hungry infantry. He would sign on for NCO training, which required a minimum twelve-year commitment, and serve as a personnel clerk on surface vessels before eventually qualifying for submarines. In the months before U-864's first patrol, he was assigned to be a member of her commissioning crew.

Willi and his pretty girlfriend, Edith Wetzler, had grown up across the street from each other, their childhood friendship blossoming into romance not long before his enlistment. The couple would spend as much time together as they could whenever he was on furlough.

Transier didn't often talk about his work with Edith, and with understandable reason. Never mind that an engine room mechanic's duties aboard a sub were classified; when a young sailor was on leave snatching some precious moments alone with his girlfriend, the last thing he wanted to do was discuss repairs to steam turbines and waterlines. But in one of his final shore leaves before the sub was to depart, Willi had hastily asked Edith to marry him and then confided to her about officials from high up the chain of command—"important people," he called them—making rounds of the submarine as she was being readied for the cruise, even mentioning that he'd overheard some of their conversations and learned their visit related to a mission involving the Japanese. If Willi knew any more about this, he did not reveal it to his sweetheart, though he would express a clear sense of unease to her, asking her to pray that he came through it in one piece.

"This mission is a mystery," he said cryptically. "Nobody knows where it's going, or how it will end." Willi also spoke to his mother before leaving Germany, asking her not to be sad if he didn't return. "I know you're too old to have another child," he told her, "or I would have said, 'Have another child so you won't be alone.'"

He contacted Edith only once after the U-boat left base, dropping an envelope addressed to her into the outgoing mailbag at Bergen. Even half a century later, reading his final letter would blur her vision with tears.

But Transier was still over a month from writing those words on the December morning that he walked the gangplank bridging the gap between the pier and U-864's upper deck, where he joined his fellow crewmen amidships—the noncommissioned sailors wearing their winter garb and toting duffel bags, the assembled officers in their blue service uniforms, bars, badges, and white peaked caps. After a brief address from Korvettenkapitän Wolfram, they shimmied down circular hatches into the belly of the sub or went to work singling up mooring lines and stowing gear and hardware.

A boat's commander was always last to go below, and Wolfram would take up his position on the bridge next to his first officer and several junior grades. Within minutes a half-growling, half-grinding noise was heard from the aft section of the ship as compressed air turned the crankshaft of her main diesels and her power plant roared to life.

Down below, Transier manned his station in the engine room as U-864's mooring lines were cast off and she put out to sea, dials, gauges, pipes, and electrical wires covering every square inch of the hull around him, the smells of diesel fuel and lubricant filling every breath.

The low thrum of her engines audible throughout her compartments now, the submarine slid from her berth into Kiel Fjord, water churning around her stern as her propellers bit into the water. From here she would leave the Baltic for the Langelandsbaelt and Kattegat Strait between Denmark, Copenhagen, and Sweden, and then sail on into the frigid waters of coastal Norway.

In the Baltic winter, a frozen collar of ice—called fast ice—tends to form in shallower waters along the coast, becoming anchored to the shoreline and nearby banks, and submarines leaving Kiel at that time of year were often preceded by armed naval trawlers fitted out as light icebreakers. They were also typically escorted from the harbor channel by a pair of small minesweepers known as *Räumboote*—or R-boats—because the 33rd was concerned about Allied mines in the Langelandsbaelt. In addition, every U-boat leaving base would have a GTB acoustic buoy slung beneath its keel amidships, and U-864 was no exception; the mine-detecting drogue would remain in place until she reached Horten.

Once the sub entered the strait, however, the escort vessels parted ways with her and went steaming back to Kiel. By then the line handlers had gone safely below, the hatches were secured, and the deck was cleared, salt water gently washing over it as she dipped her bow into the swells.

With a final breath of fresh air, Wolfram would follow his complement of officers down the ladder just before U-864 submerged, sliding beneath the ice floes adrift on the water's surface and then setting out on a course from which there would be no return.

CHAPTER ONE

BRUNO

1.

On the raw, stormy night of April 8, 1940, Operation Weserübung commenced at eleven o'clock with the Norwegian patrol boat HNoMS Pol III's sighting of unidentified vessels in Oslo Fjord, their outlines swelling out of the cold mist and snow squalls that had helped blind coast watchers to their entry into Norway's territorial waters. There had been earlier reports of German ship activities in the area, and the captain of the little patrol boat, Leif Welding-Olsen, was at his most vigilant and alert. As the vessels advanced through the swirling blackness, he and his crew heard German voices from one of them, issued a warning shot from their

76mm cannon, and gave the hailing signals to indicate the ships were trespassing on neutral waters.

They didn't back off. The Kampfgruppe consisted of an assortment of German warships: three cruisers, three torpedo boats, and eight minesweepers. Olsen sent up flares—one white, two red—to raise the coastal defense batteries, ordering a radioman to contact the naval station at Horten on their wireless transmitter. At that moment one of the German captains shone a spotlight on Olsen and ordered him to surrender. When Olsen shouted back that he refused, and the invaders continued to sail up the inlet, he engaged the torpedo boat that had turned its light on him, ramming its side. The Germans opened fire with their antiaircraft guns, wounding Olsen in the legs. The Pol III was soon in flames, her men forced to abandon ship. In the resulting confusion Olsen leaped overboard into the agitated sea to become the first Norwegian loss of the invasion.

Over the next several hours, confused, disorganized Norwegian defenders would suffer hundreds of additional casualties as the German amphibious groups struck at five other coastal cities: Kristiansand, Egersund, Bergen, Trondheim, and Narvik. Paratrooper and infantry units followed their arrival, and despite scattered and occasionally fierce resistance, Norway would be essentially under German control within a day.

The Germans would be quick to begin a conversion of the harbor facilities at Bergen and elsewhere on the coast to suit the needs of the Kriegsmarine. Seizing Norway's ports had been Hitler's primary reason for turning his acquisitive eyes upon the independent monarchy, though he would use the transparent pretext of wanting to guard its neutrality against a British-led invasion. While Germany did indeed fear the possibility of an English naval blockade that would cut off its northern supply lines—over half the vital iron ore it purchased from Sweden was shipped via the port of Narvik—protecting its ability to transport arms and matériel was a far cry from defending a foreign power's autonomy.

The real German objectives, then, were typically predatory and opportunistic. Norwegian ports would give the Fatherland's attack submarines year-round access to the North Sea and Atlantic Ocean and put them close to British shipping lanes. They also provided German supply vessels with the quickest and most direct transit routes to Eastern European outposts. Germany could not afford to have the Norwegian sea-lanes closed to it for any reason—something that was a particular concern in the winter, when incrustations of fast ice near the shore hampered the Baltic Fleet's activities. The Germans had to establish their presence in those waters before the Brits beat them to it and stifled the free movement of their vessels.

For Grand Admiral Dönitz, there was yet another consideration. His plan was to have an untersee fleet of three hundred available submarines, of which fully a third would be out on patrol at any given time, another third would be in the yard for refitting and repair, and the remaining third on its way to and from areas of deployment. This optimal disposition required a large number of U-boat bases at key spots along the the European coast, again with the twin goals of speed and ease of travel for the boats, not to mention a desire to avoid overcrowding at their ports. With the establishment of submarine bases in occupied France to cover the southern and western latitudes, Dönitz had viewed Norway not only as essential for his northern logistic, but as a place where he could manageably distribute the berthing and upkeep of his submarines among different facilities.

By the late spring and summer, Dönitz had inaugurated working U-boat bases in Trondheim and Bergen. Bergen's ancient deepwater harbor was launching patrols against British shipping by July, although the 11th Flotilla would not be established there until May 1942. Trondheim, meanwhile, became home to the 13th Flotilla in June 1940.

Anxious to shield its precious submarines from British air raids, Germany ordered the building of U-boat *Stützpunkt,* or bunkers, not long after the bases became operational. A quarter century earlier, during the First World War, it had fabricated concrete shelters at Bruges, in northern Belgium, to screen them from aerial observation. When increasingly powerful Allied bombs threatened the Kaiser's submarine fleet, the shelters were hardened with thicker concrete roofs, spurring the evolution of the World War II–era submarine bunker.

Beginning in 1940, bunker construction began—and in some cases was completed within the year—at ten different bases in Germany, France, and Norway, with several bases being designated for more than a single bunker. Later on, work would take place in three more locations, though not all the bunkers were finished before the end of the war.

The assignment of putting up the facilities was given to Organisation Todt, a consortium of construction and engineering firms headed first by longtime Nazi Party leader Fritz Todt, and then architect Albert Speer after Todt's death in 1942. OT would be responsible for a slew of massive, widespread projects across Germany and occupied Europe, among them the four-hundred-mile line of fortifications known as the West Wall or Siegfried line, the autobahn highway system, the vast underground Mittelwerk rocket and aircraft engine factory, and the U-boat bunkers in France and Norway.

As these projects grew more expansive and the German workforce became inadequate for Organisation Todt's needs, the Germans would draw on a stream of twelve million slave laborers consisting of abductees from conquered nations, prisoners of war, and concentration camp inmates. An untold number of them would die under inhuman conditions while forced to work on Todt state construction projects.

For most of the war, the Kriegsmarine's U-boat bases in France— open to the Bay of Biscay on the coast of Western Europe—saw the greatest concentrations of submarine activity. The transit routes to strategic targets had no natural choke points, no geographical barriers that would funnel the boats into easy kill zones. Following America's entry into the conflict in December 1941, the abbreviated distance they offered to hunting grounds off the U.S. coast (compared to bases in Germany and Norway) became a major consideration for Germany's submarine warfare campaign.

By 1943, submarines launched from the two Norwegian bases had become a constant menace to American and British shipping convoys bound for Russia over the North Sea. Even before Weserübung, the Germans had known that Bergen and Trondheim offered separate and distinct assets, and had determined their long-range plans for each while drawing up their blueprint for the invasion. From a strictly operational standpoint Trondheim was the plum; its coastal geography gave the submarines easy and direct access to the sea, whereas Bergen's submarines had to weave carefully through a tangle of fjords and straits, and then navigate past barrier islands, as they came and left on deployment. On the other hand, Bergen was the far busier—and readier—port, with centuries-old commercial harbor facilities in its Laksevåg section, a road and rail network, and a government naval district administrated from Marineholmen, the 125-year old base on Puddefjorden, a fast-running branch of a coastal fjord that coursed through the city center as it detoured inland.

Quick to exploit Bergen's existing infrastructure, the Germans turned Marineholmen into an administrative hub and converted the private shipbuilding and repair yards at Laksevåg, a rural area just outside the city proper, into berthing and refurbishment facilities for its growing submarine fleet. The homes of Norwegian citizens near the new Nazi base—renamed Kriegsmarinewerft Bergen–Danziger Werft—were likewise seized to house U-boat support personnel as well as engineers and technicians for the bunker construction project. Ramshackle quarters went up adjacent to the bunker for the Russian forced laborers, while at Melkeplassen, near the Laksevåg docks, the submarine crews were given spacious, pleasant barracks.

Members of a well-trained, highly valued elite, considered the cream of the German navy, U-boat sailors were accorded privileges and treatment that went far beyond the hot running water and central heating in their comfortable living quarters. At Marineholmen, where subs would return flaunting victory pennants after successful missions, the flotilla commander would meet them with marching bands and honor guards. While enlisted seamen were handed fresh fruit after months of eating canned provisions—a bonus in itself— the submarine's captain and officers would be toasted with glasses of celebratory champagne. Later, an officers' club called the Old Bull's Place would serve fresh lobster dinners to the captain and his staff in its grand banquet rooms. For entertainment there were concert halls, dance clubs, and movie theaters, a German casino on Tarnplass, and a brothel on King Oscar's Street. When out on the town, the submariners were known to be louder and rowdier than other sailors, a trait that usually seemed magnified after an extended patrol. Months of confinement at sea in an underwater "stovepipe," as they called the boats, created a unique set of physical and psychological stresses for these young men, most of whom were in their early to midtwenties; shore leave gave them a much-anticipated chance to decompress.

Throughout the war, work on Bruno, as Bergen's submarine bunker was named, was conducted around the clock under the site management of Einsatzgruppe Wiking, OT's administrative task force in Norway. The German engineering firm Wayss & Freytag had won the profitable government construction contract from Todt, and its laborers—mostly Russian POWs, with some Norwegians compelled to provide added manpower—would work in twelve-hour shifts beneath the dockside cranes, using high-intensity lights at night unless under threat of Allied bombings. The growl of machinery, the rumble of half-tracks moving their towed loads, the clanging reverberations of steel beams and support columns being lifted and lowered into place . . . these were the background sounds of life in Bergen, night and day, as the task force carried on its mammoth project.

With its imposing dominance of the shoreline, Bruno soon came to be considered an impregnable fortress by the Germans. The bunker was an immense 429 feet long and 470 feet wide, its ceiling a 19-foot thickness of solid concrete, its walls between 6 and 12 feet thick depending on what section of the complex they enclosed. Blocks of granite, along with a layer of sand and cement, were added to reinforce the roof against bomb attacks. There were seven pens, six used to house submarines, the seventh reserved for the storage of fuel, machine lubricant, torpedoes, and various types of equipment.

Despite its strategic importance to the wolf packs harrying the northern sea-lanes, however, Bruno avoided becoming a prime objective of Allied air strikes for the first part of the war. The British and Americans had ranked Bergen's U-boat facility as a lower-priority target than those in France, and with good reason: The Bay of Biscay bases gave German subs access to the entire mid-Atlantic and Mediterranean and could tilt supremacy of the oceans to one side or the other if allowed to operate unhindered. They were by far the Allies' overriding concern until the summer of 1944.

The invasion of Normandy and liberation of Paris radically altered things. After the Allied landing in August, the Germans hastily pulled their U-boat forces from France, and the Führer der U-boote (FdU) West Hans-Rudolf Rösing, who oversaw all Atlantic submarine operations, moved his headquarters from Angers to Bergen. Almost at once a tremendous expansion of the Norwegian base was ordered to accommodate the influx of personnel and submarines—including housing, berthing, and antiaircraft emplacements.

None of this had escaped the Allies' attention. Bergen's sudden upshift in importance to the Germans boosted its prioritization as a target; they were determined to knock the base out of commission even as it was being built up, and disrupt German naval activities flowing through its nearby waters. The effort would be shared by British air and naval forces, both of which were already in position to do the job. Royal Air Force bombers had already gained distinction with their roles in some of the war's pivotal campaigns; now bases in northern England and Scotland would become staging areas for raids on the Norwegian port city.

Far less prominent in terms of reputation—and deliberately so—were the Royal Navy submarines that were already haranguing German surface vessels in the North Sea. Since 1940, these had been attached to the 9th Flotilla at Dundee, Scotland. One of the best-kept Allied secrets of the war, the base was known as HMS Ambrose. As the war entered a new stage, its operations would be indispensable to stopping whatever plans the enemy meant to implement along Norway's coast.

Those plans would soon take on an unprecedented dimension for the Kriegsmarine. Right about the time FdU West withdrew from France, members of the navy's supreme command became engaged in intensifying talks with their Imperial Japanese Navy counterparts about a matter that had been on the table for some time. The discussions centered around the clandestine transport of key military and civilian technical personnel using German blockade-running submarines, something the Japanese had repeatedly requested, and that the Germans had been unwilling to seriously consider for reasons of their own. But changing fortunes for the Reich led Admiral Dönitz himself to reevaluate his position, and by August 1944 the Japanese were informed that the scheme had been okayed.

All that remained was to give it official approval and set a mutually acceptable timetable. And of course, select the U-boats that would make the long oceanic journey past Norway to the distant east.

CHAPTER TWO

VAMPIRE CLASS

1.

Prowling the North Sea for enemy traffic on September 11, 1944, the British submarine HMS *Venturer* (P68) had picked up the merchantman SS *Vang* above the Jutland Peninsula a quarter of the way through its journey from the city of Drammen, in southern Norway, to Trondheim, hundreds of nautical miles to the northwest along the country's jagged coastline.

Built in 1910, the 678-ton cargo steamer *Vang* sailed under Norwegian flag and was owned by the private shipping company Severin Lyngholm out of Haugesund. Mere weeks before the start of Operation Weserübung, in February 1940, it had hauled vital war supplies to Great Britain with Convoy HN 15, departing Bergen escorted by eight Royal Navy antiaircraft cruisers and destroyers. Now, four years later, it was carrying goods for the German occupiers who controlled Norway's ports and, in a wartime reversal of fate, had become a target of the very naval forces that once protected it.

The freighter held little chance of eluding its silent hunter. Under the command of Lieutenant James Stuart Launders, *Venturer* was the lead boat of the Vampire-class "long hull" fast-attack submarines manufactured by Vickers Armstrong at England's Barrow shipyard in 1942. Just over two hundred feet from stem to stern, a slender sixteen feet wide, it had left base with a crew of thirty-three, formidably armed with eight Mark VIII torpedoes, a three-inch 76mm deck gun, and a trio of .303 Vickers antiaircraft guns. Equipped with state-of-the-art sonars, it was the aquatic equivalent of a sleek new sports car, and sluggish old merchants like *Vang* could have been tailor-made prey.

Jimmy Launders only needed to give a single fire command to his new gunnery and torpedo officer, Sub-Lieutenant Peter C. Brand. Launched from its bow tube, a torpedo shot 1,300 yards through the water at between thirty-five and forty knots to strike the Norwegian vessel within two minutes, the powerful Torpex explosive in its warhead ripping a huge hole in its keel. Launders would spare it a second shot, speeding off even as the *Vang*'s crew scurried into their lifeboats. According to *Venturer*'s logs, the freighter's wreck sank to the ocean floor at position 58°03′N, 06°34′E off the island of Lister. Norwegian records would mention no casualties.

As for *Venturer*'s highly decorated twenty-four-year-old

lieutenant—Launders had won a Distinguished Service Cross for Mediterranean war patrols as a junior officer aboard the HMS *Umbra* (P35), and had a bar added to it since receiving his commission as skipper of the *Venturer*—he could quit the scene having notched a successful hit-and-run attack in his belt.

Based with the 9th Flotilla at Dundee, the sub was on its second patrol of northern waters since her assignment there the previous winter. Back on April 10, in her maiden patrol, *Venturer* and another British submarine, the antiquated T-class HMS *Taku,* had been dispatched to slip under the German minefields along the entrance to the Skagerrak between Kristiansand and Hanstholm, Denmark, where their mission was to seek out targets of opportunity deep within the heavily trafficked, 150-mile strait. In an effort to deny Allied vessels entry to this all-important naval route between their country and Norway, the Germans had filled the mouth of the channel with thousands of horned Einheitsmine C contact mines, turning it into a watery no-man's-land for Allied surface craft. To avoid these mines, *Venturer* and *Taku* had attempted to crawl slowly between a forest of tether cables using a special short-range mine avoidance sonar—a dicey business.

At 0248 hours on April 13, 1944, *Taku* had submerged to a depth of 220 feet and passed beneath the mine barrier on an easterly course from the North Sea into the Skagerrak. But five hours into her patrol—a little before eight o'clock GMT—she was hammered by a terrific, roaring explosion overhead. The shock wave had temporarily knocked out all her lights, mangled part of her outer skin, and cracked her pressure hull so that seawater began spraying into the boat's interior.

With his crew scrambling to plug the leaks and work their pumps to stay ahead of the water, *Taku*'s commander, Lieutenant A. J. W. Pitt, radioed base to report her condition and receive further orders. But there was really nothing to decide: She had been in no condition to carry on and would limp back to base at once. Launders was likewise instructed to abort his mission—although he'd been told he would not be heading home. Nor would he be going after more random pickings.

Under his revised orders, Launders had departed the strait and swung north up the coast toward Eitrheim, where a convoy bearing Axis war supplies was bound after setting out from the old Swedish merchant town of Gävle. Perched on the Gulf of Bothnia in the northern Baltic, Gävle had been exporting iron ore since the 1400s, and the 1,923-ton German steamship SS *Friedrichshafen* likely had been carrying a shipment from the mines in central Sweden—a valuable commodity for the Germans, and one the British very much wanted to keep out of their hands. Launders's new task had been to strike at the convoy and leave as much of its tonnage as possible at the bottom of the sea.

The intelligence he was given would have been highly accurate and reliable. By this stage of the war, Dundee, or HMS Ambrose, had been able to closely monitor and quickly act to intercept German shipping movements in the region. Along with its substation Ambrose II at Lerwick, on the Shetland Isles, it had become headquarters to one of World War II's least-known, and most successful, Allied espionage operations.

With her speed, stealth, and audacious young skipper, *Venturer* had found herself in the thick of those missions soon after her assignment to Dundee. As with the base's direct connection to the Norwegian resistance, it was no accident.

2.

Dundee is a port city on the north bank of the Firth of Tay, a narrow estuarial inlet where the River Tay meets the North Sea. The harbor had developed into a commercial shipping center in the 1800s, as local jute barons built a thriving trade with the Indian subcontinent, importing raw fiber that would be processed and woven into canvas sacking, horse blankets, and ship's sails at the town mills. But Dundee's origins as a naval facility could be traced back to 1912, when the submarine tender HMS *Vulcan* anchored in the Tay to be a floating dockyard for several Holland-class submarines—the first ever produced for the Royal Navy.

After the outbreak of World War I, the *Vulcan* was transferred to the 7th Submarine Flotilla at Leith, near Edinburgh, and Dundee reverted to its former civilian way of life. But that was to change again shortly before the Second World War. As England's diplomatic efforts to stave off a German invasion of Poland hit a wall, the Royal Navy began to prepare for an inevitable declaration of war and bolster the naval forces protecting its coastal areas. Britain's ports on the North Sea were closest to Germany's waterways, making it imperative to boost their defenses and simultaneously increase their offensive capabilities. In August 1939, the RN established its 2nd Submarine Flotilla at Dundee with the tender HMS *Forth* and nine submarines. A reshuffling of forces two months later would see the flotilla move to another port, but on April 19, 1940, the 9th Submarine Flotilla was commissioned at Dundee.

In its third incarnation, the base was finally seen as a long-term presence rather than a temporary offshore anchorage for a sub tender. Officially christening it HMS Ambrose signified that it would now be a land-based facility with personnel housing, recreation, and quayside berths. These would be established at Camperdown Dock and Eastern Wharf, where the Caledon Shipbuilding Company already had sheds and marine works that were conscripted for the Home Fleet's use. Caledon would now go from building and servicing commercial vessels to repairing and maintaining submarines.

Dundee's evolution into a home port for exile submarines made easy sense. With its resources spread thin early in the war, the RN sought reinforcements from the French navy, which quickly put a group of submarines at its disposal. One boat was sent to the base in April as its missions against enemy shipping off Norway rose in frequency. The next month saw the arrival of the French minelaying submarine *Rubris* after a separate request from the British, who had wanted to tighten their blockade in northern waters.

Arriving in June 1940, the first true exile stationed at Dundee was the Polish minelayer ORP *Wilkin;* boats from Vichy and the Netherlands followed as the Dutch and French governments capitulated to the Germans. These would be joined by the Norwegian submarine HNoMS *Uredd,* and after *Uredd* was sunk by German mines, the HNoMS *Ula* and HNoMS *Utsira.* All three were British

U-class subs built for the Royal Norwegian Navy-in-Exile, and their deployment, along with their crews, to HMS Ambrose, so close to Norway, was the obvious choice.

In the end, it was a mix of functional pragmatism and operational efficiency that led to Dundee becoming a new and unparalleled model of multinational naval cooperation. With foreign subs already there, stationing others at HMS Ambrose became a way to assure their proper maintenance: Once the mechanics and engineers at the base had gained experience working on foreign subs, practicality dictated sending the boats their way for repairs and upkeep. Moreover, if a submarine from another country required parts, it made sense to warehouse those parts in a single location for other boats of its type. And who better to navigate the country's intricate system of coastal waterways—and communicate with its organized resistance movement—than native sailors familiar with the land and language?

When FdU West came over from France in 1944, Dundee's missions in support of the underground went from being important to being indispensable to the Allied cause. By then the British Secret Intelligence Service, also known as MI6, was able to crack virtually all German naval radio communications encoded on its Enigma encryption machines. Project Ultra, as the decipherment program was dubbed, was based in Bletchley Park, a rambling country estate in Buckinghamshire, England, where thousands of men and women worked ceaselessly on the difficult and complex aspects of the code-breaking effort. After being relayed to Bletchley, intercepted radio transmissions would be decoded, analyzed, translated, and then distributed to Allied government and military leadership. In addition, the U.S. Army Signals Intelligence MAGIC program had succeeded in breaking the highest-level coded Japanese diplomatic communiqués, so that the message traffic flowing between the Axis partners was regularly decoded.

But while ULTRA and MAGIC intelligence gave Allied planners a decided strategic edge, it did not always translate into tactical advantages in fast-developing combat situations on the ground and at sea.

Edward Thomas was a British naval intelligence officer who, early in the war, managed a signals intercept station in Iceland, and would subsequently become a top cryptanalytical adviser at Bletchley. In the northern theater, his job was to take direction-finding bearings from the radio transmissions of U-boats. As he wrote in the official history of the British intelligence arm during World War II, "The British were guided by authorities in London who now had good information from the Enigma about German convoy movements, routes, escorts and patrols. Ultra was to provide information . . . up to the end of the war. But it was seldom complete and often late. That the information needed for Allied air and naval operations in coastal waters, and for the activities of SIS and SOE [Special Operations Executive, a World War II British spy group that specialized in acts of espionage and sabotage in enemy territories] was so extraordinarily full sprang from the enormous amount of information that came to hand to supplement the ULTRA. *ULTRA was, in any case, only distributed to very few recipients and was mostly used as background. Photo reconnaissance played a big part. But most of the non-ULTRA information came from clandestine Norwegian sources."*

These furtive spotters operated in different ways. Some were conscripted shipyard workers who would observe German comings and goings in the harbor from wharves and dockside buildings, and then report what they saw to their contacts with Allied intelligence. Some hid themselves at frequently traveled transit routes along the shore, tracking the movements of German vessels through binoculars and telescopes. Norwegian ship watchers also used a fleet of sixteen wooden fishing trawlers to ply the fjords and inlets near German garrisons and collect critical information about their activities.

Working hand in hand with Royal Navy commanders at HMS Ambrose, MI6 and SOE liaisons would provide the watchers, and the Norwegian resistance as a whole, with training, equipment, funding, and operational support. This included conveying supplies to occupied Norway, and slipping agents back and forth between Norway and the Shetlands aboard the supposed fishing trawlers.

Norwegians referred to this secret ferry route, and the boats that collectively made it up, as the Shetland Bus, though it was properly designated the Norwegian Naval Independent Unit (NNIU) and later, the Royal Norwegian Naval Special Unit (RNNSU). Its origins went back to the weeks between Weserübung and Norway's formal capitulation, when, on May 17, 1940, the resistance leader Sigurd Jacobsen escaped to the Shetlands aboard the trawler *M/B*

* Italics are the author's.

Vest with two of his men and four British naval intelligence operatives. After a perilous forty-eight hours at sea, Jacobsen and company arrived at the tiny port village of Lerwick, about two hundred nautical miles west of Bergen, and were given a crash course in covert surveillance and information analysis from British instructors. Three weeks later, they would return to their homeland to school members of their embryonic underground in those techniques.

Lieutenant David Howarth of the British Royal Navy, who was second in command of the unit at Lerwick, would later write that "to take the Shetland bus became a synonym in Norway for escape when danger was overwhelming," adding, "every man, woman and child in Norway knew about us."

Amid the island's scored, rocky hills, desolate shores, and swirling mists, Howarth and his superior, army major Leslie H. Mitchell tirelessly went about building the unit up from its foundations. Their bare-bones crew included a shore staff of three British sergeants, a civilian stenotypist and cipher writer named Norman Edwards, a female Norwegian cook, and two young island women who worked as the cook and housekeeper at Mitchell's farmhouse residence—and de facto headquarters—in a valley about fifteen miles north of town. The organizational office was in Lerwick with the Special Operations Executive, Norwegian Section, where secret documents and communiqués were received and stored; after the unit's first year of existence, Howarth had the SOE commandeer a seventeenth-century manor called Lunna House on the highlands above a large, secluded sound for his operational base.

The boats used for the transport were mainly small but sturdy cutters that had brought Norwegian refugees to the island after the invasion, and then been overhauled by local shipbuilders to provide for storage of extra fuel and water. These were sailed by a kind of civilian navy that grew from about two dozen Norwegian volunteers to over forty seamen who had their living expenses covered and drew modest weekly wages, with bonuses for their covert runs to Norway.

In 1943, three twin-diesel U.S. Navy SC-47 sub chasers fitted for speed and quiet running would be added to the fleet. Dundee's submarines had also become natural participants in the intrigue, conducting a series of special operations for the combined intelligence groups. Boats from the 9th Flotilla would slip into the narrow fjords twisting in from the coast, drop off agents with radio equipment and other supplies, and pick up operatives whose cloak-and-dagger missions had reached completion or been somehow compromised. In exchange they received the most current tips about Nazi maritime traffic, with the reconnaissance data provided by Norwegian coast watchers adding essential detail to the broader picture drawn from decrypted Axis radio intercepts. This allowed them to take action against enemy ship movements with far greater speed and precision than would have been afforded by waiting for Bletchley in London.

The close partnership between Dundee/Lerwick and Norway's coast watchers had been very much in play on April 15, 1944, two days after Lieutenant Launders and his crew left the Skagerrak and parted ways with the crippled *Taku* under their revised orders. *Friedrichshafen* was about fifteen nautical miles southwest of the Norwegian island of Egeroy (58°15′N, 06°00′E), steaming in convoy with two other transports and four antisubmarine escort trawlers, when *Venturer*, advised of the group's position, stole up on it at periscope depth. It was almost eight-thirty at night with darkness cloaking the water, and not even a keen-eyed lookout would have seen the feathery wake of foam behind the sub's upraised scope.

Remaining a cautious distance from his prey, Launders had given the fire order in a level tone. That was something his men would always remember about him: Launders never shouted his commands, but spoke them calmly, without raising his voice.

As the warhead blasted a hole in the ship amid heaving sheets of water, the speedy German guard boats had raced off in the direction of the British sub to retaliate. They hadn't needed to see the torpedo's wake to approximate its location; although the darkness would have created some confusion, the sub-chaser crews could retrace its path from the point of detonation. To further narrow in on their attacker, they would use their active searchlight bow sonar—the operators transmitting sonic pings, and listening for their reflections, or echoes, as the pulses bounced of their target to mark its distance and position.

But this system had its inherent limitations. The pulses could only be aimed straight ahead, blinding the trawlers to a submarine's whereabouts and movements once they were directly above it and ready to drop their patterns of depth charges. A sub, however, was not apt to loiter in place unless it had sustained damage that was preventing its escape.

Launders had no such problem as he dove deep to evade the antisubmarine boats' explosive canisters. His mission accomplished, he'd ordered *Venturer* back to the submarine depot at Lerwick. Known as Ambrose II, it was where boats from Dundee typically pulled in to top off their fuel reserves and restock provisions when heading to or from their patrols.

Venturer would spend the better part of the next two seasons undergoing shipyard overhauls and participating in naval training exercises. In June, the Allies launched the D-Day invasion with its fateful landings at Normandy, and the end of August would see American liberation forces marching into Paris beneath the Arc de Triumph.

When Lieutenant Jimmy Launders next took *Venturer* out on war patrol in September, the situation in the North Sea had changed quite a bit. With the German submarine fleet's move to Norway, and Dönitz reevaluating the role and tactics of his U-boats, things had gotten much more active and dangerous in those waters— and nowhere was this more the case than right along the coast, where the intel provided by ship watchers of the Norwegian resistance became all the more vital to the Allied naval commanders at Dundee.

The makeup of Launders's crew had also undergone a partial transformation since his last cruise. While *Venturer* was in the yard getting remedied of the wear and tear of action and seawater on its metal and machinery, an appreciable number of reassignments and completions of tours of duty had led to a 25 percent turnover of the ship's company. The task of bringing their replacements up to snuff fell largely on the shoulders of Launders's second in command, Lieutenant Andrew Chalmers, who had been with the boat since its commissioning. He would live up to the responsibility with quiet aplomb; though still months shy of his twenty-fourth birthday, the calmly efficient Chalmers was already a seasoned combat veteran. The son of an intelligence officer, he had joined the Royal Navy as a boy seaman at sixteen and gotten his first taste of action two years earlier during the British-American landings in North Africa. In recommending Chalmers for service decorations later on, Launders would specifically credit his training methods for the boat's operational successes, and emphasize that his performance "during moments of stress has been an example to all."

Despite *Venturer*'s crew reshufflings, then, her strike against the *Vang* on September 11 proved a cakewalk for Launders and his steady right-hand man. But only two days later, the sub would have an encounter in the same general area that would not go nearly as well.

Not by a long shot.

3.

The port of Egersund outside the Skagerrak had been the site of a large German garrison since their invasion, and its well-established harbor facilities were only part of the reason. The other reason, or reasons, were its underwater telegraph lines.

In the 1860s, the Great Northern Telegraph Company of Copenhagen had laid 270 nautical miles of cable between the town of Peterhead, in Aberdeenshire, Scotland, and Egersund's coastal station across the North Sea. This joined Great Britain to a system that stretched overland to Oslo, then spanned the 280 miles to Stock-holm, Sweden, where the line again ran a submerged course through the Gulf of Bothnia, resurfaced at Nystad in Finland, and traversed another 300 miles of rugged northern hinterland into St. Peters-burg. By treaties the British had negotiated with Denmark, Sweden, Norway, and Russia, the circuit formed the sole and exclusive ser-vice for telegraphic message traffic to and from England and those nations.

A prime early target of Operation Weserübung in 1940, Eger-sund had fallen to the German navy's Kampfgruppe 6 on the first night of the invasion. Control of the village gave the Germans a grip on an extended cable system that stretched across a thousand miles of land and sea, making it possible to disrupt and tap into British communications with a defiant Norwegian resistance and the Russian enemy. Egersund also could not have been logistically more advantageous as a shipping center, situated as it was along the main coastal route between Norway and Sweden, and providing a convenient point of embarkation to Germany.

For years after they swept into the village, the Nazis had manned existing Norwegian shore emplacements largely without upgrading their gun batteries. The reason came down to a simple allocation of resources: The French and Belgian coasts across the English Chan-nel were the likeliest areas for Allied landings, and buttressing them took precedence. Still, the occupation commanders had constantly requested that their outdated weapons be replaced, and even before FdU West Rösing and his battered U-boat fleet moved to the North Sea, the Germans had committed to strengthening Norwegian defensive positions with newer and better armaments.

Although the improvements to Norway's segment of the Atlantic Wall were never fully completed, the years 1943 through 1944 saw many installations bolstered and modernized. Germany would soon make a deliberate effort to pull its shipping convoys closer to shore within reach of their artillery barrages . . . but if the hope was to deter Britain's harrier subs from their hunts, the daring makeup of their captains had been greatly underestimated.

And so at five o'clock in the evening on September 13, 1944, the merchant DS *Force* and two other cargo ships—probably the larger *Karmoy* and the *Vederngon* both of which were documented as leaving Egersund for Germany that day—were steaming southwest of the village harbor when *Venturer* came up on them and their antisubmarine escort. The convoy was hugging the coast in shallow waters and Lieutenant Launders, sweeping for enemy convoys, ordered his helmsman to make a close approach, even though it meant bringing the sub dangerously within range of the coastal batteries.

Though the Wehrmacht soldiers stationed at Marine Küsten Batterie Egersund—or MKB 4/503—had seen little action until now, the emplacement had been reequipped with four big 12.7-cm SK C/34 naval guns, two flak guns, powerful spotlights, and a state-of-the-art Zeiss Entfernungsmesser 6M rangefinder on a hilltop mount. To complete the MKB's makeover, pillboxes for machine guns, antitank artillery, and flamethrowers had been built nearby to stave off a possible amphibious assault.

Gliding up to within twelve hundred yards, *Venturer* launched a spread of three torpedoes at the *Force*—but they never connected with the freighter. Launders would report that all three exploded, one detonating prematurely. According to him, the other two torpedoes simply missed their intended target.

Several things, alone or in combination, could have gone wrong; even veteran torpedomen considered handling the MK VIIIs a challenge. A small freighter like *Force* would have had a shallow draft in the water, so the torpedoes easily could have swum under its keel and struck a sandbank or sunken debris—porpoising, or running deeper than their desired depth, was a common problem in shallow water. Near-shore waves could have also thrown off the depth controls or tumbled the weapons' internal gyroscopes and resulted in their straying off course. Or more than a single torpedo could have detonated too soon . . . the submerged blasts occurred in swift succession and sound bounces around a lot underwater, causing the auditory equivalent of optical illusions. Launders could have been mistaken about only one of the three explosions being premature.

In any event, Launders now had to make a snap decision. Despite the misses, the *Force*'s deckhands were jumping overboard or clambering into lifeboats, leaving the Nazi merchant vessel a sitting duck for a second go at it. But *Venturer* was in a tight predicament of her own. At that hour, there was plenty of daylight left for the enemy sub chasers to see three white wakes roping back across the water to her position. Because the convoy had escaped any harm, the trawlers had nothing to distract them from pursuing her. And she was close by—very close—in shallows that radically decreased her evasive capabilities.

Launders could flee and hope to elude the trawlers, whose depth charges would likely sink his boat if she was overtaken. Or he could continue his attack and try to sink the ship and its abandoned cargo.

He opted for the latter and ordered *Venturer* to the surface, ordering a party to open fire with her 76mm deck gun. Again it was Sub-Lieutenant Brand who was in the thick of things, leading the men topside as water sloshed around the soles of their boots and went streaming down over the submarine's gunwales. Not only might the deck gun's explosive shells down the transport, it would give the German trawlers something to worry about as they closed with *Venturer*. And buy the latter some time.

She would need every moment of it. Almost as soon as the submarine emerged from the chop to open up on the *Force*, MKB 4/503's shore batteries had abruptly roared to life. At the 76mm gun, the men continued to take aim at the steamer, slamming the vessel's flanks with armor-piercing shells, Stoker John Norman Standley feeding cartridges into the breach loader's barrel. But the fire from the shore had quickly thickened, a fusillade of artillery whistling through the air at the submarine, the incoming rounds sending up great gouts of spray as they struck the water nearby. *Venturer* was now under heavy attack.

In the control room, Launders realized he'd done all the damage he could to the freighter and ordered the gunnery crew back belowdecks. Fortunately, their heroics had held the escort at bay long enough for a hurried getaway. As *Venturer*'s chief navigation officer, Ensign John Frederick Watson recalled, "our boat could maneuver very well, it could very quickly turn and dive." Which was clearly put to an extreme test as she made a full-rudder turn toward deeper water, then submerged and arrowed off at flank bell.

Venturer would return to base unharmed and spend a few weeks going through another round of maintenance and refurbishment, with her grateful crew getting in some highly coveted shore leave. But this interlude came to an end by November, when the submarine was again pressed into action.

Conceived jointly by HMS Ambrose and Lerwick, the mission was intended to penetrate deep into enemy-controlled fjords and channels in aid of a resistance movement in critical need of supplies. For *Venturer,* it would take a sudden detour into the unexpected.

CHAPTER THREE

HOLEN SCHOOL

1.

Tholthorpe was the definitive "two-egg base." This was entirely thanks to Mrs. Mudd, the kindhearted old woman who'd taken the servicemen at the airfield under her generous care. She called them her boys and considered herself their fairy godmother and wanted very much to make them feel right at home in Yorkshire, England, though they were of course many thousands of miles away from their real Canadian homes.

In sharp contrast, a one-egg base was a station where you could not expect to be very well fed. The joke was that you knew you'd been assigned to one when you asked for a couple of three-minute eggs at the mess, and the breakfast cook told you he was low on supplies, and then boiled up a single egg for six minutes instead.

Yorkshire had several bases of that ilk, without question, although the men of No. 420 and No. 425 Squadrons would not have hesitated to say they preferred the most miserly of English rations to the dust, flies, bad water, and dysentery of North Africa, where they'd flown their Vickers Wellingtons on desert sorties until the end of 1943.

At Tholthorpe, the meals were hearty and delicious by any measure—second, perhaps, only to the food available at the American air-force bases, and that was primarily because of their wider assortment of desserts. Mrs. Mudd took unsurpassed delight in cooking for the squadrons' fliers, ground crews, and engineers; it was her way of being hospitable and showing she appreciated their brave contribution to the war effort. While the local constabulary might have argued that her appreciation had gone too far when they learned she'd been poaching fresh meat for the young airmen, the Canadians felt nothing but appreciation, and covered the fines she had to pay with their own modest wages.

Along with East Moor's runways, ordnance dumps, repair hangars, barracks, and makeshift tennis court, Tholthorpe was one of two substations of Beaver Base No. 62 at Linton-on-Ouse a short distance to the south. Together they all fell under the control of the highly decorated Royal Canadian Air Force Bomber Group 6, the only foreign air group to serve as a distinct operational unit under the RAF Bomber Command. There were seven other stations and substations: No. 61 at Topcliffe, with substations Dishforth and Dalton; No. 63 at Leeming, with substation Skipton-on-Swale; and No. 64 at Middleton St. George up in Durham County, substation Croft.

On the morning of October 4, 1944, while HMS *Venturer* was at Lerwick for overhaul and resupply, Group 6's Halifax bombers flew west on a mission that would be the first in a long, fateful series of events that eventually led Jimmy Launders and his crew to their most important accomplishment of the war—one that would mark them in history forever.

Bound for Norway that day were Tholthorpe's Squadrons 420 and 424, Skipton-on-Swale's 433 and 431, and Croft's 434 accompanied by thirty-nine larger Avro Lancaster bombers of Squadrons 419 and 428 out of Middleton St. George. A dozen Mosquitoes of Bomber Support Group 100, their cockpits bristling with radio countermeasures equipment, served as long-range escorts, and eight Lancasters of the elite RAF Pathfinder Force Group 8 joined them to mark their targets: the submarine bunker and docks at Laksevåg, where the massive buildup had been under way since September.

The flight across the North Sea from Yorkshire took about two hours and fifteen minutes. At 9:05 A.M., the planes came roaring in above the ocean at altitudes between twelve thousand and fourteen thousand feet and then banked north along the coastline toward Bergen to drop their explosive loads.

The tragedy that unfolded over the next hour was one the people of Norway would never forget.

2.

The sky over Laksevåg was clear and bright as a diamond on October 4, plentiful sunshine cutting through the autumn crispness, windowpanes gleaming with frost in the still, cold air. While most of the city's inhabitants welcomed this respite from the dreariness of a typical autumn day, there were others who later claimed to have held it suspect, as if the weather had been too good to be true. The Norwegian climate was not known to be so kindly, not without exacting a price.

According to Trygve Freyvald Guldbrandsen, that ominous feeling had a more tangible basis for the mothers who sent their children off to school for the first day of the fall term. Three weeks earlier, in September, the floating dock of the Bergen Mechanical Workshop around the headlands in the south bay had been mined and destroyed by a British mini-submarine. Then, the day before, on October 3, a British Mosquito had overflown the Laksevåg area on a reconnaissance run, buzzing above the range of German anti-aircraft batteries as it made its passes over the docks and then swung away to the west.

Unaware of the plane that had been sighted by many in the area, Guldbrandsen had nevertheless felt his mother's tension before leaving for school. In Nora Harbor outside Bruno, the Bergen Steamship Company's construction and repair shipyards had been appropriated by the Kriegsmarine, renamed Danziger Wharf, and expanded to ease the traffic congesting the docks around the headlands. These were prime targets of the British, and Guldbrandsen's school was on Holen Kringsja Road just a few hundred yards from the bunker site.

When the Kockum air-raid horns blared at 9:05 the morning of the strike, some people were at home, but a large number were at their jobs—this was a Wednesday, the middle of the week. If it had been an isolated occurrence, it might have sent the city into a panic, but the early warnings were familiar and had never before been followed by the second wave of alarms that signaled an imminent attack. Anxious mothers aside, the populace initially thought it was just more of what had become almost normal over the past four years, a recurring fact of life in the strange, even surreal condition that was being a citizen of a conquered land.

But five minutes later they would hear the horns again. As hearts froze around Laksevåg, the Allied squadrons appeared overhead, their thunder countered by the repetitive chop of antiaircraft fire. When the first bombs fell, people living high on the slopes nestling the city's inland side would feel the hills tremble under their feet.

The suddenly terrified citizens had almost no time to dash for safe havens, though only a comparative few would have been able get to them anyway. Their German subjugators had outlawed neighborhood evacuations under the harshest of penalties—including death—and that had restricted people to taking cover wherever they happened to be. If someone was fortunate enough to have a bomb shelter on his immediate premises, he could try to scramble into it. If he wasn't, he had to find whatever nearby safety he could and pray for the best.

As if that hadn't presented enough risk to innocent Norwegian lives, the danger was greatly compounded because the Germans had commandeered and installed themselves in so many of the industrial and residential structures near the docks. An aircrew had to release its load from a high altitude while taking heavy flak and peering through the smoke of bombs that had already struck their targets. It would have been difficult if not impossible for them to distinguish civilian buildings from military targets at the base.

An expansive three-story building with a stone foundation and high gambrel roof, the newly completed Holen School was considered the largest and most modern primary school in the municipality. In fact, even the Germans had been impressed as the schoolhouse went up and made a play at turning it into naval quarters. But they had already grabbed another local school, the Damsgård, for Einsatzgruppe Wiking's supply committee and community outrage prompted them to reassess their plans. Finally they had backed off and it had opened its doors as scheduled for the start of classes.

When the air-raid alarms sounded, most of the Holen school's 350 eight- through eleven-year-old students were shepherded along into the basement by their teachers. Although part of it had been built with thick concrete walls to serve as a bomb shelter, a large section on its south side was allocated for use by a local volunteer Red Cross auxiliary.

In orderly fashion, the kids were brought downstairs. As was customary in Norway at the time, boys and girls were taught separately and, class by class, some of the boys and all the girls and their teachers in the basement retreated to the bomb shelter. But the shelter wasn't large enough to accommodate the entire group of children, and the boys and teachers from two of the classes—fourth and fifth graders—rushed into the large space on the building's south side with sixteen Red Cross workers.

The bombs struck ten minutes later. All around Laksevåg, the ground quaked, power lines were severed, and buildings collapsed into rubble. Each Halifax carried twelve thousand pounds of general-purpose bombs: a dozen thousand-pound bombs or a mix of thousand- and five-hundred-pound bombs. Three thousand-pound bombs dropped on the Holen School, the first scoring a direct hit on the space where the two boys' classes and emergency volunteers had taken refuge.

All sixty boys in the basement room were killed along with their teachers and the first-aid workers. A girl in the adjacent shelter died as a dividing wall buckled and then came toppling down on her. When firefighters extricated the children's corpses from the rubble later on, some were still clutching their teachers' bodies so tightly it was difficult to pull them apart.

Trygve Guldbrandsen, a seventh grader, was among many students who had been transferred to the Holen School from the Damsgård School after the Germans helped themselves to it, turning it into an adjunct for their bunker construction facilities. His class had started its morning in the large, skylit art room on the top floor near the school kitchen and craft room. One moment he was working on his sketches, and the next he was interrupted by the harsh, startling wail of the air-raid alert.

The teacher quickly led Guldbrandsen and his classmates down to the science room on the ground floor, where they crammed themselves in with students from several other classes, including a group of seventh-grade girls. Guldbrandsen would always wonder why they weren't brought to the basement. If they had been, he knew, he would almost surely have wound up with the students in the part that had taken the terrible first hit.

Once downstairs, the teachers and students in the science room could do nothing but wait and listen to the crump of detonating bombs across Laksevåg, the blasts creeping closer and closer until the building's wide stone foundations began to shake. Guldbrandsen remembered that he was standing near the windows with some other kids when he told a pair of frightened girls to lie down on the floor. He would later guess that he'd intended to join them. But "if I got that far, I have no idea."

The next thing Guldbrandsen knew, there was a blue flash and "great ringing, and I was thrown across the room and landed [on my back] under a wooden table." The table's legs had snapped just above where they were bolted to the floorboards, the heavy tabletop slamming down on him, its edge pressing into his chest. His legs, meanwhile, were bent at an unnatural angle under a mound of stone, laths, and fallen beams.

As Guldbrandsen lay pinned and helpless under the rubble, "There were shrieks from falling bombs, flashes and crashing sounds when they exploded, the deep boom of large caliber anti-aircraft guns and the barking of machine guns . . . and above all the intense, threatening, physically sickening roar of the two hundred and fifty heavy planes above us."

At one point during his ordeal, another boy who was able to move about gave Guldbrandsen a soiled handkerchief to hold over his nose and mouth so he wouldn't inhale the lime dust filling what was left of the room. Between the gritty haze of dust, acrid smoke, and lack of oxygen, the men picking their way through the ruins—German submarine crews had joined frantic Norwegian rescuers in an effort to dig out surviving children—found it difficult to breathe or even light matches to help them see.

Four hours passed before they were at last able to grope their way through the smoking wreckage, lift Guldbrandsen clear of it, and get him onto a stretcher. He would be brought to a military barracks and given a bed beside a boy he knew from school and several wounded Russian slave laborers. After a while the doctor came and pulled a sheet over the other boy's face. Guldbrandsen noticed that it did not puff up with breath over his nose and mouth, but lay flat and still, like the boy himself.

He was luckier; he'd suffered deep cuts on his legs and been badly skinned over his entire body, but had escaped serious injury.

Almost miraculously, he would not be alone in his good fortune. As teenager Anna Duus recalled, a young neighborhood boy named Reidar was standing in the doorway of the classroom where his group had sought shelter when the world came crashing down in smoke and flames; only the entryway's heavy crossbeams protected him from being buried under an avalanche of debris. Moments later, he had looked up and seen an expanse of blue sky where the ceiling had been obliterated. Bombs were still raining onto the street and quays from overhead.

In the middle of the floor, shocked and disheveled, a teacher sat among the bloody, dismembered bodies of dead children reciting the Twenty-third Psalm. As her surviving students screamed and cried around her, she assured them they would soon be in heaven.

That memory, above others, would forever haunt the days and nights of fourth grader Ragnhild Bratt Tveit and several of her classmates.

The death count at the Holen School would come to eighty—sixty-one children, sixteen rescue workers, a janitor, and two teachers. And that would not account for all the civilian fatalities that day. At the Kleivdal leather factor near the harbor, thirty-six employees perished when its bomb shelter took a direct hit, with another worker eventually succumbing to injuries. Eleven more were killed in the bomb shelter of a nearby bucket factory.

Overall, 193 Norwegians and a still-uncalculated number of Russian slave laborers were killed in the bombings, with 700 more left homeless. Not even the dead were untouched by the destruction: In a local cemetery, the scattered white bones of long-interred corpses poked from the churned-up soil after explosions ripped into their grave sites.

Although the air strike lasted just eleven minutes, the devastated civil infrastructure would complicate rescue attempts throughout Laksevåg for hours after the roar of the planes faded away. The bombs had downed power cables and burst water mains under the cratered streets; government records indicate that pressure levels were so low in some areas that firemen's hoses sputtered drily when they tried to use them . . . and that firefighters in places where the water continued to flow hesitated to open their hoses for fear of drowning people trapped in the carnage.

Ironically, the Damsgård School just two miles to the south of the Holen School—the one that had been converted into a supply center by the German bunker builders—escaped being bombed and was left intact.

Fortress Bruno also remained standing, but for a different reason.

3.

The Royal Air Force Bomber Command's official campaign diaries for Bomber Group 6 declared that the October 1944 raid on the Bergen pens "appeared to be successful," but that was true only by a profound interpretive stretch—or viewed in terms of the relatively light RAF losses. A single Lancaster from Squadron 419, Flight VR-V, plunged from the sky over Scotland on its return to base, sending all seven members of its aircrew to their deaths; the rest of the flights returned safely.

But if the operation's success was measured by damage to the intended target, or interruption of German submarine activities, then little of real significance was accomplished. Not one of the seven thousand-pound bombs that struck the bunker penetrated its concrete roof, and although the campaign diary claims "the electrical wiring system in the pens was completely put out of action," that intelligence—even if accurate—failed to mention that it at best caused a hiccup in the bunker's normal activities. The diaries state that three U-boats in open berths were "damaged by the bombing but did not sink"; the Germans, for their part, would acknowledge the losses of two Type VII U-boats, the U-228 and U-993, the latter of which suffered two casualties. Of the "three small ships" that were hit, the two that sank were a tugboat and a cargo vessel. The third was a freighter that the British said carried arms and ammunition and that the Norwegians said was loaded with coal and had already been partly sunk in the harbor's shallow waters. Three Norwegian vessels were also destroyed: a ferry that had been commandeered by the Germans and two cargo ships.

About a dozen German military personnel were lost in the raid.

The assessment of the RAF war diaries notwithstanding, this was a poor return for what came to between 700,000 and 1.3 million pounds of high explosives dropped on Laksevåg during the strike . . . and for the devastation that the massive bombing caused to civilian lives and property.

It was January before the RAF struck at Bruno again. In the interim it would undergo a comprehensive process of evaluating the autumn strike's mistakes and take a series of steps to correct them. Very tellingly, it would assign its most elite precision bomber squadron to the second mission, which was staged with a major alteration in tactics, aircraft, equipment, and weaponry. The main reason for the change—and the mission itself—was a German submarine on a search trip to Japan, one that had come into Allied sights as a high-priority target.

All this led to very different results. As it turned out, however, no one could have predicted what they would be.

CHAPTER FOUR

EAGLE, LONG KNIFE, MONSOON

A large submarine compared to others in the German fleet, able to travel long distances without refueling, U-864 was still designed to be an attack boat, not a transport, and its standard complement of fifty-seven sailors, provisions, weapons, and fuel placed considerable demands on interior space. Bring aboard a higher-than-average number of regular personnel, her special passengers, and the secret crated cargo for delivery to Japan, and scant room remained for any more freight inside her forward and aft compartments. But space would have to be found—or more correctly made—for the large, heavy load of mercury she was to carry.

The trip to the Far East presented a technical and logistical challenge, albeit one that did have precedents in earlier missions. Japan and Germany had engaged in maritime commerce on and off since

1869, with slowdowns and interruptions throughout the twentieth century due to shifting geopolitical circumstances. By the 1930s, their governments had begun to form closer and more stable economic ties, however, and in September 1940, the two, along with Italy, became signatories to a document called the Tripartite Pact that was, in the words of its preamble, "calculated to promote mutual prosperity and welfare of the peoples concerned." In essence the agreement laid out the three Axis powers' respective geographic claims to a "new order" of dominion in Europe and East Asia, as well as the broad principles of future military and technological cooperation between them.

Largely insisted upon by the Japanese to overcome resistance to the treaty by factions of the armed services, one of six "supplementary" protocols signed confidentially between the two nations stated:

> The Contracting parties undertake to exchange from time to time without delay all useful inventions and devices of war and to supply one another with war equipment, such as airplanes, tanks, guns, explosives, etc., which each Party may reasonably spare, together with technical skill and men, should they be required. Furthermore, they are prepared to do their utmost in furnishing one another with and in aiding one another in the efforts to procure minerals as well as machinery for war industries and various requisites for livelihood with machinery of all sorts employed in the production of such requisites.

Another secret protocol read:

Germany will use her industrial strength and her other technical and material resources as far as possible in favor of Japan . . . to enable her to be better prepared for any emergency. Germany and Japan will further undertake to aid each other in procuring, in every possible way, necessary raw materials and minerals, including oil.

Finally, an extraordinary document based on relevant sections of the Tripartite Pact was drafted at Hitler's headquarters in Berlin on March 5, 1941, nine months before the Japanese bombing of Pearl Harbor and America's entry into the war. Issued to members of his military high command, the Führer's Directive No. 24 on Cooperation with Japan began with this paragraph:

On the basis of the Three Powers [Tripartite] Pact, the object of collaboration must be to induce Japan to undertake positive actions in the Far East as soon as possible. This will tie down strong British forces and the center of gravity of the interests of the U.S.A. will be shifted toward the Pacific.

In a second clause, Hitler's directive went on to stipulate:

. . . To this end, the high commands of the three services [army, navy and air force] are to meet Japanese requests for information about war and battlefield experiences as well as for assistance in military, economic, and technical matters in a comprehensive and generous fashion . . . Priority should naturally be accorded to those Japanese requests that could have some impact within a short time on the conduct of the war.

In special cases, the Fuhrer reserves the right to take decisions himself.

Together these papers formed the diplomatic basis of a trade in raw commodities, secret technology, and specialized personnel that lasted the entire war. At first air passage was discussed as a means of import and export, but the nonstop flights to Japan desired by the Luftwaffe required that its cargo planes take off from German-held sections of the USSR—an idea rejected by Tokyo, which had signed a nonaggression treaty with the Russian Goliath to its north in April 1941, and was determined to avoid any hint of being in violation of it. Slower overseas shipments were eventually carried out, but within two years of the first such delivery, Allied bombers out of bases in Great Britain, the United States, Iceland, and Canada were regularly intercepting German merchantmen and disguised passenger liners that were attempting to run their cargo and scientific experts past the American and British blockades. Whatever the program's early successes, intelligence from ULTRA, MAGIC, and covert observers in occupied countries tipped its balance too far toward the loss side for either Axis partner to find it sustainable.

Even so, Admiral Dönitz was far from eager to oblige when the Japanese proposed submarine transport as a contingency. His objective was to win the battle of the Atlantic. He saw his U-boats as warships, not underwater freighters, and to him sending them to the Pacific in that role would spread an already overtaxed fleet even thinner around the globe. He also hardly appreciated the Japanese asking for a pair of workhorse IXC U-boats on which they hoped to model a new class of submarines for the imperial navy.

But Tokyo continued to press Berlin for the exchange of resources set out in the Tripartite Pact, a deal that both parties agreed was to their mutual benefit—albeit sometimes grudgingly, and with internal differences of opinion about the precise nature and extent of their cooperation. Germany's voracious war machine demanded the consumption of rubber for tires, oils for food and industry, and tungsten ore for the manufacture of mines and armor-piercing shells, among other supplies produced in Japanese territories. Japan needed bulk shipments of steel, lead, optical glass, and especially mercury.

Above and beyond all else, the Japanese emperor wanted the military technology that Germany had produced under the coordination of the Forschungsführung (Fo-Fü), Hitler's armament research commission in Berlin. This program had been carried out on a massive scale throughout the war at a host of black project installations, spurring scientific broad jumps in the fields of pyrotechnics, ballistics, chemistry, rocketry, and aviation/aeronautics. The latter had produced an innovative aircraft engine that worked on the concept of jet propulsion, a technology the British pioneered in the late 1930s but had then somewhat neglected. The Junkers 004 and BMW AG's 003 were the first operational gas turbine—or turbojet—engines ever built, designed to power a new class of revolutionary high-speed planes that would come to be known as jet fighters.

These jet-powered aircraft were themselves in the experimental stages. The model to receive the Junkers engine was the streamlined, twin-engine Messerschmitt Me 262 Schwalbe, or Swallow, a powerful and highly maneuverable warplane that could be armed with 30mm cannons and air-to-air rockets. At the secret Flugzeugwerke Reichsmarschall Hermann Göring, or REIHMAG, production center, twenty-seven Me 262 prototypes were assembled using Jewish slaves, hundreds of whom would die of disease and starvation deep inside a mountain complex that had once been a porcelain sand mine.

Similarly, BMW's first combat jet, the Heinkel He 162 Volksjäger (People's Fighter) was built in extensive salt mines outside Magdeburg on the Elbe River. A light single-engine plane with an airframe constructed almost entirely of plywood and flown by a one-man crew, it had been developed to be quickly and inexpensively run off the line by semiskilled labor and was categorized as an interceptor aircraft—a fighter that could defend against the large British and American bombers inflicting heavy damage on the Fatherland with their continuous sorties.

The facilities responsible for development of the secret weapons were scattered and hidden across Nazi Germany. In the woodlands outside the centuries-old city of Braunschweig, a thousand specialists worked on advancements in ballistics and armor at Luftfahrtforschungsanstalt Hermann Göring, the rooftops of its fifty to sixty buildings concealed under branches and planted trees. At the giant Heeresversuchsanstalt Peenemünde rocket research center on the Baltic island of Usedom, and later the subterranean Nordhausen-Bleicherode factories, thousands of scientific personnel, again transforming concept and experimentation into reality, had developed the V-2 missile and V-1 flying bomb (a forerunner of the cruise missile) along with several winged combat craft that fused rocket and aviation technologies. Together the sites were a military-industrial dynamo of prodigious output, primarily resting on the backs of a slave labor force made up of Jewish inmates from the Buchenwald and Dora-Mittelbau concentration camps.

The Me 163 Komet rocket fighter may have been the most ambitious of the hybrid aircraft. Less than nineteen feet long with an approximately thirty-foot wingspan, weighing just nine thousand pounds, the short, stubby, hornetlike Me 163 was designed by rocket-glider expert Alexander Martin Lippisch. His radical fighter utilized a more powerful variant of the Walter rocket motor that fellow inventor Wernher von Braun had developed at Peenemünde and was first produced at Messerschmitt's fighter works in Regensburg, Bavaria, with later versions coming out of the Klemm aircraft factory near the Black Forest and elsewhere in Germany and Austria.

The Komet's Walter Mark II rocket motor was fueled by hydrogen peroxide and "C-stoff," a liquid cocktail of methyl alcohol, hydrazine hydrate, and water that gave the little interceptor sufficient thrust for a steep, powered seventy-degree zoom climb of 10,000 feet per minute to an altitude of up to 29,689 feet, which was about fifteen times faster than the best Allied fighter of its day. In the hands of a skilled pilot, it could streak through the air at close to Mach 1—the speed of sound—and fly circles around conventional aircraft. The Komet's undercarriage was jettisoned on takeoff to eliminate the drag of exposed wheels and the bulk of retractable landing gear, taking the greatest possible advantage of its lightweight airframe.

The German plan for the Komet was to set up rings of defensive squadrons around Germany along the aerial paths of enemy bombers, each ring twenty-five miles from the next so they were in gliding distance—a thousand interceptors in all. With the huge American B-17 Flying Fortress designated as its chief target, the maneuverable rocket fighter's attack profile called for it to engage the bombers at high altitudes and open fire with its 30mm MK 108 cannons, weaving through the formation before enemy gunners could bring their weapons to bear.

The Komet had problems, however: The slow firing rate of the its MK 108 guns gave its pilot no more than two or three seconds to hit his target as he shot past at blazing speed—a tough challenge for any but the most skilled veteran fliers. Another issue was that wind resistance and gravity quickly pulled the heavy 30mm shells into downward parabolic arcs, making the gun accurate only at short range. But four, five, or even six hits might be needed to down an enormous B-17, and with just sixty cannon shells stowed aboard, this demanded gunnery skills that were beyond many pilots.

An eventual solution was to arm the Me 163 with ten 50mm Jagdfaust launchers mounted in the wings and angled upward at their targets. As a Komet pilot came soaring up beneath the fuselage of an enemy bomber, a photocell wired to the tubes would detect the dark silhouette of the bomber against the sky's brighter background and send out an electronic pulse to fire the mortar shells. This system greatly reduced the importance of a pilot's marksmanship and, because of the simultaneous firing of the launchers, allowed more shells to strike their target before they were pulled into a downward trajectory.

There were more hurdles for the Komet before full-scale mass production could be authorized, among them the brief duration of its powered flight, which lasted just six to seven minutes before the rocket fuel burned off. After exhausting its fuel, an Me 163 might have to make subsequent passes of the bombers with controlled glides. In these unpowered dives it was still able to achieve an impressive five hundred miles per hour, maneuvering through the bomber formation before most enemy gunners could bring their weapons to bear. As many as three or four passes were possible depending on the response time of the squadron's escort fighters, but sooner or later the small glider had to land. And once a glider committed to a landing, there was no turning back—alighting without engine power, it was easily picked off on descent and touch-down.

It was the rocket fighter's test pilots rather than the designers who addressed this vulnerability. Diving for their airfields, the pilots would pull out close to the ground and run a series of tight, evasive high-speed circles over the field, staying within the defensive perimeter of their antiaircraft batteries. The fighter's spring-loaded skids would absorb shock and cut on friction as it met the ground, but landings were bumpy, uncomfortable, and overall very tricky: An approach that was too fast could lead to overshooting the field, one that was too slow to a collision with a tree or fence.

Irrespective of its bugs, the Me 163 held a potential that could not be dismissed by the Germans—or by Japanese observers in Germany. Keenly aware of the destruction Allied bombing raids had brought its European partner, Tokyo wanted to bolster its air defenses against similar assaults, and of all the *Wunderwaffen*, or so-called wonder weapons, available for purchase from Hitler's workshops, the jet and rocket fighters held the greatest appeal.

The Komet in particular was a good fit with Japanese resources, production capabilities, and tactical needs. Despite wartime scarcities, they had ample supplies of the wood that composed much of its airframe, and believed they could create an adaptation with even more wooden segments. Their Mitsubishi, Nissan, and Fuji aircraft plants had the means and competence to work off the original German design, while Yokosuka Arsenal undertook the manufacture of its rocket engine.

The Me 163 was, in short, the one Fo-Fü aircraft that could be cheaply and efficiently rushed off the assembly line and was suited to an interceptor role against bombers and their escorts—either with cannon fire, or if necessary by kamikaze suicide attack.

Although Hitler himself was adamant about his 1941 directive to strengthen Japanese war capabilities as a means of keeping America busy in the Pacific, not all his subordinates were so anxious to hand them the prized fruit of German technological research. This sentiment was shared by civilian armaments developers who were profiting tremendously from the Nazi weapons program, and wanted to see that Japan purchased their hardware and blueprints under negotiated financial licenses.

Still, the two nations' overlapping agendas made it imperative that they work things out, and Dönitz was eventually persuaded to commit some of his submarines to the operation . . . which didn't prevent him from trying to put checks on how many were used to fulfill Germany's obligations. The question in his mind was how to limit their allocation.

While Dönitz hedged, and Fo-Fü arms developers bargained, the IJN took the lead with the exchange in June 1942, sending one of its own transport subs to occupied France loaded with 3,300 pounds of mica used in electrical insulation, 1,452 pounds of shellac for pyrotechnics such as flares and tracers, and schematics for an advanced aerial torpedo. Code-named Sakura, the imperial battle cruiser I-30 arrived at the Lorient submarine base in August and was met in impressive manner by Grand Admiral Erich Raeder, Dönitz (who would follow Raeder as commander in chief of the entire navy), and Captain Yokoi Tadao, Hideo Kojima's predecessor as Japanese naval attaché to Berlin.

At the Lorient submarine pier, the submarine's commander, Shinobu Endo, and his officers received a heroes' welcome normally accorded German U-boat captains returning from patrol. Brass horns blared a military fanfare. A pretty girl gave Endo a flower bouquet. Gathered to witness his arrival was a crowd of submariners, infantrymen, doctors, nurses, smartly uniformed female signals auxiliaries, and curious French civilians, the entire spectacle served up with theatrical flair by Nazi propagandists to send a message of exaggerated unity to the Allies: The Japanese submarine fleet was now operating out of European bases, binding Axis naval power across continental and oceanic divides.

Over the course of an eventful three-week visit, Endo would be personally honored by Adolf Hitler in Berlin and stroll through Paris along the café-lined Champs-Élysées. Amid the galas and sightseeing excursions that kept the submarine's commander and his officers busy, a small Yokosuka E14Y1 floatplane carried aboard the I-30 for reconnaissance missions was filmed in flight above Lorient, again with the goal of signaling that the IJN and Kriegsmarine had solidified their operations. Then on August 22, I-30 finally departed for Asia with a cargo haul of German torpedoes, targeting and fire control equipment, assorted bombs, antitank and antiair-craft guns, a million yens' worth of industrial diamonds, and, most valuably, fifty Enigma encryption devices.

As a whole, I-30's visit was a triumph for Germany and Admiral Raeder in particular: it had yielded significant international public-ity, and a fair return in goods and war matériel, without giving up any highly prized modern aircraft and weapons designs. But the Japanese would never reap the benefits of the deal. On October 14, I-30 sank with most of its cargo aboard when it ran into a British minefield outside Singapore, where it had made a port call en route to the submarine base at Kure, Japan.

Raeder was nevertheless satisfied and relieved by this new stage in the two powers' wartime trade relationship. He'd fully bought into the notion of using the Pacific war as a strategic diversion for America, and had at last demonstrated movement on the trade ini-tiative with Japan to Hitler and the Wehrmacht's high command, or OKW—all of whom had grown irked with its slow progress and expected him to start pushing it along at an accelerated pace. But although the hoopla surrounding I-30 blunted some of their impa-tience with the grand admiral, it did nothing to diminish Hitler's growing personal infatuation with Karl Dönitz.

Dönitz had very adeptly cultivated his image as the innovative mastermind of submarine warfare and bold chief of the U-boat aces idealized in director Günther Rittau's *U-Boat Westward!*, further impressing it on the public with his brief appearance as himself in the movie. At the same time Raeder's surface fleet continued to be pounded by air attacks enforcing the Allied blockade, sustaining losses that progressively diminished him in the Führer's estimation despite the relative success of the I-30 initiative. It was almost to be predicted that one officer's rise would, sooner or later, converge with the other's fall.

I-30 would be the first of five Yanagi—"long knife"—boats to set sail for Europe from Japanese bases in the Pacific and Indian Oceans over the next two years. The three submarines that followed were likewise converted cruisers: I-8, I-34, and I-29. An enormous submarine by the standards of the time, the fifth, I-52, had been designed specifically as a long-distance cargo hauler, although I-29 alone would make the round trip without falling victim to Allied interdiction.

On January 31, 1943, Dönitz was elevated to the rank of grand admiral, replacing Raeder, whom the Führer had furiously blamed for a major defeat of the navy's surface fleet by British forces in the Barents Sea. Dönitz had literally written the book on German submarine warfare and his appointment to the Kriegsmarine's top post was a clear and direct reflection of Hitler's confidence in his strategies and tactics—and a very deliberate statement that the Reich was about to spearhead a reassertion of naval power with its U-boat fleet.

Dönitz guaranteed that the Allies got the message with a German radio declaration that made overnight newspaper headlines in Britain, America, and Canada. Their strident, alarmist tone had exactly the result he'd desired.

WARNS OF BIG U-BOAT EFFORT: DOENITZ TAKES POST, read the *Milwaukee Journal.* NAZIS OPEN U-BOAT WAR ON ALLIES, asserted Florida's *St. Petersburg Times,* which described Dönitz as "Germany's wily submarine warfare wizard." Declared a headline in Canada's *Windsor Daily Star:* SAYS U-BOATS TO HIT HARD: CHALLENGE IS ISSUED BY NEW COMMANDER TO ALLIES.

The *Daily Star* article went on to read:

London, Eng, Feb 1—Germany menaced the Allies today with the threat of a greater submarine war, backed by the total power of the Nazi navy . . . Her warning of what the Allies were expecting, a desperate effort to win the war by an all-out campaign against Allied supply lines, came with the weekend elevation of Grand Admiral Karl Doenitz to commander-in-chief of the German navy.

Doenitz, master of submarine warfare, hoisted his new flag—a black cross on a white field—over his headquarters yesterday and the German radio broadcast his declaration.

"I will put the entire concentrated strength of the navy into the submarine war, which will be waged with still greater vigor and determination than hitherto. The entire German navy will henceforth be put into the service of inexorable U-boat warfare. The German navy will fight to a finish.

Despite the article's dire tone overall, its concluding section was fascinatingly accurate in its characterization of the German submarine fleet's own possible bête noire :

The pace of Allied sinkings of U-boats has presented Germany herself with a desperate problem in the matter of qualified submarine crews.

Already boys as young as 16 and 17 have been reported being taken into the service and observers said the concentration of the entire German navy in the service of U-boat warfare might entail the transfer to submarines of sailors from battleships and cruisers.

The suggestion that teenagers were serving aboard U-boats was a deft bit of verbal embroidery that may have been spoon-fed to journalists by the Allied wartime publicity arm. Germany had relaxed its mental and physical fitness standards for naval applicants—and, in fact, had done the same for men entering all branches of the service. But submarines were complicated machines on which every hand knew he might at some point have to rely on a shipmate for his survival. As the war progressed, younger men were taken into the service, and the training for submarine duty was unquestionably accelerated. Any sailor younger than eighteen who'd been assigned to a U-boat would have been a rare exception to the rule, however.

What was true was that Dönitz had mounting concerns about his fleet being stretched too thin. His rise to chief of the navy did nothing to make him want to oblige Japan's appeal for a pair of German submarines, or to convert him into a proponent of using U-boats as long-distance transport ferries. His abiding conviction that they could win the war for Germany if used principally to cut off maritime lines of supply had not changed. "At the request of German Naval High Command the Japanese had started work on the technical preparations for a [submarine] base in Penang, and in the spring of 1943 had again expressed a wish for the dispatch of German U-boats," he would write. "But as long as opportunity to sink ships in the Atlantic existed I had refrained from accepting the Japanese offers."

Hitler himself was the final arbiter in that decision. The same month Dönitz got appointed to his new post, the Führer and his OKW war staff aligned against the grand admiral's protestations and ordered that Japan's emperor Hirohito was to be gifted with the German submarines. It was their belief that the IXC boats were superior combat vessels to any in the Japanese fleet, and that by reverse engineering them the imperial navy would have an increased capability to disrupt Allied shipping in the Pacific and Indian Oceans.

The first boat they sent was the U-511, which sailed for Japan in May 1943 on what would be her fourth and last patrol as a German naval vessel. Almost three months to the day after her departure, she pulled into Kure Harbor, where she was subsequently transferred to the IJN. On the last day of August, the Japanese imperial submarine I-8 arrived at U-boat base Brest, France, with a cargo of rubber, tin, and quinine, advanced Type 95 torpedoes and torpedo tubes, as well as plans for a Japanese aircraft and submarine trim system and two civilian engineers. Also aboard was a full secondary crew of forty-eight Japanese sailors. They would train on the next submarine Hitler had promised the emperor, U-1224, a new Type IX C40 tagged for transfer to the Japanese before she was even commissioned. Dönitz had stifled his objections and gone along with the scheme, although the idea of Aryan and Japanese crews working together on the same boat was less than ideal for him. "Our crews, who were used to European food, would not be able to exist on the types of food preferred by the Japanese," he would later write.*

---

*While Dönitz's claim that his submariners could not "exist" on Japanese food was both an exaggeration and a revealing insight into his cultural bias, there were indeed

In February 1944, the U-1224's specially trained Japanese crew sailed from Kiel for their homeland, but they were still in Atlantic waters—near the Azores archipelago—when an American destroyer sent them almost three thousand feet down to the abyss with mortar and depth-charge barrages.

Still, the U-511 and U-1224 were only two of the boats Dönitz saw as part of a broader stratagem. Long before the first of them set sail, he'd implemented a plan that would satisfy Hitler's demands for an ongoing submarine trade with Japan, and simultaneously spare any more U-boats from being designated as cargo bearers or production models for the imperial fleet. Although he'd seen no way around using submarines for the program, it had occurred to

---

profound differences between the German and Eastern-Pacific diets. In the 1940s they would have been considered mutually alien, unwholesome and incompatible.

The U.S. War Department Technical Manual TM-E 30 Handbook on Japanese Military Forces, 1 October 1944, lists the following foods as basic infantry rations; they would not have differed much, if at all, from submariners' fare:

Cereals and staples. Rice, wheat, barley, canned rice cakes, canned powdered rice dumplings, canned rice boiled together with red beans, biscuits {kanpan, a hardtack cracker}, vitamins, sugar, soy bean flour.

Canned meat and seafood. Beef, salmon, sardines, mackerel, seaweed, clams, trout, tuna fish, cod livers, seaweed and beans packed in layers, crab meat.

Dried meat and fish. Flounder, salmon, bonito, squid, cuttlefish, laver meat.

Canned fruits and vegetables. Tangerines, pineapples, bamboo sprouts, bean and burdock, boiled lotus, sprouted beans, arum root paste, spinach, bean flower, mixed vegetables, carrots.

Vegetables and fish in barrels. Pickled salted plums, pickled radishes, sea cucumbers in curry powder, smelts in oil.

Dried Fruits and vegetables. Apples, carrots, Chinese greens, red beans, onions, potato chips, mushrooms, squash, kelp.

Seasonings. Soy bean sauce, dehydrated soy bean sauce, soy bean paste, vinegar, curry powder, salt, ginger.

Beverages. Tea, sake, condensed milk.

him that they might not need to be of German origin. The Royal Italian Navy, it seemed, had provided him with convenient and viable substitutes.

Built as combat cruisers in Taranto's naval shipyards, Italy's twelve new Romolo-class subs had proven technically inferior to German boats—incapable of speedy dives and with bulky hull forms that made them easily detectible to Allied radar. Dönitz had hoped to deploy them with his Atlantic wolf packs but soon abandoned the thought, while acknowledging that they were too large to viably maneuver in shallow Mediterranean waters where Italy's Regia Marina (royal navy), operated. As he pondered how to some-

---

A contrasting example of the typical chow eaten by U-boat sailors may be taken from the U.S. Naval Intelligence Division's declassified Interrogation of Survivors of the Type V IIC submarine U-70 in April 1941. Appendix 1 of the document is a translated menu for the boat's expected 42-day combat patrol. For closest comparison with Japanese staples, which were mostly preserved, the three daily menu excerpts shown here were selected from the tail end of U-70's deployment, when the majority of fresh foodstuffs would have been exhausted, leaving canned and dried supplies, and whatever cured meats remained uneaten, as the primary ingredients. There were generally two prepared meals a day. All entries are for 1941, the year of the submarine's capture by the British.

Sunday *30 March* Corned beef, turnips, potatoes, fruit.

Cooked ham, bacon, one pickled cucumber, dripping ersatz {a kind of bread made of potato starch and low quality flour soaked in gravy}, bread, tea.

31 March Egg-flip {a mix of eggs, potatoes, and salami the Germans called hoppel poppel}

Tinned sausages, salt fish, butter, bread, tea.

1 April Lentils and bacon, one sausage, stewed fruit.

Sausage, cheese, butter, bread, cocoa.

It is no wonder, looking at the wide dissimilarities in Japan and Germany's respective seafood and meat-based cuisines, that neither country's sailors and passengers were eager to share berthing aboard long-range transports.

how withhold his U-boats from the transport program, Dönitz came up with a creative idea involving the Romolos.

Dönitz made his bid at the same late February naval conference in which he'd vainly objected to gifting Hirohito with IXC submarines, attempting to persuade Hitler that the best possible use of the Romolos would be as blockade runners. Ten of the subs were already operating out of German bases in France, so the process of converting them into transports could start almost at once, and be completed, he argued, within six weeks. To convince the Italians to agree to his plan, Dönitz suggested that Germany offer them an even exchange that guaranteed the replacement of each Romolo with a brand-new IXC boat.

Hitler initially balked at this proposal, insisting the Italian submarines were unreliable, and that the deal would fall lopsidedly in Rome's favor. Yet Dönitz's persistent lobbying soon led him to reverse his decision, with the caveat that the boats were to be manned by Italian crews. This, it was reasoned, would eliminate delays that would arise from having to retrain German personnel. The grand admiral, who prized his elite sailors almost as much as his U-boats, could not have been more in favor of that stipulation.

In March of that year the Italians agreed to the swap, and modification quickly commenced on seven of the boats. Two more that had been earmarked for the program were sunk before they could be refitted, while another was withheld because it was scheduled for patrol.

Starting out with sixty-ton cargo capacities, the seven Aquila—or Eagle—subs that received makeovers in dry dock at Bordeaux gained the ability to carry an additional 150 tons from German engineers. The alterations were finished right on target, and Aquilas I, II, and III—respectively the *Enrico Tazzoli,* the *Reginaldo Giuliani,* and the *Commandante Cappellini*—would all leave France in May, the very month U-511 left on her voyage to Japan. Aquilas V and VI—the *Barbarigo* and *Luigi Torelli*—followed in June, but that would be the end of things going smoothly for the program.

The departures of the remaining boats were stalled throughout the summer and fall, the first hitch coming when Italian dictator Benito Mussolini's government resigned in July, the second when Italy surrendered to the Allies in September. One submarine, the *Giuseppe Finzi,* was subsequently deemed unfit for the journey and scuttled. The *Alpino Bagnolini* did finally embark in 1944, but with German hands at her controls.

In the end, just three of the five original transoceanic submarines succeeded in reaching their Far Eastern destination, and none returned to Germany. Like the Yanagi boats, they were either sunk or captured by the Allies, making Dönitz's scheme a near-total disappointment from a German perspective.

By early 1944, this would leave him with a flock of nettlesome, interconnected, and somewhat contradictory problems. Paramount among them was Hitler's unrelenting demand to carry on the arms and technology trade with Japan and, indeed, intensify it with the delivery to Tokyo of parts and blueprints for Germany's most revolutionary secret weapons.

With the Allies closing in on Fortress Berlin, the Führer and his high command were more zealously adamant than ever about sidetracking the Americans by ratcheting up the pressure in the Pacific.

They had even agreed to send German engineers and technicians to Japan in order to jump-start the production of wonder weapons there—particularly aircraft such as the Komet that could present a heightened threat to U.S. air and naval forces.

Japan's sense of urgency was also reaching a crest. It had watched with trepidation the building of large airstrips in China and the Mariana Islands capable of supporting the deployment of long-range American B-29 Superfortress bombers, and feared its island nation might soon suffer similar attacks. Those misgivings were realized in late November, when 111 B-29s from the 21st Bomber Command at Saipan staged a daylight raid on the Musashino aircraft factory in Tokyo.

Although the strike was largely unsuccessful due to tactical miscalculations, the Japanese government viewed it as a sign of worse things to come and continued to lobby hard to procure German weapons technology, prioritizing design contracts for advanced jet- and rocket-fighter aircraft, and making it evident that it was willing to pay handsomely in gold, coin, and precious gems. If the speedy winged harriers were available to imperial armed forces, Japan believed it might yet reassert air supremacy over the Americans in the Pacific and win the war.

With German and Japanese goals meshing so completely, the German high command was adamant that the deliveries proceed apace, leaving Dönitz no choice except to carry out its orders. In fact, he had gradually come around to agreeing that a strengthened Japan could indeed divert the Americans, and that Germany might reap benefits from sending over technical and military personnel to study Japanese expertise in those same areas. He still hesitated to use German submarines for the job, but the failures of the Italian and Japanese boats had pared away his credible alternatives—and shaped new questions in his mind about why so many of the transport missions had met with Allied interdiction.

Dönitz had become wary of the Enigma code being compromised after the sinking of the *Bismarck* in May 1941, having learned the British had intercepted the great battleship's escort and supply convoy. His apprehensions would deepen following a second incident in early October, when a Royal Navy submarine seemed to materialize out of nowhere to disrupt the rendezvous of three German submarines in Tarrafal Bay, off the west coast of Africa. The unexpected British appearance in Tarrafal struck Dönitz as no accident, and led him to worry that the Brits had located their targets by deciphering coded ship-to-ship radio transmissions.

Immediately after that attack, Dönitz instructed his chief of naval communications, Rear Admiral Eberhard Maertens, to determine whether there had been a breach of Enigma security. Within three weeks, Maertens would issue a blanket dismissal of that theory in a report to Dönitz and the naval high command, blaming the success of the British strikes on the enemy's superior aerial reconnaissance. But Dönitz clung to his suspicions despite Maertens's reassurances and promptly began seeking out ways to upgrade Enigma's capacities.

The code machine itself looked like a cousin of a manual typewriter built into a wooden box. It was meant to be carried by a single person, though early models weighed over a hundred pounds, and subsequent variants weren't much lighter. The first Enigmas utilized removable hard rubber Bakelite print wheels, or rotors, that slotted into the device and transferred the ciphertext characters on their rims to a paper ribbon. A selection of between five and eight rotors was provided for the machine's three available slots, and Dönitz's naval protocols stipulated that their installation remain the sole duty of men with officer's rankings.

The rest of the procedures were delegated to the radiomen, who had fairly long checklists for each and every transmission. Enigma operators were issued codebooks with key settings for a specified time period; changes were initially made once a month, but their frequency increased over the course of the war. The key settings indicated which rotors were to be used, their order of insertion into the units, and the starting positions for each of the rotors in its respective slot. A grooved outer finger wheel was used to turn the rotors into position.

Before a coded message was sent, the settings also had to be changed on an external electric plug board, or *Steckerbrett,* that bore certain similarities to telephone operators' switchboards of the day. The plug board's pairs of alphanumeric characters were connected by patch cables with jacks at either end, and the operators would manually switch the jacks to change the connections between characters, again using settings specified in their code manuals. A radio operator patching the letter *A,* say, into the letter *T* meant that *T* would be substituted for *A* when he typed in a message, giving it an added layer of encryption.

In February 1942, Dönitz had exponentially strengthened the

Kriegsmarine's encryption security with his introduction of the Enigma M4, a four-rotor model the admiral reserved for use by his U-boat command. Even before it was put into operation, improvements had been made to the three-rotor version, increasing its selection of rotors from five to eight. But that alone had not satisfied Dönitz, who'd demanded and gotten more comprehensive modifications.

The M4 variant's arrival marked the start of better days for the Kriegsmarine, and Dönitz was too bright to dismiss it as simple coincidence. In his mind there had to be a link between the implementation of his new Enigma machine and the enemy's sudden blindness to his submarines' patrols and convoy attacks.

As it turned out, however, that reprieve wasn't to last. By December, and heading into the winter of 1943, the Allies once again seemed to be aware of every move his wolf packs made in the Atlantic. For the second time in less than two years, Dönitz looked toward a breach of Enigma's security as the reason.

Maertens still refused to accept the possibility. This time he would attribute Allied successes to coast watching and intelligence sharing by the French underground, along with a new precision air-to-surface radar that had been jointly developed by British and American scientists—and discovered aboard a downed RAF Pathfinder bomber whose wreckage had been picked apart in the Netherlands. He assured Dönitz that the situation could be remedied by employing proper tactical and procedural countermeasures, especially with an advanced generation of streamlined, snorkel-equipped XXI and XXIII "Electroboats" (so called because they used arrays of large and powerful batteries to push their engines to high speeds) under construction at Bremen and Danzig, and snorkel retrofits available for the IXC and IXD long-range submarines. Once the ultramodern Electroboats were integrated into the fleet, and the older boats received their snorkel upgrades, it would represent a total overhaul of the submarine force. With their sleek contours and reduced radar silhouettes, the XXI and XXIII E-boats would be nearly undetectable to radar and elusive targets for sonar. Beyond that, all the snorkel boats would cover vast stretches of the ocean without having to surface to draw air into their diesels.

In the end, the Pathfinder evidence mollified Dönitz. He would accept Maertens's latest findings, which gave him a basis for confidence that his IXC and IXD boats could be employed as round-trip transports to Japan.

Now, in 1944, Dönitz also had a fresh angle to play. In his negotiations with Tokyo, he had arranged for a technical section to be established in Japan, and laid the groundwork for the arrival of officers who would study Japanese air-navy tactics and technology. Always quick on his feet, the "wily submarine warfare wizard" had reassessed his once-firm position based on changing circumstances. If his submarines must be sent to Japan, he would see that Germany's naval forces drew the maximum benefit from it. With the war at a critical stage, he knew what was necessary to cut his losses and protect his fleet against British and American attack.

It was what Dönitz did not know—or more correctly what he did not know about what the enemy knew—that would eventually hurt him.

2.

Her snorkel installed, U-864 would now have to be prepared to store the mercury coming aboard for her voyage.

The shipment was of the greatest possible value to the Japanese. Used as a primer in their explosive detonators and other military and civilian devices, the mercury had been part of the expected cargo for I-52's never-to-occur homebound trip, and the delay in receiving it had left them increasingly impatient. With virtually no natural deposits of mercury-bearing minerals, Japan had become reliant on the Germans for its supply, and between 1944 and 1945 purchased 927 tons that were exported to the Far East on submarines sent to bases in Singapore and Indonesia (although barely more than a third of what was shipped would reach its destination due to Allied air and naval interdiction).

The amount to be placed aboard U-864 was only a fraction of the three hundred tons Japan desired to buy from the Germans, who had in turn purchased an even larger quantity from the miners of northern Italy. Fearing its availability would diminish as Axis fortunes in Europe worsened, Tokyo's goal was to acquire as much as possible with all due urgency.

The preparatory work on the boat, and perhaps the loading itself, was begun in Stettin on October 19, 1944 after she left the Bay of Danzig, where U-boats would be put through a series of rigorous acceptance and approval drills before being certified as seaworthy— among them torpedo firing trials and tactical workouts such as rudder and speed tests, timed crash dives, and mock convoy attacks. At about this time, Commander Wolfram and his closest officers received their operational orders—that is, were informed of their imminent trip to the Far East and the cargo they were to deliver. While the boat's noncommissioned officers and seamen would not be told of their destination until after she had departed from Kiel, many picked up clues through circulating rumors, as Willi Transier would divulge to his new fiancée in their private interludes.

The Type IX D2 submarine, while a formidable battle cruiser, was suitable for a dual role as a transport, having been designed with a stowage hold in the keel between the boat's hydrodynamic outer skin and the inner pressure hull that enclosed the crew, machinery, and torpedo rooms. This keel hold ran for more than two-thirds of the submarine's length and had a removable side that allowed for the loading of eighty to a hundred tons of rectangular lead weights used in normal ballast.

There were limitations to what the hold might carry; it was unpressurized and therefore not watertight, so anything that could be damaged by seawater—food supplies and machinery, for example—would have been stored inside the pressure hull. That left it available for raw metals and ore; diamonds, gold, or coins delivered for payment of received matériel; and goods such as rubber and tin that would have been brought aboard on a return trip.

The U-864's surviving *kriegstagebücher,* or war logs, give no specific details of how the hold was altered to accommodate the outbound mercury, stating only that she received "remaining shipyard work and installation of the Monsun load container." But the bricklike iron ballast weights that typically sat stacked on flat platforms in the keel would have had to be removed and replaced with cargo, and this left some technical issues to consider. The substitution had to be carefully done; the amount of fixed weight needed to keep a submarine level in the water was determined by using a precise set of buoyancy ratios, and these were scrupulously calculated by professionals. In Stettin, it would have been handled by the AG Vulcan shipbuilding firm, which had been based there since the 1800s.

As a further consideration, the ballast had to be properly distributed and stabilized so it didn't shift around within the hold and cause the boat to tip forward or backward. This was simple enough with the uniformly stackable iron bricks, but the mercury had been stored in 1,857 molded and welded steel canisters, many of them cylindrical, others flask-shaped.

It is possible that racks or some other means of keeping the canisters steady were installed at the Stettin shipyards. But the sunken wreck of another German submarine suggests that the mercury canisters rode in steel chests called box lockers and stood upright, held in position by a special strap rigging. The box lockers could then have been preloaded and put aboard the sub fairly quickly with a minimum of trouble.

Located on the banks of the Oder River, Stettin, a Polish city by origin, had been part of the Prussian Empire for the better part of a millennium. In the 1940s, it became an industrial center for the Reich, home to a motorized infantry division and its third largest port after Hamburg and Berlin. While under Gestapo control, it would come to have more than a hundred slave labor camps where members of the city's Polish minority, Jews, Russians, Belgians, and French POWs were forced to work in its factories or serve as prostitutes for the German military.

By winter 1944, Stettin, like most German naval ports, had become
the target of repeated Allied air strikes, and their poundings had left its
medieval squares bombed-out ruins. But if the years when it had been
a lure to visiting sailors had passed, the submarine crews could still find
places for entertainment after the completion of arduous maneuvers.
Sailors were typically given leave while their boats underwent work at
the base, and U-864's hands were no exception to the rule. Whether
the sub's keel hold was altered, filled with box lockers of mercury, or
both, the yard stay would give her crew a few weeks to drink and carry
on at local bars and brothels while MPs looked the other way, then
sleep off their hangovers in the relative comfort of barracks ashore.

On November 4, Korvettenkapitän Wolfram left a note of
appreciation in the 4th Flotilla's guest book, as was traditional for
a visiting U-boat commander on behalf of his boat and crew. With
his large, bold signature written above those of his leading officers,
Wolfram's words seem to reveal that the danger of the mission to
Japan was already bearing heavily on his thoughts.

If we now go on patrol into uncharted regions, then we want to
say "Thank You" to the 4.U-Flottile for your hospitality. With the
crew of U-864:

Ralf-Reimer Wolfram Korv.Kpt.uKmdt
Franz Eckhardt Kptl.(Ing)u.L.I. [WI Lt (Ing.)]
Hubert Freiherr von Loe Ob.Ltnt.u.1.W.O.
Friedrich Reeay, Dr Stbs.Arzt (MarSt Arzt)
Heinz Sauerbier Ltnt.z.S.u.2.WO.
Wolfgang Auerbach Ltnt.(Ing) [WI: Lt (Ing.)]

November 7 saw the completion of the work on U-864's hold, after which the submarine moved on for flak training in the nearby Swinemünde antiaircraft school's offshore practice range. A new twin-barreled 37mm AA cannon was fitted onto her conning tower's railed wintergarten deck, probably replacing a single-barreled gun, but the flak crew became ill with diarrhea and their exercises were cut short.

On November 11, after being away from her home port for several weeks, U-864 left the Swinemünde training grounds for Kiel and pulled in later that day. There she technically remained under the administrative umbrella of the 5th Unterseebootsflottille, a submarine training group, while gearing up for her January mission to East Asia.

That same day, a Type VIIC attack submarine designated U-771 was returning to Narvik after a failed strike on a large British-American convoy steaming from Loch Ewe, Scotland, to Murmansk in northern Russia. U-771 was normally tasked with patrolling Norway's coastal waters to defend against possible Allied invaders, but had forayed after the convoy with the ad hoc Wolfpack Panther, which had been hastily assembled to take out the Arctic-bound vessels.

Before it could reach base, U-771 was picked up by a British sub in the middle of its own special operation in the area. Lieutenant Andy Chalmers, Jimmy Launders's second in command aboard the HMS *Venturer,* had quite unexpectedly sighted her through his periscope.

Only one of the submarines would survive their meeting.

CHAPTER FIVE

HANGMAN

1.

Oberleutnant zur See Helmut Block was just a week shy of his one-year anniversary as commander of U-771 when he'd brought the boat in toward Narvik after a long, rough turn at sea.

Commissioned on November 18, 1943, U-771 had undergone six months of training maneuvers before she was finally assigned to the 9th Flotilla at Brest in northwestern France. But soon after reaching the base in late June, Block was ordered to sail her north to Norwegian waters and join Gruppe Mitte as a reinforcement.

Mitte itself had only been in existence a short time. On the heels of his promotion to commander in chief of the navy, Admiral Dönitz had made it plain that he felt an Allied assault on Norway would precede their invasion of Western Europe. His thoughts were not unsound; Dönitz's intelligence sources had long warned that British prime minster Winston Churchill would view this as the best way to cut off lines of supply and communication to Germany's vital Baltic ports. Back in 1940, in fact, that very belief had led the Germans to launch their takeover of Norway with Operation Weserübung.

In anticipation of the invasion, Dönitz had decided to create two underwater shields around the probable enemy landing zones. But the grand admiral had by now lost faith in the ability of nonsnorkel boats to conduct successful operations in RAF-patrolled western waters; Rear Admiral Maertens had fully persuaded him that without snorkel retrofits and the introduction of Electroboats, the German submarine fleet would remain vulnerable to the British precision radar on which he blamed their earlier defeats.

The problem was that Dönitz could not dock all his VIICs, the workhorses of the fleet, for upgrades at once. His temporary solution, then, was to optimize their deployments until his improvements could be fully implemented. Deciding that the nonsnorkel versions would be best suited to shorter patrols in the northern theater of operations, he had created Gruppe Mitte in February 1944, sending ten of the boats to guard the Norwegian coast. A month later, he'd ordered the formation of a second defensive patrol in the Bay of Biscay, calling this concentration of fifteen submarines Gruppe Landwirt. Both groups would soon be strengthened, with the number of boats in Mitte swelling to twenty-two and in Landwirt to thirty-six or thirty-seven by late spring. A day after the completion of her training maneuvers in Hamburg, U-771 would be assigned to the 9th flotilla at Brest, then join the U-boats sent to tighten the defenses around Norway in relief of snorkel boats that had been shifted out to Biscay.

Dönitz had meant to provide all Landwirt boats with snorkels and enhanced radar detection capabilities before the Allies struck, but his goal was not to be realized. On June 5–6, the Allies surprised him and the rest of the Wehrmacht with their assault on Normandy, leaving the admiral with no choice but to hasten the subs into action. In the Bay of Biscay, Gruppe Landwirt and nineteen other boats were ordered into a defensive line between the French ports—and U-boat bases—of Saint-Nazaire, Lorient, and La Pallice. Meanwhile, Group Mitte was told to stay ready in port for possible invasion forces. As the German tactical command's war log for that period stated, "An L.S.T. [Allied landing craft] sunk in the invasion area is . . . more important than a Liberty ship sunk in the Atlantic."

Near the end of June, U-771 left the southern Norwegian city of Stavanger on her first war patrol. In contrast to the organized, cohesive wolf packs that had been Dönitz's greatest tactical innovation, the group's submarines were instructed to range widely along the coast to avoid Allied antisubmarine flights while searching out supply and attack convoys. Late on his fourth day of patrol, Oberleutnant Block would see his only real combat before the fateful encounter with *Venturer* that coming fall.

It happened shortly before midnight on June 26. On a reconnaissance flight out of Tain in the Scottish Highlands, a Consolidated Liberator III sub hunter from the RAF Coastal Command's No. 86 Squadron had spotted the U-771 off to its east, moving in loose tandem with the U-317, a second Gruppe Mitte VIIC submarine. Without snorkels to allow them to recharge their batteries while submerged, the U-boats were on the surface taking in air under cover of night.

The Liberator, coded N, had been scheduled for a morning sortie, but there was a maintenance problem an hour into the mission— its starboard wing tank was leaking fuel. At about 0700 it had returned to base to get patched up, and then left the runway again at dusk with a new pilot, Lieutenant G. W. T. Parker, in command of its crew of eight.

At 2320 hours Parker had sighted the U-boats from about five miles off. His Leigh searchlights beaming from their wing nacelles, he brought the aircraft down over the U-371, his gunners strafing her with their 7.7mm Browning nose and waist guns. Although neither German submarine attempted a crash dive, the bright circles of the plane's oncoming carbon arcs had given their flak teams ample time to man their guns.

Opening fire, flak teams on both submarines struggled to lock onto the British aircraft in the blinding glare of its Leighs, their guns swiveling back and forth to send up wide bands of tracers and ammunition. With the AA volleys pecking at his flanks, Parker pulled sharply up out of range of the weapons and ordered his crew to prepare their depth charges.

On his second pass Parker dropped a rack of three 250-pound charges to the U-317's starboard from low overhead. Their detonation slammed the boat with a pressure wave that rolled her to port and plunged the flak gunners on her bridge overboard into the black, churning sea. Within moments she began to spiral into the depths, taking the rest of her fifty hands down with her.

Aboard U-771, Oberleutnant Block was informed that the British aircraft had taken multiple hits—and though he could not have known it, the volleys had inflicted a grave wound. One of the Liberator's major design problems was the nearness of its fuel tanks to exposed upper sections of the fuselage, and Lieutenant Parker's number three tank had been punctured beneath the plane's lightweight outer skin. With his plane hemorrhaging gasoline and oil, Parker knew he would have to head home to Tain at once or crash into the same dark waters that had swallowed the German submarine.

Banking west as he departed in haste, Parker had glanced down at the spot where the depth-charged U-boat had capsized, his carbon arcs lensing through the mist. Their ninety-million-candle brilliance revealed bodies afloat on the water's surface in a large, spreading patch of oil. The submarine was no longer in sight.

With near-whiteout conditions outside his cockpit windows and his tanks continuing to bleed fuel and oil, Parker had been forced to abort his return to base and nursed the crippled Liberator to an emergency landing at the RAF station in Stornaway, in the Outer Hebrides, where the aircraft was judged to be damaged beyond repair. In the confusion of the firefight—perhaps due in part to limited visibility—he'd mistakenly thought only the U-317 had struck him with antiaircraft fire. But Block's war diary would record the role his submarine played in disabling the English bomber.

A few weeks after that engagement, the Allied aerial harassment of German submarines along Norway's coast would cause more problems for U-771. On August 2, she and yet another Mitte boat, U-1163, were being transferred from Stavanger to Kristiansand, moving on the surface under escort, when they were attacked by a pair of de Havilland Mosquitoes from the RAF No. 333 Squadron.

Flown by exiled Norwegian air-force pilots based in Banff, Scotland, the RAF outriders came swooping down on the subs off Obrestad in the North Sea. Beset by heavy flak from the escorts, one of the planes dove in too low, clipped U-771's extended radio mast, and went veering out of control into the ocean, where its pilot and copilot perished in the crash. The other Mosquito aborted the strike and returned to base.

By German accounts, neither U-boat was seriously damaged. But repairs on U-771 must have been needed and were probably what kept her close to shore until October 14, when she was sent out with the Wolfpack Panther on her second war patrol.

The Allied convoy designated JW 61 was composed of twenty-nine cargo ships along with two oilers and a rescue vessel to sustain them en route from Great Britain to Russia's Arctic reaches. Their supplies were going to Stalin through U.S. president Franklin D. Roosevelt's lend-lease program, and many of the steamers had in fact originated in New York City, harboring briefly in England before they embarked with the convoy.

With the Mitte U-boats presenting an increased threat in northern waters, a group as massive as JW 61 demanded an accordingly formidable escort. Seven destroyers, three corvettes, two sloops, a dozen frigates, a light cruiser, and three aircraft carriers were assembled—the carriers bearing a mix of Wildcat and Swordfish attack planes and Grumman Avenger torpedo bombers. The Russians would add a half dozen of their BO-2 sub chasers—heavily armed and equipped with their latest radars— to the protective shield.

Over the next two weeks, JW 61 would pass directly through the teeth of Wolfpack Panther, which harried it across the Arctic Circle to the Kola Peninsula. But its defenses were too much for the U-boats to penetrate and the subs were repeatedly thwarted. On October 28, the convoy safely reached the Kola inlet and the U-boat pack was spread over a wider patrol range. In the Barents Sea about a week later, U-771 and two other Mitte boats attempted raids on a much smaller Allied convoy but were again repulsed by its escorts, likely the same BO-2s that had guarded JW 61.

Oberleutnant Block and his crew turned back toward Norway on November 8 and within three days reached the northwestern coast, where they would surface on a course for the U-boat base at Narvik. Unshaven and rumpled, pale as ghosts after almost a month in the submarine's cold, airless confines, exhausted from the stress of their patrol and a lack of fresh food and exercise, they would to a man have had nothing on their minds but the prospect of some coveted shore leave as they approached Narvik under a thin sliver of moon, preparing to wend their way to base through the narrow coastal channels.

They did not suspect that they had come very near a submerged British submarine as they entered the Andfjord, off the mainland . . . or that the enemy boat, there on its own clandestine business, had spotted them from a near distance and was already gliding in for its kill.

2.

Dundee-Lerwick was calling it Operation Hangman, and its purpose was to choke off German shipping in the northern theater once and for all.

For years the Shetland Bus had been shuttling supplies and landing agents to assist Norway's underground resistance, of which the coastal observers were an indispensable and irreplaceable component. At Lunna Ness, the sound provided a sheltered, tucked-away anchorage for the fishing boats, while the manor itself gave Lieutenant Howarth and his sailors lodging, and its outbuildings stored equipment for the boats and what Howarth later described as "a small standing stock of sabateurs' [*sic*] implements—explosive, fuses and firing devices of different kinds, incendiary bombs, hand grenades, and such things as knuckle dusters [brass knuckles], Benzedrine tablets, compasses, torches, maps and Norwegian clothes." There was also a stockpile of radio transmitters, batteries, and spare parts, as well as Norwegian currency and items like cigarettes and plug tobacco that had become scarce wartime commodities for the captive public and could be exchanged for various necessities.

The Benzedrine pills were used to help tired Norwegian agents stay alert under dangerous circumstances, but Shetland Bus crews also popped them to stem fatigue during their runs. From the beginning, these were conducted in the dead of winter, when the Scandinavian nights offered long hours of darkness as cover. A motorboat would depart the slips at Lunna Ness, navigate the reefs and sea stacks beyond the entrance to the sound, then head out to sea for a two-day journey to Norway. Once there, it would putter into the maze of grooved, whorled inlets along the coast, lower anchor, and release a dinghy or lifeboat. A light flashing out of the blackness on the shore, a prearranged response from the boat, and the sailors aboard would silently make their delivery to the resistance members awaiting their arrival.

The Germans were fully aware of the surreptitious drops, just as they knew the supplies were brought over from the Shetlands by camouflaged fishing boats. But the innumerable watery channels used for the runs cut into hundreds of miles of shoreline and were difficult if not impossible for the occupiers to effectively patrol.

Over time their countermeasures came to include building up coastal defenses and intimidation of the Norwegian populace. By 1944, the Germans had set up watch posts at lighthouses and other sites traveled by the Shetlanders. What was more, they had assumed some of the chameleon's colors and converted civilian fishing trawlers into *Vorpostenboote,* or outpost boats, to guard the likeliest marine approaches to the coast.

With Dundee submarines using part of Lerwick's North Ness as a refuel and provision depot, it was almost inevitable that the Ambrose commanders and RNNSU would join forces for their operations. Being on the same side was the plainest reason, but working together offered important reciprocal benefits for the two service arms. A submarine was able to elude enemy lookouts as no surface craft could, making the supply deliveries and personnel landings easier as the Germans tightened security. Meanwhile, the firsthand observations of coast watchers could be relayed to Dundee's subs almost at once as opposed to information taking days or longer to come over from London. And the speedy receipt of intel wasn't the only plus; it would have been difficult to imagine a more accurate and reliable tracking of ship movements than the sort done by spies on the ground and water who could keep close visual tabs on the loading, arrivals, and departures of convoys and patrols.

On November 4, Jimmy Launders took HMS *Venturer* out of Dundee on Operation Hangman, stopped at Lerwick for supplies to be delivered to the observers, and then sailed on across the North Sea toward the Norwegian coast. The sub's area of resupply was Narvik, where the surveillance of German merchant and Kriegsmarine vessels was a particularly important and dangerous affair.

For a pair of reasons, the city of Narvik had become a highly strategic center of maritime goings-on for the Nazi invaders. Since the turn of the century, its Ofotbanen railway had been a direct, nonstop link to the iron ore fields of Kiruna, Sweden, far to the snowy north, with the city's ice-free harbor having been the impetus for the line's construction. In a watery cul-de-sac that protected it from freezing over, the port allowed the Nazis to transfer their freight from Ofotbanen railcars to cargo ships year-round, and then bring them on from there to end points in Germany. The sheltered harbor also spared navy warships from having to endure the worst of the northern elements—and screened them from Allied surveillance and sabotage.

By 0735 on the night of the eleventh, *Venturer* was moving submerged near the Lofoten Islands as she arrived for her rendezvous outside the vital port city. Upon reaching the drop point, Launders would surface and have one of his men flash a signal from the submarine's deck, then await a response from shore for a predesignated interval. If it came, he would order the landing to be conducted as planned. Otherwise, he would assume the resistance members had either been delayed or assessed conditions onshore as being too hazardous for the drop, in which case *Venturer* would slip back underwater and return after sunset the next day. These attempts could be repeated through the new moon cycle, after which the brightening night sky would force them to be called off.

Venturer was near the entrance to Andfjord, a fifty-five-mile-long body of water running between the Lofotens' craggy bluffs, when Sub-Lieutenant Peter C. Brand spotted the conning tower of another submarine through the search periscope. He'd been taking turns at the viewer with First Lieutenant Chalmers, who was officer of the watch, and Chalmers quickly stepped over to relieve him. With the moon on the wane and sheaths of fog drifting over the water, it was a challenge to discern anything even at that close distance, but Brand's experienced eye managed to identify the sub as a 740-ton German U-boat. It was a few thousand yards away, moving on the surface at a good clip.

Alerted in his quarters, Launders hurried to the control room, snatched a look at the sub, and then quickly requested estimates of its speed, range, and bearings from his first officer. Chalmers judged it was doing a brisk thirteen knots as it traveled south entering the Andfjord in the darkness and mist—putting it at close to top speed.

Its course indicated it was heading toward Narvik . . . or perhaps Kilbotn, a speck of a village to its south that the Nazis were using as a submarine depot.

By now Launders's cool, level composure under pressure had bred incredible confidence among his crewmen. But many senior hands were especially impressed by another of his traits: a head for mathematics that translated into a special knack, even genius, for plotting out trajectories and firing positions.

Launders set about the calculations at once, ordering Chalmers to handle the boat and close with the German sub.

Venturer quickly knifed to within about two thousand yards of her. Peering through his viewer, Launders listened to Telegraphist John S. Byrne, the periscope assistant, give him a final set of bearings as the U-boat was aligned in his crosshairs. Meanwhile in the torpedo room, able seamen Harry Plummer and John McDougall had readied the torpedoes under the direction of their crew chief, hastily resetting their depth controls for the fjord's approximate water level and loading them into their bow tubes. All they had left to do now was await the skipper's firing command.

It came just six minutes after the target had been sighted. On Launders's typically calm orders, a spread of four torpedoes launched from *Venturer*'s bow tubes traveling at speeds that ranged between forty to forty-five knots. Ninety seconds later a loud, rumbling explosion was heard through the British sub's hull and ASDIC* sonar receivers.

---

* British sonar. Its name was taken from the Allied Submarine Detection Intelligence Committee that developed it.

The detonation was followed by what World War II submariners would describe as the most gruesome of sounds—the rending metallic groan of a boat breaking up, and then the smaller crackles of her batteries blowing apart in her flooded compartments. Chilled to a man, the members of *Venturer*'s crew knew that they were listening to the death throes of a submarine and all hands aboard.

And that it could as easily have been them.

3.

Oberleutnant Block would have had virtually no time to react, no realistic possibility of ordering evasive maneuvers or a crash dive. Likelier than not, his hydrophone operator didn't have a chance to warn him of the incoming torpedoes.

Each Mark VIII carried a 750-pound Torpex warhead, and when they struck U-771, its crew would have been deafened by the roar of the blasts as the submarine's pressure hull was breached and the explosive shock waves threw them off their feet. As seawater came rushing through the sub's compartments, washing over the men in icy torrents, most would have suffered an immediate loss of consciousness. With cold shock the heart's temperature plummets, the contractions of its chambers stop, and the victim perishes even before drowning. If the gasping reaction is triggered and the lungs fill with water, death will be significantly quickened.

Few if any of the fifty-one casualties of war aboard the boat would have known what hit them.

4.

Lieutenant Launders held *Venturer* in position underwater for a short while after the lethal strike, Chalmers making 360-degree scans through his periscope in the cramped control room. It wasn't long before he noticed fishing trawlers off to their south, a serious concern for his skipper. Although Launders wanted a close-up look at the German boat to verify its destruction—and see if there was anything interesting in its wreckage—he knew the trawlers would be indistinguishable from the outpost boats seized as booty from conquered Norwegians. The Germans also had dedicated sub chasers called *Kreigscutteren* in the area; modeled after the durable civilian trawlers, they, too, could easily have been mistaken for harmless fishing vessels.

Deciding an inspection would be an unacceptable risk, Launders finally ordered his submarine to leave the fjord on a swift northward course. His foremost priorities were the safety of his crew and their still-to-be-made supply run to the coast watchers.

The wind had departed, and the fog fled with it, when *Venturer* returned to Andfjord the next night, surfacing in the darkened waterway chosen for the rendezvous. A brief exchange of signals confirmed that their resistance contacts were waiting in readiness. Then an inflatable dinghy dropped into the water from the submarine's deck, the sailors assigned to carry out the drop quietly slipping down into it.

Byrne, the leading telegraphist and periscope attendant, was in charge of the small landing party, with Lieutenant Brand, whose courage and resourcefulness under fire had by now earned his captain's deep trust, joining him as second officer.

After the crated supplies were lowered into the dinghy, the group untied their mooring rope and paddled ashore in the clear, cold darkness. Behind them, lookouts on the bridge of the submarine stood with binoculars raised to their eyes, watching for signs of German patrol craft or movements beyond the water's edge.

Nothing of that nature occurred. The dinghy's occupants made their landing, transferred their load to shore, and returned to the submarine. Getting into and out of the rubber craft, a tricky business in the darkness and frigid currents, left several of the crewmen soaked and shivering in their clothes, but that was the worst of it for them. Their mission successfully carried out, they returned to *Venturer* without incident, and were soon homeward bound for Lerwick.

It was now the night of November 12, the day after U-864 arrived in Kiel.

On opposite sides of a conflict that was rapidly coming to a critical juncture, the subs would spend the next few weeks in separate harbors being readied for their upcoming patrols.

CHAPTER SIX

IN STRICTEST SECRECY

1.

Although Lieutenant Sven Plass was among the core group of German naval officers assigned to the new Japanese technical office, he hadn't been slotted to make the trip with U-864. It was, in fact, only his country's rapidly declining wartime fortunes that put him aboard her.

Admiral Dönitz's bid to install Plass in Tokyo was cabled on December 13, 1944, eight days after the submarine left Kiel, and four days after its arrival at Horten for deep-diving and snorkel certification trials. Because Dönitz wanted a comprehensive study of the imperial fleet's procedures and technological expertise, he had personally selected ten Kriegsmarine officers—eight fleet commanders and two engineering officers—on the basis of their diversified service histories and fields of expertise. These men were listed as Lieutenant Richard Bulla, naval aviator; Lieutenant Hans Reimer German, navigation expert; Lieutenant Commander Robert Kopp, communications expert; Lieutenant Jobst Hahndorf, fire control specialist; Lieutenant Heinrich Peter-Pirkham, torpedo boat tactician; Lieutenant (jg) Heinrich Hellendorn, antiaircraft specialist; Lieutenant Commander Kurt Ziegler, diesel-motor specialist; Lieutenant Commander Karl Nuber, high-pressure steam specialist; and Lieutenant Plass, who is called an ordnance specialist in the surviving communiqués.

Plass's background alone indicates that more went into Dönitz's selection process than first meets the eye. Christened Sven Otto Nils, he was born three months before the end of the First World War on August 12, 1918. His first name had been chosen to honor his Swedish mother, Maja, and his second name, Otto, was taken from his maternal grandfather.

Sven's father, Dr. Ludolf Plass, was the executive director of the AG and Lurgi Metals Company in Frankfurt, which had been engaged in cooperative industrial projects with Japan since before the start of World War II; Lurgi's expanding patents involved the production of diesel oil, gasoline, and advanced synthetic fuels, all of which were of great interest to the Imperial Navy. So close was Lurgi's relationship with Japan that it had a branch office in Tokyo, where it had formed a partner group called Nippon Lurgi Goshi KK. After the war, Lurgi was targeted for investigation by the Combined Intelligence Objectives Subcommittee of the United States and United Kingdom, formed to share and analyze information about Germany's secret munitions programs, which included the development of biological, chemical, and atomic weapons of mass destruction.

Growing up in the prosperous, countrified village of Schönberg outside Frankfurt, Sven, the second of three children, was an intelligent, quick-witted boy—"easygoing yet purposeful," his father called him—whose popularity and good grades came almost effortlessly. Ludolf's international business dealings brought many foreign guests to his home—and with them regular offers to visit their families abroad. Coupled with those invitations, Sven's parents placed great emphasis on broadening his horizons, and he'd spent six months at a high school in Switzerland on an exchange program, vacationed in England and France with his parents, and often visited relatives in Sweden. Besides his native German, he spoke all three of those nations' languages and would become fluent in Spanish during his naval officer's training.

That training began in 1937, when Plass, then nineteen, joined the Kriegsmarine as a petty officer, urged by a friend whose father was a highly ranked commander in the fleet. His experiences as a cadet would take him on sailing voyages that spanned the Atlantic Ocean and led around Africa to the Far East.

After the outbreak of World War II—and the death of his mother after a protracted, painful illness—Plass quickly rose through the naval ranks with promotions to second and then first lieutenant, receiving decorations for action against the British as a chief gunner on the battleship *Scharnhorst*. In February 1942, under heavy bombing, the *Scharnhorst* and another battle cruiser of its class, the *Gneisenau,* made a daylight breakout from Brest, France, to Germany with a bold dash through the English Channel that earned Plass the Iron Cross First Class and a promotion to commander.

He was subsequently stationed in Kiel, where he met his future wife, Elisabeth Grauhan, the daughter of a prominent surgeon and professor at Kiel University. Lilly was studying physical therapy at the time, and Plass, a dashing sight in his crisp, beribboned officer's uniform, would quickly snag her attention with his lively sense of humor and rousing stories of naval combat.

According to her sister Antje—the youngest of four siblings—Lilly and Sven's early mutual attraction would flower into romance one day when they were boarding a sailboat for a pleasure cruise around Kiel Harbor. "Lilly got her foot caught between the boat and the pier, Sven picked her up, and there the spark was ignited," she recalled over half a century later.

On June 27, 1943, Lilly and Sven were wed in the small town of Senftenberg near the Polish border, where the Grauhan family had resettled because of increasingly frequent and destructive RAF air strikes on Kiel. As fate would have it, the *Scharnhorst* was sunk by the British six months later in the Battle of the North Cape—coincidentally the same humiliating defeat that would result in Hitler's furious dismissal of Grand Admiral Raeder, and his replacement by Karl Dönitz as head of the navy. Plass, who had been on leave at the time, was transferred to an upper-echelon ground post at Kiel, where he and his bride rented an apartment in the home of married friends.

But the war was drawing closer and closer to them. British planes would storm overhead with increasing regularity, day and night, their sorties leaving large sections of the city in bombed-out, fiery ruins, the smoke sometimes shrouding the dockyards from sight. When Lilly discovered she was pregnant, she and Sven reluctantly decided it would be best that she go stay with her mother and father in Senftenberg.

It proved a wise, almost premonitory decision: Shortly after she left, their residence and everything they owned was obliterated by an air strike; Lilly would hear afterward that the couple who owned it were killed in the bombing.

Once again, Plass had the good luck of being elsewhere when the catastrophic blow struck. Over the next six months he worked diligently at the expanding spectrum of responsibilities that had come with his advancement, taking leaves whenever possible to visit his spouse and in-laws in Senftenberg. In a letter written after the war, Plass's father mentions his "wide-ranging education, his knowledge of languages and his ease in dealing with people," as reasons why Sven was particularly suited to this new administrative career. He also wrote that his son was on several occasions summoned to the ministry in Berlin—probably referring to the Foreign Office. No records exist to explain why Sven was called on for those visits, but he was informed during this period that he was in line for an appointment to the diplomatic service, an opportunity he very much felt would bode well for his future.

As Ludolf Plass recollected: "Sven welcomed this idea, since in the long term this sort of work was more important to him than purely military activities." A proud father, the senior Plass perhaps felt his son was being groomed for a diplomatic post entirely on his own merits. But Sven's family connections to Lurgi and the state-controlled Japanese fuel and chemical technologies industry must have been influential in making him an attractive candidate—especially in light of the pressure being applied on Admiral Dönitz to ramp up the pace of the exchange program with Japan.

While Plass tended to his duties, Lilly carried their child to term in Senftenberg. Their daughter Maja, named after Sven's late mother, was born on June 28, 1944, almost exactly a year after Lilly and Sven had their large, festive wedding celebration at her parents' home. Because of its relative seclusion, the village had been spared the ravages of the war to that point, and this allowed Maja to spend, in Dr. Plass's words, "the first half year of her life in tranquillity. Sven came from Kiel and Berlin several times to visit his small daughter. He always felt particularly happy in the family circle of his in-laws and their many children."

Toward the end of November, Plass took an extended leave and came to spend the holidays in Senftenberg with his wife and newborn child, remaining with them until after New Year's. As someone in the "upper command echelons" at Kiel, he would have been well aware of the preparations U-864 had been undergoing for her voyage, and almost certainly knew that he was a strong candidate for the assignment to Tokyo—although negotiations between Dönitz and the imperial navy, surviving as ULTRA intercepts, do not mention German line officers going to Japan before the December 13 cable, and the first reference to Plass by name is the IJN answer to Dönitz dated January 13, 1945.

Most likely Plass had only been awaiting a finalized agreement between the two countries, and was granted his prolonged family leave with the understanding that official confirmation, and his selection for the mission, were imminent.

Throughout December and January, meanwhile, Dönitz had reevaluated and downscaled his plans. He'd first hoped to send five submarines to Japan between January 10 and March 15, but the relentless Allied surge toward the Fatherland, the demands for replacements and redeployments in the Atlantic, and the Baltic and North Seas, the escalating number of boats grounded for repairs after sustaining combat damages, and the heightened risks entailed in running them through enemy choke points, had compelled him to cut back on both the number of subs and naval personnel he would commit. Unhappy, the Japanese naval attaché in Berlin, Vice Admiral Katsuo Abe, kept urging the necessity of sending more boats from "the general standpoint of Japanese-German joint strategy."

Dönitz hedged. Shortly after the New Year, he told the Japanese that only three sailings could be firmly scheduled, with U-864 being the leadoff boat, and the others to follow later in the spring. He also halved the original number of naval officers assigned to the technical branch, so that ten was reduced to five.

Of this small handful, Dönitz had chosen Lieutenants Plass and Hahndorf to leave on the first transport, and it can be safely assumed it was not a random selection. Dönitz never acted without thoughtful consideration, and the importance he placed on their assignment may be gleaned from the fact that he'd wanted to meet with Plass face-to-face in Berlin rather than have him briefed via subordinates.

To Lilly, Plass gave nothing but the sketchiest of information about his impending mission; it would have been a breach of official confidentiality to do otherwise, and was unacceptable from a good husband—military men shared as little about their duties as possible with their spouses so as not to burden them with worries for their safety. Besides, no firm date had been set.

It was another matter entirely for Sven to confide in his father. The telegram from the OKM enclosed with his letter to Dr. Plass was lost or destroyed during the war, but Ludolf's own four-page, typewritten letter to his granddaughter Maja—composed in February 1955, but not given to her until decades later—reveals that his son had discussed his pending trip with him in some detail.

Sven anticipated sailing to Japan aboard a U-boat "in strictest secrecy," Ludolf wrote, "in order to establish closer relations with the Japanese navy." He would elaborate by saying that "since there were also high-ranking Japanese officers on the craft, there was no question of it taking part in any sort of combat."

Dr. Plass's knowledge of the broad purpose of U-864's mission to Japan a quarter century before the declassification of British ULTRA decrypts, and his awareness of the Nipponese passengers he called "officers"—a designation that was technically correct—reveal that he and Sven privately shared information outside the margins of their surviving correspondence and Sven's oath of secrecy. How much Ludolf's position with AG and Lurgi may have entered into his son's appointment, and what exact benefits the Kriegsmarine, Sven's Asian hosts, and Lurgi might have expected to derive from his stint with the projected technological liaison office, remain unknown and perhaps unknowable. But these factors were surely on Dönitz's mind when he made his personnel selections.

In the end, Dr. Plass's letter raises as many questions as it answers about Sven's final voyage. Still shy of her eleventh birthday when it was written almost as a dry, formal report, Maja had by then been torn from her homeland and was being raised by adoptive parents. Plass himself would never give her the letter, which would be kept with other family documents until after his death. It was not until 2003, decades later, that Maja was even made aware of its existence.

Reading it would open the doors to a lost, haunted past marked by wartime devastation, and start her on a journey across land, sea and sky to her father's watery grave.

2.

About seven hundred miles north of Senftenberg as the crow flies, in Horten, Norway, U-864 spent most of December having her snorkel and dive systems—and to some extent her crew's stamina—put through a series of repetitive, arduous trials.

Simple in principle and design, the snorkel was really just a metal tube that projected above the waterline from the boat's submerged conning tower. It permitted her to remain underwater while she drew in oxygen to feed her diesel engines, which would then drive a generator to recharge her batteries. With the sub running at a shallow depth, air flowed down the tube through an intake pipe, while a separate exhaust pipe expelled the toxic fumes produced by engine combustion. In the manner of snorkels used by skin divers, the intake pipes were fitted with cutoff valves that would automatically close when the vessel went deep to prevent seawater from pouring down into them.

As the snorkel descended into the conning tower, it was coupled to another series of ducts that snaked back through the U-boat's interior compartments. Rather than feed into her engines, the ducts would vent out into the pressure hull to provide air to both the crew and diesels. This assured that water passing through a faulty cutoff valve could not flood the combustion chambers inside her engine and lead to a total shutdown of her power plant.

Despite repeated and careful inspections, things could and often did go wrong with the snorkel. At Horten, U-864's crew was familiarized with its assembly and taught to remedy problems that might arise under demanding—or even hostile—circumstances.

When a boat snorkeled in rough seas, the heavy wave action often resulted in water sloshing down into the intake pipe. Usually the positive air pressure inside her hull counterbalanced the flow, but greater difficulties would arise from the failure of an intake or exhaust valve. An intake valve that locked shut after the snorkel dipped under a wave would quickly cause the sub's engines to suck up its interior oxygen and deprive the crew of their breathable air. An exhaust valve that jammed in its closed position was even more dangerous, since the engine smoke would be trapped inside the hull and fill the crewmen's lungs with stifling black soot and noxious carbon monoxide fumes.

In January 1945, the U.S. Navy's interrogation of German POWs yielded an account of a IXC-class U-boat's recurring snorkel problems during its Horten trials. Once, when the head of the snorkel was undercut by waves, the engine choked off and "all the men aboard the control room were affected and eight of them lost consciousness. The U-boat immediately surfaced to ventilate and the crew went on deck, three of them being carried up on stretchers. The U-boat remained on the surface for thirty minutes. Some difficulty was experienced in getting the diesels started."

In another incident that beset the same IXC submarine, the diesels ran for several minutes after its snorkel's intake valve closed, consuming so much air inside the hull that the "crew experienced extreme discomfort, all had violent nosebleeds and some of them ran around as though bereft of their senses. The negative pressure [a vacuum effect created as the oxygen inside the sub was used up] was so great that several of the cans of food broke open. All of the milk cans were 'popped,' destroying at a blow the entire milk supply."

These potential problems were why stringent testing of the snorkel installation was always conducted before a lengthy war patrol of the sort U-864 was about to undertake.

In the waters of Oslo Fjord, an immense glacially carved bay that cut into the Norwegian mainland for sixty miles off the Skagerrak, Korvettenkapitän Wolfram and his crew repeatedly practiced running on snorkel. It required operating the boat at a shallow depth for much longer periods than they were used to, and adjusting to changes the apparatus made in her performance. The procedure was to submerge below snorkel depth, raise the mast, and then come up to snorkel depth. After trim was established, the boat would then, lower the mast and surface. This was repeated many times during the course of the trial.

While snorkeling, U-boat sailors often reported feeling nausea and having clogged ears and sinuses due to the pressure variations of wave crests and troughs near the surface; their distress was said to be greater when waves ran parallel to the boat's track than at right angles. Consequently Wolfram's helmsmen learned to move on a zigzag course—a pattern already practiced by U-boat commanders who wanted to make their boats more evasive targets when traveling on or near the water's surface.

Diving, and diving angles, were drilled time and again in the offshore practices grounds. A submarine's hydrodynamic design and winglike dive planes enable it to fly beneath the waves like an aircraft through the sky, but its trim, or balance, is difficult to maintain at a shallow depth.

Like all snorkel boats, U-864 would run just beneath the surface twice each day, two and three hours at a time, and still had to be ready to dive in haste during a close encounter with the enemy. Her snorkel had a drum-shaped aerial around its head for high-frequency radio communications, and any alteration to a boat's superstructure could affect its crash-diving time. U-864 would have to sharply descend from snorkel depth, or about 60 feet underwater, to about 400 feet, and then level off, approximating the 650- to 750-foot crash dives she could make in the open sea.

Rising from a dive brought its own dangers. One of the greatest threats a U-boat faced as she surfaced (or traveled at shallow depth while snorkeling) was broaching—part of her hull breaking the surface of the water because of an internal weight or pressure imbalance. The bow or stern of a submarine suddenly thrusting up above the waterline could be detected with ease by a hostile observer, and the enormous wake it created only increased the risk that it would be sighted.

For this reason, the flasks of mercury that had replaced the iron ballast blocks in U-864's keel would have claimed special attention during her sea trials. For a vessel to remain steady, its ballast had to be properly distributed, but although the engineers at Stettin were considered reliable experts, it was imperative to assure the stability of the containers under running conditions. If they loosened or shifted from their fixed positions, the problem would have to be resolved before U-864 was cleared for her voyage.

Another trial typically performed before completion of the exercises at Horten was the *Meilenfahrt,* or measured mile, designed to put the submarine through timed speed runs along a set training course. Vessels equipped with hydrophones clocked the boat at opposite ends of the course; U-864 was expected to achieve nineteen knots an hour on the surface, and almost seven knots submerged.

Although her stint at Horten lasted a week to ten days beyond the norm, suggesting bugs may have cropped up with her snorkel system, U-864 met the necessary benchmarks for certification by the end of the month, when she was at last declared battle ready. Sometime on the night of December 27 she left Horten with just one scheduled detour in her journey to the Pacific—a stop at the submarine depot at Kristiansand South, where she would top with fuel and pick up as many extra provisions as she could carry.

It was a short trip down the coast. Sailing out of Oslo Fjord into the Skagerrak, then hugging the shoreline to evade British aerial and naval stalkers, U-864 bore southwest for the old Norwegian harbor, where she landed in the early hours of December 28 accompanied by the Type VIIC submarine U-825, which had also received snorkel certification at Horten prior to her war patrol—an assignment that would keep her roving local Norwegian waters with Gruppe Mitte.

Port calls at Kristiansand were generally brief, and U-864 pulled in through the dreary fog at Sølyst, the small island village across a cable bridge from the city center. There she made fast alongside the VIIC and other U-boats floating opposite the corn silos, not far from the railway station and hostel where her men were given beds overnight.

At the hostel, the German sailors would double up in their rooms, while the Japanese guests asked for and received individual accommodations, as was their custom. Even within the submarine's narrow confines, Nakai and Yamato had arranged for berths that were set apart from the German crewmen and each other, their heavy canvas hammocks slung in different passageways.

Perhaps the two Japanese engineers thought of reunions with home and family on the eve of their departure; their absences had been long, and Yamato's extended by continual delays. It is possible that Willi Transier, unsure when he would see his Edith again, would have relived their final romantic moments together in his memory, the back of his head flat on his pillow, his eyes turned toward the ceiling, wide open and distant. With darkness pressing at his window, and ice glazing its cold glass panes, did the engineer Rolf von Chlingensperg reflect on his last great adventure, the expedition to scale Nanga Parbat, Germany's *Schicksalberg,* or mountain of tragic destiny? Frowning down from unassailable heights, alluring and treacherous, its slopes had demanded sacrifice upon sacrifice from all those who would have made their ascent.

Whatever thoughts swirled around in the minds of these men and their shipmates, it is likely many remained wakeful into the night contemplating what the future held in store . . . a pensiveness that lingered on for Willi Transier. Days after U-864 left Kristiansand, he would express his longing for Edith in a message scribbled on the back of a photograph, mailing it when the submarine was forced to make a stop that was in none of the men's plans—and that would change everything, irrevocably, for all of them.

3.

Crammed with food, fuel, and supplies, U-864 left Kristiansand South on December 29 to begin her passage to the east, cruising on the surface with two patrol boats as escorts. They soon parted ways, the U-boat slipping down to periscope depth as she left the Skagerrak.

A short while later, however, Korvettenkapitän Wolfram radioed out word that something was wrong with her snorkel. It is unknown whether the failure was related to issues that might have held up the boat's certification at Horten. But whatever malfunction Wolfram reported was considered serious enough for operational command to order him into Farsund, a minuscule fishing village about fifty miles west of Kristiansand just outside the entrance to the strait.

With its century-old lighthouse, striped red and white after the colors of the Viking banner, Farsund was naturally sheltered by sea stacks and harbor channels cutting between high, slablike granite palisades. It had been used as an emergency transit port long before the German occupation, but now a coastal battery at Fort Varnes formed part of the Westwall defenses and added to the protection of U-boats and other vessels arriving for repair.

For Wolfram, the problems were unexpectedly about to compound. He had no sooner ordered a slow turn to port when a loud grating shudder was heard and felt throughout the entire boat. Shaken up by its sudden halt, every crewman aboard knew they had grounded the instant it happened. Wolfram had misjudged the depth or contours of the harbor channel, ordering a submerged approach at forty meters, or about 130 feet.

This second mishap since leaving Horten probably resulted from Wolfram's limited command experience and unfamiliarity with local waters. Fjords are essentially near-shore valleys, filled with seawater, that had been carved into the terrain as huge glacial masses of ice retreated in prehistoric epochs. The walls of these rugged depressions are steep, their bottoms sloping and actually becoming shallower in the direction of the glacier's laborious movement, where the rock and soil it dragged along was pulverized and compacted by its immense weight. The mouth of the fjord, then, often rises in a flat sill of underwater moraine before dropping off behind it into a deeper body of water.

Within moments of striking the embankment, Wolfram ordered his crew to conduct a systematic check of the boat's condition. Their gauges didn't show any ruptures of the diving tanks. They reported no signs of the leaks or major flooding that would have meant sea-water was pouring in from breaches in the exterior hull. The sturdy inner pressure hull also seemed fine—there was no drop in pressure within it, no appreciable loss of power to the equipment. Further evaluation showed the hydroplanes to be functional, but Wolfram would have to wait until the boat reached port before they could be thoroughly inspected for damage.

Wolfram had gotten lucky. If the submarine had struck a hard rocky outcrop or sideswiped the wall of the channel, his situation might have been very different—and disastrous given the precious cargo in the keel hold. Still, he could not just assume the integrity of the sub's thin outer skin was uncompromised; it would have to be carefully examined topside along with the snorkel and dive planes.

His damage assessment completed, Wolfram next had to free the boat from the sandbank. On a submarine that has grounded, the commander will typically have his helmsmen shift weight to the rear of the boat, reverse engines, and then ease off the bottom. Wolfram would have quickly followed these procedures and brought U-864 to the surface. Then, as the war logs indicate, he had his wireless operator call out for a pilot to bring her into Farsund.

A pilot was literally what his job title described—a local captain who shuttled out of port and took command of the vessel's bridge. A small harbor boat bore him alongside; then the pilot climbed aboard and guided the vessel in, issuing all orders for course and speed and pulling it toward the dock.

In this way, U-864 passed through the channel into Farsund's naval station, where its engineers and mechanics confirmed that the grounding had done her little structural harm. At the same time they were unable to solve the problems associated with the snorkel. Wolfram would have to sail her into Bergen, where the fleet's technicians had the expertise and equipment to undertake comprehensive repairs to the apparatus with the boat dry-docked in Bruno. Although a reinspection of the hull would have been done there under any circumstances, the length and importance of U-864's mission sealed the decision. There could be no chances taken with her safety.

On January 1, 1945, U-864 put out of Farsund for the large Norwegian city to the north. Because of her snorkel breakdown, she was forced to travel on the surface under escort and made sluggish progress, once again tracing the coastline. New Year's Day was spent mostly at sea, and whatever celebrations her crew might have shared began and ended with the realization that another holdup—possibly a lengthy one—had now become unavoidable.

For Nakai and Yamato, this setback must have seemed only one in a string of disappointments, a new, unwanted twist they could add to the dilatory wrangling and reversals that had stalled negotiations for their return home over many frustrating months.

Willi Transier's feelings would have been much more conflicted. Again, he must have thought of Edith, and the blissful moments they had stolen together during his shore leaves. Although they had not yet married, that was, in a sense, just a formality, something they knew would happen when the war allowed them to gather their families for a proper wedding ceremony. Before leaving Germany, he had asked that she do her best to contact him if she discovered she was carrying his child, explaining that, no matter his fate, it was his hope that something lasting could come of their love, a seed of life and renewal, a part of him that would remain with her in the event he failed to return from his journey.

Now, as the boat left for Bergen, Willi could not have known if its stop there would mark an early end to that voyage, or was just another interlude in which to measure his yearning for Edith against his dedication to service and country.

In Berlin, meanwhile, Admiral Karl Dönitz would soon conclude that the submarine's latest delay was a blessing in disguise—that it might yet be turned to his decided advantage. With the reduction of sailings to Japan and his frequent reshuffling of their departure schedules, two of the key men he had hoped to send over early in the program, Lieutenants Plass and Hahndorf, had been left off U-864's list of nonregular passengers. Although he'd still fully planned for them to make the trip aboard a second submarine that winter, the repairs to U-864's snorkel would unquestionably keep her in Bergen for several weeks. That would allow him the opportunity to call the officers to Berlin for a personal meeting, give them their secret mission orders, and then have them fly to Oslo aboard a military transport. On their arrival, Norway's ample ground and railway connections would enable them to link up with the submarine at Bergen with time to spare. Then, finally, U-864 could embark on her mission.

British intelligence and the Royal Air Force, however, had very different plans. And owing in part to the code breakers at Bletchley Park, and in part to other sources of information, they were several crucial steps ahead of Dönitz in putting them into action.

PART TWO

EVERYTHING FALLS APART

CHAPTER SEVEN

CODE BREAKERS, BOMBES, AND DAMBUSTERS

1.

Bletchley Park really wasn't the best of spots for a code-breaking operation of the scale and importance of Project ULTRA, as the British secret services dubbed it. Sitting about fifty miles northwest of London on what had once been a small cattle farm, the mansion offered the advantage of being close to a major railway hub and the Watling Street section of the Great North Road. But its easy accessibility created a security risk, and the physical layout of the house itself presented drawbacks.

In an attempt to throw off foreign spies—German agents foremost in mind—a real-estate buyer for the British government had claimed, rather vaguely, to a newspaper reporter that Bletchley was to become a training center for its air defense ministry. This was in 1938, when Admiral Hugh Francis Paget Sinclair, a founder of MI6, purchased the estate from a developer named Faulkner, who had bought it from Sir George Leon, who had inherited it from his deceased parents, Sir Herbert Samuel Leon and his wife Lady Fanny, who'd owned the property since 1882 or thereabouts.

A wealthy stockbroker and investor, Sir Herbert had acquired the title of baronet late in life and, seeking to make the estate a shrine to his social and financial ascendance, expanded the original redbrick farmhouse in an eyebrow-raising collision of mock-Tudor, Victorian, and Gothic architectural styles. The furnishings were pretentious and showy, and the arrangement of rooms, with expansive halls, chambers, and parlors spilling off one another in a manner that often left visitors baffled and disoriented, made the estate less than ideal for the vital business taking place on the grounds

Bletchley did provide its two hundred original cryptanalysts with several outbuildings converted from tack rooms and feed sheds in the stable yard—brick cottages where they could work in the organized and compartmentalized environments they preferred. But at its wartime peak between 1944 and 1945, the staff would swell to almost nine thousand, the greatest number of whom were clerks and operators on home-front duty with the all-female Auxiliary Territorial Service and Women's Royal Naval Service, or WRENS.

The code breakers of Project ULTRA were an interdisciplinary mix of intelligence personnel and civilian employees. As author Jerome M. O'Connor wrote, "Arriving daily were crossword puzzle experts, university mathematicians, literature dons, classicists and librarians. Tapped from newspaper advertisements, musicians, language instructors, historians, accountants, bankers, and newspaper and publishing executives passed through the gates. Topping the odd aggregation, even philosophers and pedagogues from museums, and rare book store owners applied and were eagerly accepted."

Bletchley's facilities would expand over time to accommodate its growing task force. Even before the outbreak of hostilities with Nazi Germany, prefabricated slat-wood huts began sprouting up around the mansion. Sweltering in the summer, bitter cold in the winter, these utilitarian structures were where thousands of men and women labored round the clock to fill in specific pieces of the code-breaking puzzle.

Eventually there would be seventeen functional huts, some of them linked by tunnels, on the estate grounds—plus an eighteenth, recreational one where the stiff, fatigued cryptographers could retreat to work out mental and physical kinks with exercise, table tennis, and various card and board games. Huts 3, 4, 6, and 8 were used for the German Enigma decrypt teams, Hut 7 for Japanese codes and intelligence, the rest for other types of intelligence, codes, and communications. Later on, the huts would be supplemented by eight brick-walled blocks with reinforced concrete frames and flat concrete-slab roofs. Known only by letters of the alphabet (*A–H*), the long, single-story structures were for the most part identical and had thirteen spurs running off their main corridors. The spurs on one side of a corridor contained watch rooms for military guards, and those on the opposite side were boxy little office spaces—the appendage-like appearance of the spurs earning the buildings the name "spider blocks."

Block H housed the wall-size Colossus computers used to decrypt German OKW messages encoded on a machine called the Lorenz, which was capable of a far higher level of encryption than the Enigma. Their electronic brains made up of row upon row of hot, humming, electricity-guzzling vacuum-tube arrays and wires, the Colossi were the world's first programmable digital information processing machines. "Messages faced almost immediate discovery by Colossus," wrote O'Connor, "with solutions automatically printed on an IBM electric typewriter—and in the original German."

The bulk of the decryption, however, was done by Enigma teams using smaller electromechanical decoding units known as bombes—for all intents and purposes "counter-Enigma" machines whose existence owed a great debt to the Poles. Long before the war, Poland and France had grown jittery about German intentions in Europe and begun pooling intelligence about their vaunted cryptographic device. In 1932, Marian Rejewski, a Polish mathematician and cryptologist, received German Enigma documents from the chief of his cipher bureau; they, in turn, had been slipped to him by a French spymaster named Captain Gustave Bertrand, whose operatives obtained them for a price from a traitor inside the German cryptographic office. This web of espionage and cash-lubricated duplicity gave Rejewski and his associates the informational tools to design replica Enigma machines that could read German ciphers—although they had known this was only the first step in a process.

In order for the Enigma's encryption system to work, the settings, or cipher keys, on the sender and recipient's machines had to be identical. Provided to Enigma operators in their codebook entries, the keys at first changed monthly, then weekly, then daily, then three times a day, until they were eventually reconfigured with every coded transmission. Without access to the keys, or the ability to quickly generate their own, the Poles had to determine them by slow trial and error, turning the wheels and jacking in plug-board cables by hand—and there were 105,456 possible combinations for each setting change.

Rejewski's accomplishment was a precursor of what might someday be achieved, but given the prodigious volume of German message traffic, any intercepted and decoded transmission was the equivalent of a single captured fish out of a vast school that could go freely swimming through the net. Far from satisfied, Rejewski pushed forward with his work in earnest, knowing much more had to be done before Enigma was cracked in any meaningful sense.

Developed in late 1937, the Polish *bomba* was the upshot of another six years of committed, methodical effort by Rejewski's task force. Rejewski would insist that the device was named after a gelato dessert he'd been savoring in a Warsaw café when the idea for it flashed into his mind, although the rhythmic, ticking time-bomb-like noise it made was alternately offered as an explanation. Whichever is accurate, the *bomba* consisted of six Enigma copies that were wired together and could run through thousands of possible setting combinations in about two hours. Although successful, the *bomba* did have certain shortcomings, which would eventually lead to the creation of a system that utilized six *bombas* working together for increased tabulating speed and power.

Soon after its creation, this aggregate *bomba* was, according to reliable accounts, able to decipher three-quarters of the German radio message traffic intercepted by Polish eavesdroppers. Then, in the summer of 1939, when Germany again upped the ante for the code breakers by giving Enigma operators a fourth and fifth interchangeable rotor—and adding new patches to the *Steckerbrett*—Rejewski found himself confronting a whole new slate of problems. The cryptologist still believed he could tackle them if provided enough time, funding, and manpower, but all these things were in scarce supply. With German tanks and infantry having already stormed into Czechoslovakia and massing at Prussian bases across the border, Rejewski's contacts in the government cipher office took a very different recourse.

On a July visit to Warsaw, a coterie of top British and French intelligence people was brought to a secret facility in the city's wooded outskirts, shown the *bomba,* and given a detailed rundown of its capacities by Rejewski and the head of the Polish cipher bureau. "At that meeting we told everything we knew and showed everything we had," Rejewski later recalled. Arrangements were hastily made to send their copied Enigma machines and *bomba* design schematics to London via sealed diplomatic pouch.

At Bletchley Park, cryptographers Alan Turing and Gordon Welchman built upon Rejewski's achievements to develop a third-generation *bomba*—or bombe, as it was redubbed after its migration to the United Kingdom. Turing would introduce the idea of working with "cribs," words and phrases that were liable to recur frequently in military and diplomatic transmissions—salutations, officer rankings, similar types of orders, even language that reflected the personal habits and verbal tics of the German code clerks.

With the cribs extracted by Bletchley's code-breaking teams, the Turing-Welchman bombes, which were a dozen times speedier than Rejewski's, would match the translated characters to others embedded within a message, enabling strings of words and sentences to be deciphered. These repetitive word packets gave Turing and Welchman the keys to the settings on the sender's machines.

The process was not without snags and delays, but by 1941 Bletchley's code breakers were deciphering nearly all encrypted German army, naval, and diplomatic communications with ease. The transmissions were snatched out of the air by signals intelligence posts, or Y (for cryptology) stations, at remote sites across the British coast and countryside, then relayed to Bletchley via motorcycle courier, landline, and teletype, and decoded on the eight-foot-high iron bombes. Generally working in small huts bristling with radio aerials, Y-station operators—or wireless monitors, as they were called—ranged from MI6 agents to army, navy, and RAF personnel, to WRENS and women's Auxiliary Territorial Service conscripts, to volunteer ham radio buffs.

Working on a need-to-know basis and sworn to secrecy, the men and women at the listening stations diligently went about their business, spending long, exhausting shifts at their radio equipment, living close by in spartan bungalows. They were never told the destination of the messages or informed of their importance. They referred to the recipient of their intercepts only as Station X, the British code name for Bletchley Park, and had no information about what was being done there. But ULTRA would have starved and withered without their steady flow of intercepted communications.

While the introduction of Dönitz's four-rotor Enigma in 1942 did nothing to staunch that flow, it did bring Bletchley's ability to decode the messages it acquired to a near standstill. If the Allied cryptographers had any edge, it was that they'd gleaned an awareness of the M4 months before it became standard issue for the Kriegsmarine. Their tips were extracted from multiple sources: decrypts mentioning the enhanced device, an Enigma lid with four windows seized from a captured submarine, and finally a repeat transmission by a sloppy code clerk who'd used the four-rotor machine before its first scheduled date of operation, then caught his gaffe and duplicated the identical message using the three-rotor format. A comparative analysis gave the code breakers a clear picture of the fourth rotor's wiring and aided their eventual solution of the M4—which they had come to call Shark.

By February or March 1943, Bletchley's code breakers were largely back on track. They had taken many creative approaches to identifying the crypto keys and tightened up their cooperative efforts with U.S. cryptanalysts, who had broken the Japanese diplomatic codes with their own Project MAGIC years earlier. During the ten-month "Shark blackout," one of Britain's leading intelligence officers, John Tiltman, traveled to the United States on a tour of its cryptographic facilities, and later successfully pushed for his country to share its blueprints for the Turing bombe with American officers at Bletchley Park.

Around the middle of 1943, the American bombe went into production at the National Cash Register Company in Dayton, Ohio, where seventy-five "super high-speed" units, as author Hervie Haufler described them, would be run off over the next six months.

Thereafter the United States would take over the lead role in Shark decryption. According to Haufler, who served as a U.S. Signal Corps cryptographer in the war, America's superior manufacturing capabilities, and speedy output of bombes, made it "better equipped to deal in a timely fashion with the vast numbers of permutations that had to be run through to reach Shark Enigmas' settings."

That summer, an advance party of U.S. army crypto specialists reached England to lay the groundwork for three major Signal Security detachments that would follow in the first three months of 1944. The 6811th (Haufler's unit) and 6812th arrived in February, with the 6811th taking over radio intercept operations at Bexley, a creaky old mansion in the suburb of Kent on the Thames River. The eighty cryptologists of the 6812th, for their part, bivouacked at a former WRENS barracks named Eastcote in the greater London area, where they operated almost a hundred Turing bombes at the outstation's U.S. wing. Meanwhile, the 6813th went to Bletchley and was integrated into every facet of the code-breaking effort. Altogether the units totaled three hundred men, who remained in England for the duration of World War II.

It would not be long before ULTRA and MAGIC intercepts, cryptanalysis, and the information they revealed about Axis submarine movements were streaming between Bletchley in England and the U.S. Navy's communications intelligence section (OP-20-G) and Combat Intelligence Section across the Atlantic. By 1944, the Allies had decoded and translated a large volume of Japanese-German diplomatic communications about their blockade-running schemes and negotiations regarding the exchange of scientific experts, military personnel, leading-edge weapons, aircraft technology, and essential war supplies. They had used intercepted radio transmissions to chart the progress of the Japanese imperial Yanagi submarines I-8, I-34, and I-29—as well as U-1224, Hitler's personal gift to the emperor—and target them at sea. They knew about the decision by Hitler and his high command to provide modern U-boats like U-1224 to Japan for cloning in its dockyards, and they knew of Dönitz's gradual softening on the idea of using his fleet submarines as transport vessels. They knew the names of the outbound German military and scientific personnel assigned to train with the IJN, and they knew the identities of the Japanese technicians who were being given passage home. They knew the code names of the imperial and Kriegsmarine boats tabbed for the program, knew their approximate schedules of departure, and in many instances knew their stated cargo loads, although they realized it was possible some of the manifest listings had been falsified as cover for transfer of supersensitive payload items.

The shipment of high-tech munitions to Japan was of grave and imminent concern to the Allies, who had relied on a plethora of covert sources to follow the progress of advanced Nazi weapons development programs. In late February, British and American planes had struck at hundreds of German aviation factories, conducting almost four thousand sorties over a six-day period to knock them out of commission.

The operation, called Big Week, was meant to prevent the introduction of rocket- and jet-powered aerial marauders into the European theater, but the possibility of the Japanese military-industrial machine getting hold of them was an even greater threat to American troops in the Far East. Although Japan's airpower had declined in the Pacific, U.S. strategists believed the coupling of kamikaze tactics with the innovative Fo-Fü aircraft could prove lethal to their naval carriers, give control of the skies back to the imperial fliers, and tilt the course of the war back in the enemy's favor.

And then there was the grimmest wartime specter of all for Washington—the dark, hovering fear that Nazi Germany might provide Japan with the materials to build, and launch, an atomic bomb. MAGIC decrypts going back to 1943 had clued the Americans into the fact that Japan was trying to procure uranium oxide from Germany and have it dispatched to its shores via submarine. While U.S. intelligence experts knew Japan had been pursuing an atomic research program since at least the late 1930s, they had no way to determine how far along its scientists had gotten in their work. But they were very aware that the program was headed by Dr. Yoshio Nishina, one of the world's premiere nuclear physicists, whose Riken Laboratory had purchased a nuclear accelerator from the University of California, Berkeley, in 1938. And there was no doubt that the V-1 and V-2 rocket technology the Japanese had procured through the transport program would give them a long-range delivery system that, if armed with fissile nuclear material, could virtually assure their victory over American combat forces and perhaps even be used in a cataclysmic nuclear strike at mainland America.

It likely wasn't a coincidence that Big Week launched on the very same day that British-trained Norwegian saboteurs sank the ferry SF Hydro, which had been loaded with large drums of deuterium oxide—or heavy water, a component in the uranium enrich-ment process—from the Vermork hydroelectric power plant as it was being carried across Norway's Lake Tinnsjø en route to Ger-many. Two German scientists had split the atom in 1938, showing the world that fission led to a massive release of energy, and within months the nuclear arms race had been on between the Axis and Allied powers. The Allies saw no evidence that Hitler drew a dis-tinction between the nuclear bomb and his other *Wunderwaffen;* if anything, he seemed openhanded about sharing whatever military technology might help defeat the Axis powers' common enemies.

From late 1943 to September 1944, a series of Shark decrypts involving the Yanagi imperial submarine I-52 brought anxieties over the arms-and-expert transfers to a head. Processed by Bletchley and OP-20-G, the intercepts opened a broad window of insight into the accelerated pace at which Germany and Japan planned to move forward, the commitment both Axis powers had to the venture, and their belief that it might succeed in countering Allied gains.

In the summer of 1944, the bounty of message traffic about the submarine began to reveal Axis suspicions that it had been sunk while bound for a German port (it had in fact been destroyed in June by American torpedo bombers). Rear Admiral Kojima, the naval attaché, would now issue an appeal to Germany for a contin-gency plan to send out, via U-boat, the cargo and special personnel originally slated for I-52's return trip to Asia.

The selection criteria for those personnel had been laid out to Kojima in an August 6 dispatch from Tokyo instructing him to "please restrict them in view of the war situation to those who are absolutely requisite to the direct strengthening of the war effort." Just over a week later, the attaché cabled his application for "nondepartmental passengers" to his superiors for approval. Fully eighteen of them were Japanese expatriates who were listed by name; another eight were Germans that Kojima applied for on the basis of their particular areas of technical expertise. Mindful that placing so many of his countrymen on the list was a tall order—and that Dönitz might balk at too extensive a roll—the attaché had asked that the transport be kept to "one to two persons at a time, one to two ships per month."

Kojima's full wish list had read:

    I.   Navy

        1. Paymaster Commander Inaba

        2. Technical Commander Shooji (special course on the construction of the MK 163)

        3. Technical Lieutenant commander Tomonga (research in submarine mass production)

        4. Technical Commander Kuroda (he may be able to stand the long voyage, having recovered from his illness)

        5. Technical Lieutenant Tarutani (special course in the "TL" power plant)

        6. Technical expert Yamato (specialist in electric apparatus of acoustic torpedo)

        7. Unofficial expert Nakai (chemical expert for the "R" power plant)

II. Army (those ordered in your dispatch to return to Japan immediately)

    8. Major Suematsu

    9. Technical expert Kawakitka

   10. Colonel Kootani

   11. Technical expert Suzuki

   12. Major Kingoshita

   13. Major Kigoshi

   14. Colonel Uchiai

   15. Major Kobayashi, aeronautics expert?

   16. Major Yoshinari, aeuronautics expert?

   17. ——Ogawa, ordnance expert?

III. Foreign Office

   18. Komuro (Commerce Ministry)

IV. German Technicians

   19. One Messerschmitt expert (specialist in airplane and rocket plane designs)

   20. One person, same as above

   21. Same (specialist in construction of the fuselage of rocket planes)

   22. One Junkers expert (specialist in handling assembly of "TF" power plant)

   23. One BMW expert (specialist in construction of the above)

   24. One Heinkel expert (assistant to technician Schmidt in Japan)

25. One Daimler-Benz expert (specialist on the NW-501)
26. One Seimens expert (specialist in torpedo control)

Total 26 Persons

Tadao Yamato and Toshio Nakai, the sixth and seventh men on the list, were later chosen to sail with U-864, the first German submarine to leave on the program, demonstrating the importance the Japanese placed on their return. Admiral Kojima's top two requests under the section for German technicians perfectly matched the credentials of Rolf von Chlingensperg and Riclef Schomerus, who were also passengers aboard U-864. The third position, a "specialist in construction of the fuselage of rocket planes," was filled by the somewhat enigmatic Franz Türk.

A thirty-seven-year-old professional carpenter and model maker from the city of Wuppertal, in the Rhineland, Türk was four years the senior of Korvettenkapitän Wolfram and a dozen years older than the average seaman aboard U-864. He had entered submarine school in 1943, at age thirty-six, making him ancient for a recruit at that stage of the war. And he had only managed to attain the rating of *Gefreiter*—the lowest a submariner could hold—despite having started his training before many other crew members.

Franz Türk was much too old to be doing what he was doing. His age and modest rank raise immediate questions about his eligibility for submarine service—and in particular his desirability for a mission as highly prioritized as U-864's. But his background as a woodworker and modeler would seem to hold the answers to those questions. Kojima's call for a "specialist in the construction of rocket planes" like the Me 163 Komet, which was largely fashioned of balsa wood and required unique manufacturing techniques, would have called for someone of Türk's precise professional skills. It remains the only logical explanation for his presence on the boat.

Türk's assignment to Japan, then, must have preceded his admission to submarine school, and been decided upon long before Schomerus and Chlingensperg were chosen to make the trip. That would have given him added time to receive full submariner qualifications rather than be accorded honorary rank as they were—although his training was, in reality, no less a cover. Had the Kriegsmarine originally wanted him to depart in advance of the rest? Were the Japanese geared to put the Me 163 into hastened production as early as 1943? Had they perhaps finalized agreements for it well before closing on their deals for other contracted technology? The answers are undetermined.

In those waning days of summer, U-864 was itself still unknown to the Allies and had not even begun preparations for its voyage. But an early September intercept—once again sent from Kojima to his naval higher-ups—put them on the alert that German vessels were about to be used in place of the Yanagi submarines. Reporting on a personal session with Dönitz, he wrote:

I acknowledged that I was finally forced to conclude that the SATUSKI #2 [Japanese code for U-1224, which the Allies had sunk off the coast of Portugal in May] had been lost and further that I was unable to think otherwise of the GINMATSU. The Empire had had great hopes for them, but now it will require German submarines for cooperation in the transport of personnel and goods. If these were assigned to the Indian Ocean operations defense sector, I suggested, it would be advantageous from the point of view of both Germany and Japan. The Admiral agreed and said that three transport submarines were scheduled to be completed by the end of this week.

Whatever Dönitz had pledged, the desperate circumstances facing Germany as it was besieged on two major war fronts would soon alter the terms of the bargain. With the Soviet Red Army marching in from the east, and the Americans ready to forge their way across the Rhine, plans were being scuttled as quickly as they were put together. In Brittany, the Germans were clearing out the U-boat bases vacated by FdU West and conducting wholesale destruction of records and material in their dockside warehouses—including consignments earmarked for the Far East—before any of it could fall into the possession of Allied troops.

Amid this whirl of confusion, the information that Japan was receiving about U-boat departures had become spotty and inaccurate. On December 18, Japan's chief naval inspector in Germany sent this cable to Tokyo, reporting on the status of outbound (to Japan) or inbound (to Germany) goods over the past several months, and his understanding of the schedule for future U-boat shipments:

We have endeavored to return to Germany as many as possible of the goods loaded in the four "YANAGI" ships and the "AKIRA" No. 4 [Japanese code for the Italian Aquila submarine *Giuseppe*

Finzi, deemed unseaworthy by the Germans] whose departure from Bordeaux was suspended, as previously reported, also of the considerable number of purchases which could not be shipped by them, and which remained behind in warehouses there, except for those which it was thought possible to load in German submarines and on the "GINMATSU." However, while this transfer was as yet incomplete owing to the work of discharge not proceeding and in addition the transport in France being extremely congested, the enemy's second front developed rapidly. (We finished sending back to Germany about 130 machine tools . . . In fact, the following goods were left behind in Bordeaux at the time of the enemy army's penetration into the port, but according to later reports from the Germans three German submarines which were being equipped in the port at the time, left hurriedly for Japan, taking with them a considerable amount of mercury, lead and optical glass from the goods left behind as ballast. Apart from this it appears a considerable amount [of additional cargo] may be loaded on board, but as details are obscure, please let us know on arrival [of the U-boats to Japan] the names, numbers and quantities of good shipped. The rest are presumed to have fallen into enemy hands or to have been blown up.

The cable goes on to detail some of the items of freight, with deletions that its U.S. Navy translator explains were made because they "enumerated only cargo numbers and amounts of various undescribed articles." The translator also adds, "The three German submarines which left Bordeaux in late August, 1944 are unidentified."

And now a summer of turbulence and defeat for the Reich had turned to bleakest winter. As December drew to a close, Admiral Dönitz had reduced the transfer program to three submarines, with U-864 as his lone outrider for the year and the uncertain goal of following through with two more boats in 1945. For their part, the Allies still knew nothing of U-864, but their signals intelligence operations had scored enough information from radio intercepts to confirm that the Germans were heavily invested in providing their most dangerous *Wunderwaffen* to Japan. Despite massive losses in the Atlantic, there was no doubt the Kriegsmarine was still capable of pursuing that goal and had promised to send over submarines stocked with plans and components for the "futuristic" arms and armaments, accompanied by a cadre of technical advisers schooled in their production. The Allies knew they had to prevent this, but actually doing so was a problem.

"One subject on which ULTRA could not be relied on to provide timely warning, or sometimes any warning at all, was the movement of Germany's main naval units," wrote the distinguished British Sigint officer Edward Thomas. "Reports from the ship watchers were often the first to be received in London."

By 1944, Thomas's star with the navy had soared; he had gotten reassigned from the listening station in Iceland to Bletchley Park, and then been made adviser on signals intelligence to the commander in chief of the Royal Navy's Home Fleet. In that post he would play a central role gathering intel about German naval operations in Norwegian waters and along the Arctic convoy routes. Through repeated experiences, Thomas had found that the time it took to decrypt and translate German naval communications captured from the front, then distribute them to Allied commanders in London and Washington, then formulate plans based on that gathered information, and then wait for their orders to be relayed back to the theater of operations . . . all this resulted in impracticable holdups for tactical leaders.

This was no truer at any stage of the war than the winter of 1944. As the Kriegsmarine scampered to elude Allied blows, the departures of its vessels were often decided at a rapid clip that was difficult to anticipate and counter.

With BdU West relocated to Norway, the Allies would need to lean heavily on the men and women who had been watching the nation's coast, transmitting radio updates on German ship movements, damages, repairs, and even changing sea and weather conditions. And British intelligence would now collect a handsome payoff for its formation of the Shetland Bus, and the daring missions of the 9th Flotilla's submarines in support of the resistance.

Only two months after Operation Weserübung, the fugitive Norwegian cabinet had implanted itself in London, where, said Thomas, their joint efforts with MI6 "almost entirely lacked the friction experienced with other governments in exile. They agreed on an early division of labor, the SIS [MI-6] obtaining information from the ship-watchers, and the Norwegian government political, military and static information."

It was "well-placed Norwegians," Thomas wrote, "backed by much fuller information from PR [photographic reconnaisance, shorthand for the British Film and Photo section], the Norwegian High Command and local SIS sources" who had led to the successful actions against the Vermork hydroelectric plant. "Bombing of

Norwegian ports assumed high priority towards the end of 1944 when ULTRA and PR showed that the Germans intended to continue the U-boat war from Norway after the evacuation of their French bases, now employing a new type of ocean-going U-boat whose formidable characteristics were disclosed by decrypts of Japanese messages from Berlin to Tokyo. These revealed the high hopes pinned on these monsters by Hitler and Dönitz. . . ."

The veteran spy was of course referring to IX D2 submarines, the class to which U-864 belonged. And after her departure from Trondheim, U-864 herself had left a highly conspicuous trail up the coast.

In Kristiansand, the entrenched Norwegian resistance was a constant problem for the occupying forces, its subversive activities triggering rashes of Gestapo arrests, tortures, and executions. But despite those bloody reprisals, the opposition had not been uprooted. U-864's loading of sufficient stores and fuel for a long, six-month journey would have seemed curious at the very minimum to ship watchers monitoring the dockyards . . . as would a pair of Japanese men in imperial navy officer's uniforms when they took overnight accommodations at the town railroad hostel.

The ship watchers could not have missed the submarine's grounding off Farsund within hours of her departure from Kristiansand, the dispatch of a pilot to steer her into the village harbor, and the hurried inspections and repair attempts at the village shipyard. Again, the Japanese passengers would have raised eyebrows. The submarine's referral to Bergen for repairs, and passage on the surface because of her faulty snorkel would also have been observed. And with visits to local taverns the norm during port calls, and pretty girls to impress, odds were slender that none of the young men aboard the U-boat let a word slip about their exotic destination.

All things considered, there was too much to notice about U-864 for it to go unreported—and the intelligence would not have been harvested from ULTRA intercepts, but by an underground network MI6 and Lerwick had trained, organized, and supplied for over half a decade.

The question for the British was, how to stop the U-boat?

The answer lay in its stop for repairs at Bergen, and with the Royal Air Force trying to finish a job it had botched the previous autumn.

2.

The British sometimes called it the bouncing bomb, and sometimes the Scampton Steamroller after the airfield from which it was first deployed—but their official code name was Upkeep. Housed in a big cylindrical container that resembled a spinning oil drum, Upkeep was devised to skip across the water's surface like a stone across a pond, hop over the torpedo nets that protected German dams, then roll down the dam wall into the sediment at its base. Because the bomb would be right against the wall, or very close to it, when its pressure fuze mechanism triggered its detonation, the water behind it had a tamping effect that directed nearly all its explosive wallop at the target. This handily turned an impediment into an asset, since the normal effect of water on a bomb that fell shy of its target was to scatter its destructive energy to the point where it became ineffective.

The invention of Upkeep roughly coincided with two other developments. One was the introduction into service of the Avro Lancaster bomber, a thirty-ton giant, with a hundred-foot wingspan, a fuselage measuring almost seventy feet from nose to tail, and four supercharged, high-octane radial engines powering it through the air. The other was an RAF plan to strike at Germany's hydroelectric storage dams in the industrialized Ruhr Valley.

British air marshal Arthur Harris's theory on bombing raids was straightforward if cold-blooded. Discrete targets such as munitions factories, oil production facilities, or military command centers were difficult to take out with precision, and could be put back in commission within a fairly short period after they were hit. It was Harris's contention that strikes at the widespread area that included the target would destroy the roads, public utility grids, government offices, and workers' homes needed for its rebuilding, and batter the morale of the civilian populace.

The Ruhr industrial centers were geographically well-located for this stratagem, spread out downstream of a system of twenty colossal dams that channeled river water throughout the valley. In the view of Prime Minister Winston Churchill and his most trusted military advisers, the production of steel for German armor and weapons would be seriously impaired if key dams were breached.

Ironically, Harris, the leading proponent of this type of raid, had reservations about the British being able to pull the strike off. The newfangled bombs were meant to be dropped at a low-level altitude, and he felt that flying at night, and swooping between the hills over enemy territory, the Lancs would be perilously exposed to thickets of German antiaircraft artillery.

At length Harris's objections were overruled, although he hesitated to commit an entire Lanc squadron from his main bomber command for the mission. Thus, in late March 1943, a separate squadron was formed from RAF No. 5 Group at Scampton, Lincolnshire, in northeastern England. The unit was originally called X Squadron, and later given the number 617. Operating under the umbrella of the RAF Bomber Command, flight crews from the Australian, Canadian, and New Zealand air forces were assembled to conduct the raid, which would require a slew of modifications to the aircrafts and a tactical repertoire specially drawn up to utilize the bouncing bomb—among them refined pathfinding reconnaissance and targeting techniques. An elaborate training program for its initial mission, Operation Chastise, was conducted in tight secrecy over the rolling countryside.

Less than two months after the 617 was born, three waves of Lancs—nineteen in all—took to the air from RAB Scampton, winged across the North Sea over Holland and Belgium, and struck at the Eder, Möhne, and Sorpe dams. The 145-foot high, granite-block wall of the Eder held over 400 million tons of reservoir water in check, the 120-foot Möhne wall 140 million tons, the Sorpe 70 million tons. For their Upkeeps to achieve the proper backspin to reach and blow their targets, the daring pilots had to dive down into the valleys through soupy fog, skim the treetops at 60 feet on their approaches, and drop the bombs between 400 and 450 feet from the dam walls.

Although complications to the Sorpe attack forced it to be aborted, the raid was very close to an unqualified success overall, earning the 617 its soon-to-be-famous Dambusters moniker and an emblem depicting a breached dam and floodwaters above the motto *Après Moi le Deluge*—After Me the Deluge. As the war raged on, the 617's well-earned reputation as a crackerjack elite would peg the group as the bomber unit of choice for the RAF's highest-value targets.

In August 1943, the Dambusters moved to the RAF air base at Coningsby, with its extensive support facilities, permanent hangars, and hard runways built for heavy-lift bombers. The squadron would remain there for over a year before it once again relocated, this time to its final home, a satellite aerodrome in the nearby farming village of Woodhall Spa.

Early on New Year's Day 1945, the 617's group captain John Emilius "Johnny" Fauquier left his quarters in Tattershall Thorpe Parish south of the airfield, trudged to his jeep through the blowing wind and snow, and, with his driver at the wheel, set out directly toward Coningsby, where Fauquier had been summoned by Air Chief Marshal Elsham Wolds, Hugh Alex "Connie" Constantine, Group 5's newly appointed commanding officer.

Bumping and slipping over three miles of narrow, white-sheeted dirt road, the thirty-six-year-old, Canadian-born Fauquier arrived at the base's Wing Operations Center to meet with AOC Constantine and other Group 5 section commanders about a directive that had come down from Bomber Command headquarters. HQ, he knew, had received information from London about an urgent new strategic objective . . . and in the words of Air Marshal Harris, *stra-*

tegic objective was "generally a euphemism for targets chosen by the Admiralty."

With the officers gathered around a conference table, Constantine revealed that Bomber Command had sent down orders for another strike at the German submarine base at Bergen. The Kriegsmarine had continued to build up the size of its U-boat fleet there while continuing to expand the already enormous submarine bunker on the headlands at the east end of the harbor. Their French bases abandoned, the Germans had determined that Norway would now become the central staging area for their campaign against Allied shipping convoys—and Bergen was now the fleet's seat of command.

But all that was, in a sense, only background. Most germane to the current mission, ULTRA and MAGIC intercepts indicated the Norwegian bases were now to be used as waypoints for long-range transports that were dispatched to ferry military hardware and other materials to Japan. Decrypts about the nature of their cargo were of great concern to London and Washington, and local sources had informed them that one such boat—believed to be the first of several that would make the journey—had left Farsund within the last seventy-two hours and was sailing into Bergen for repairs. Presumably it would be entering the pens, which were prime targets of the attack, but no chances could be taken. Additional objectives would be the harbor's restored floating dock and whatever submarines and other vessels might be within sight.

First and foremost, however, it was imperative that the transport be taken out of commission.

In outlining the mission's parameters, Constantine would make it plain that there could be no repeat of the missteps that had led to the bungling of the October 4 raid. Civilian casualties were almost inevitable, yes. But the scores of five-hundred- and thousand-pound bombs dropped by the Canadian Halifax and Lancaster Squadrons had brought about horrendous collateral damage and loss of innocent Norwegian lives, while the U-boat bunker had been left virtually unscathed.

To ensure that this failure was not repeated, Constantine had decided that the crack 617 and 9 Squadrons would be conducting the strike this time around. The previous November, they had collaborated in a terrifically successful operation to sink the battleship *Tirpitz,* the heretofore indestructible pride of the Kriegsmarine, an armed floating fortress that had been the nemesis of Allied shipping in the North Atlantic for over two years. On that mission they had used the new five-ton Tallboy bomb, a weapon as imposing as its target. It consisted of an aerodynamic, torpedo-shaped steel case filled with 5,200 pounds of Torpex explosive that was twenty-one feet long, thirty-eight inches in diameter around the middle, and had been designed to bury itself deep inside armor, tunnels, and reinforced concrete without breaking apart. These bombs had decimated the nearly eight-hundred-foot-long battleship, blowing its lofty gun turrets free of the hull and capsizing it in the ocean.

Now the Tallboy was designated the primary weapon for the raid on Bergen, which would be carried out in daylight for the highest level of accuracy.

To the surprise of no one at the table, bad weather would be a factor. This was, after all, the frozen heart of the Norwegian winter. Meteorological reports were for heavy snow, fog, and occasional gale-force winds to persist over the next several weeks. But they could not wait for the Arctic fronts to clear the map. The Lancs would fly at the earliest possible opportunity—as early as the next morning, if a forecasted break in storm activity panned out.

It did not. Instead, the snowfall intensified throughout the afternoon and night, grounding the flights. Rather than drive out in the blanketing whiteness, the squadron leaders slept over at Coningsby and lunched with the vice admiral at his residence. When Fauquier left for Woodhall Spa on the afternoon of January 2, Constantine told him to be on standby and assured him he would be constantly kept in the loop.

The poor conditions held on for the next two weeks. Each morning between January 4 and 7, Lanc crews at Woodhall and Bardney were called into their operations rooms for preflight briefings, and each morning the mission had to be scratched. Shrieking winds and blowing snow pounded the area hard for several days and did away with any thoughts of getting planes into the air. On January 11, though, an early lull in the snow again raised hopes for the mission, and plows rumbled out to clear the buried concrete runways. But the weather soon worsened again and left the airmen on the ground.

When January 12 dawned cold and gray, they must have hunched over their breakfast eggs and tea mugs half expecting yet another cancellation. But soon the sun poked through the clouds; on that day the storm system had finally relaxed its grip long enough for the operation to commence. Sixteen Lancasters were taking off from Woodhall, accompanied by a Mosquito Pathfinder flown by Group Captain Fauquier and his navigator, Squadron Leader George Ellwood. With another sixteen Lancs leaving Bardney, and seven men to a bomber crew, a total of 234 RAF fliers would participate in the raid.

Just before seven o'clock in the morning, the 617s' aircrews at Woodhall Spa exited the corrugated steel Nissen hut where they had assembled for their briefing, stepped aboard a bus, and were driven out to the airfield's austere gray T2 hangars. There, under bare incandescents, the men carefully made their exterior inspections of the planes, then climbed ladders toward the rear on their starboard sides, ducked their heads under the low cabin roofs, took their stations, and went through their preflight systems checks. The Lancs' bomb bays had already been loaded owing to the false starts of recent days, making them all but ready for takeoff.

Soon the planes were taxiing out onto the runways. At Woodhall Spa there were two exceptions due to mechanical problems. Flight Leader B. J. Dobson's plane, wing number LM 485, and Squadron Leader Tony Iveson's NG 181 both had to play catch up with the rest of the squadron—although Iveson's late start was hardly the worst problem he and his crew wound up facing before everything was said and done.

But apart from a handful of last-minute snafus, the operation was a go. At 8:25 that morning, after a week of weather-imposed delays, the first planes climbed into the air from the snow-cloaked fields of Lincolnshire and roared out over the ocean toward their target.

Not all would have the good fortune to return.

CHAPTER EIGHT

FORTRESS NORWAY

1.

On January 9, 1945, while the 617 Dambusters and 9 Bomber Squadron labored to dig themselves out of the snow in rural Lincolnshire, Korvettenkapitän Ralf-Reimer Wolfram and his crewmen were waiting out repairs on the U-864 in much more comfortable fashion. That Tuesday night Wolfram, a group of his leading officers, the ship's physician Friedrich Reuss, and their two German guests aboard the bunkered submarine had ventured forth from their quarters to enjoy a scrumptious lobster dinner, beer, and conversation at the German officers' club in Laksevåg.

Once a lavish banquet hall, the room had lost none of its well-appointed charm since the Nazi invaders seized it for their leisure use. Gracious, hardworking people, the Norwegian waitstaff was always professional and courteous to the men at the tables. They knew no other way to do their jobs . . . and, beyond that, understood that the best thing for themselves and the ongoing welfare of their loved ones was to conceal their resentment behind proper smiles.

Before returning to their quarters, Wolfram's party showed their appreciation for the considerate treatment they had received by making entries in the club's guest book—a plain binder with a swastika-and-eagle insignia on the cover. Passing the book around the table, they would fill two of its large white pages with their messages.

Commander Wolfram accepted the guest book first, writing his personal motto: "Great Heart, Clear Horizon." Then he paused contemplatively with pen in hand. Things could have turned out worse for his boat and crew. They had, after all, skirted disaster at Farsund, and wound up in a very hospitable place for their extended stopover. "We were lucky again," he added gratefully to his inscription. "Heartfelt thanks to the officers' club."

After Officers Eckhart, Aurbach, Sauerbier, and von Loe left their signatures under Wolfram's, it was Rolf von Chlingensperg's turn. He flipped the page to a blank leaf and jotted down an impromptu bit of verse:

Bergen was not in our program
The U-boat Captain Wolfram *
This unexpected misfortune,

---

* The Kriegsmarine customarily referred to a U-boat by its commander's name; hence U-864 was called Wolfram.

We handle its bad luck as good luck
And don't let it ruin
Our enjoyment of this Bergen* stay
When wisdom swigs like a drunkard, and stupidity gorges,
Both have to be lucky.
May we in our future be humble enough
To look back enviously at our present selves.

Having published an autobiographical account of his adventures at Nanga Parbat, Chlingensperg may have had an exaggerated view of his writerly skills. But what he'd meant to express with poetic flourish—the German lines were rhyming couplets and contained several deliberate wordplays—was the very same point Wolfram had made moments earlier. It surely must have been on his mind that, for many a countryman, this was the grimmest of times. At home people shivered in their beds without food and supplies. On the Western Front, the fighting in the Ardennes was at a fever pitch, with the German offensive stalled at Alsace, and thousands of soldiers reddening the snow with their spilled blood. And in the east the Soviet army was on the inexorable march toward Warsaw.

Here in the northlands, however, Germany was still conqueror, and the wear on one's spirit could be salved with laughter, talk of past adventures, and brave words about the challenges to come. Chlingensperg could have almost pretended these were the days when he'd

---

* Chlingensperg used the word *Berge,* which translates as "mountain" in Old German, instead of the city's correct name in the third couplet—a nod to his mountaineering expedition, which was obviously in his thoughts that night.

been preparing to climb the great mountain with his fellows, their quest the very symbol of a strong and ascendant Reich. The submarine might have gotten held up under far less agreeable circumstances.

After completing his poem, he dated it, turned the book lengthwise, and signed his name from bottom to top along the left margin—he'd filled nearly the entire page—and then passed the book to his colleague Riclef Schomerus. Scarcely as prolific as Chlingensperg, but also clearly in good humor, Schomerus jotted down his brief entry at the bottom of the page, using a crimped hand to record his name in its available space rather than turn to a new leaf. Below it he wryly commented, "At this festive affair because of transport."

In German military tradition, guest books were signed before men took leave of a place that had hosted them, and it is clear from the parting tone of their words that Wolfram and his officers assumed this would be their final gathering at the club. The dinner had been their send-off to Bergen, and indeed the West, before they took sail for what their captain had once called "uncharted places."

Enjoying their meals, drinks, and camaraderie beside the glow of a snapping fireplace, untouched by the stormy night outside, they could not have known that, as with nearly all aspects of their voyage, nothing would go as planned.

2.

It was 9:09 A.M., when Tony Iveson and his crew finally got into the air almost forty-five minutes after the 617's mission commenced.

There had been mechanical problems with the Lanc they were supposed to fly, and they'd had to scramble to take a reserve—tail number NG 181, radio call sign M for Mike—and then attempt to close the distance separating them from the rest of their squadron.

Every schoolboy knew the shortest distance between two points was a straight line, and Iveson's navigator, Flight Officer J. D. Harrison, had not forgotten his basic math lessons as he plotted a tape-measure course over the North Sea. Almost four hours later, Iveson spotted the other planes flying in the loose daylight formation the Brits called a gaggle. When Lancs sortied in large numbers, the spread-out gaggles allowed for evasive flexibility if they were attacked by ground barrages or enemy aircraft. Planes could move up, down, or laterally within the group, and it was only as they neared their destination that they would tighten up to make faster passes and heavier bombardments.

"After a few trips," related Iveson, "one got used to the idea of a Lancaster just ahead and above with its bomb doors open and the twenty-one-foot Tallboy bomb in sinister view."

Those in the target area might have agreed with his characterization of the Tallboy. *Sinister* was a good word. Near misses with it had caused railway bridge collapses and landslides that blocked the entrances to subterranean rocket facilities, validating their designation by creator Barnes Wallis—the same man credited with inventing Upkeep—as "earthquake bombs."

As with the Upkeeps, the Tallboys had required modifications to the Lancs. The aircraft's bomb-bay doors were bulged outward so they could close around the bombs, and special chains were used to hold their massive weight securely in place. Because they had to be dropped from a significant altitude to accrue the terminal velocity needed for penetrating their targets, a precision bombsight was designed to allow their deployment from twenty thousand feet or higher.

Today the Number 9 was designated the high section at seventeen thousand feet; 617's Lancs would be the low section and come in at between fifteen and sixteen thousand feet, with Fauquier's little Mosquito staying down at about seven thousand feet to coordinate air strikes, scout for shipping targets, and assess the success of the hits. Fauquier had split the bombers into three teams: Six planes would rove for ships, Flight Officer Phil Martin in Lanc DV-393, R for Roger, would lead a group of three aircraft against the floating dock at the north end of the harbor, and Squadron Leader J. F. Brookes in NG 228, V for Vera, would head the seven aircraft that constituted the main U-boat bunker detail.

M-Mike was among the flights assigned to Brookes. Slotting into the gaggle from the rear, Iveson was instructed to orbit his target until he had it in clear view and only then make his drop. It was a strong reminder that Fauquier was determined to minimize collateral damage at all cost. Normally the bomb would be released as the Lancs made rapid passes and getaways; an orbital drop would leave the plane vulnerable to barrages of German AA fire from below. But orders were orders, and the Norwegians deserved to be spared more needless destruction.

Iveson prepared for his first pass, realizing there was still no sign of the expected escort—Mustangs from the 315th Polish Fighter Squadron that had participated in the *Tirpitz* raid. Hopefully they'd show, Iveson thought. Without them to run cover, the Lancs would be circling unprotected.

Stationed in the nose of the plane, scrunched over the optical panel of his Mark IIA Stabilizing Automatic Bombsight, the bomb aimer, Flight Sergeant Frank Chance had taken over navigation duties from Harrison and was calling out course alterations to guide Iveson's approach to the bunker. A sophisticated tachometric sight issued to the 617, the SABs calculated the exact differentials that wind conditions created between air and ground speeds, allowing the bombs to strike with unprecedented accuracy.

Now the colossal U-boat shelter was visible below and ahead of the Lanc. Clenching the bomb release lead in his gloved fist, Flight Sergeant Chance poised his thumb over the toggle button and continued to rattle off revised headings. And then the plane was nearly over its objective, antiaircraft, tracer, and smoke rounds pouring from gun emplacements around the bunker and the decks of flak ships in the harbor.

Finally the aircraft reached its target. A wiry tension hummed through its cabin as Chance shouted a bombs-away, pressed his release button, and the Tallboy dropped from its bay toward the bunker, the abrupt jettisoning of its weight rocking the plane in the air, making its crewmen's stomachs lurch violently.

Within moments the earthquake bomb detonated to raise a cloud of dust, soot, and debris that, recalled Iveson, "hovered stationary over the U-boat pens in the still wind conditions, mixing with the haze of the smoke screen laid by the Germans." Steadying the Lanc, he gazed down through his canopy and tried to get a visual estimate of the damage to the bunker. But it was screened from sight by the heavy pall, leaving him with no choice except to follow orders and orbit until the smoke dispersed.

Meanwhile, Iveson had yet to notice any sign of the Polish escort and wondered what could have delayed its arrival—or if it was even going to show at all. But he "hung around waiting" for the dust to clear per his group commander's instructions, circling the pens, growing increasingly nervous about his position. The longer the Lanc stayed put over the bunker, the greater the odds of Nazi ground artillery knocking it out of the sky.

Then, all at once, he heard his rear gunner, Pilot Officer Ted Wass, shout out from the tail section: "Okay, Skipper, I see the fighters!"

The words gave Iveson's spirits and confidence an instant boost . . . but it was a fleeting one. As the planes came within closer eyeshot, the hum of their engines rapidly growing in volume, he felt his relief leak out of him like the air from a punctured balloon.

It wasn't the escort that Pilot Officer Wass had spotted, not by a long shot, but a group of German Focke-Wulf 190 fighter aircraft coming in for their attack.

3.

Down at his low altitude, Fauquier was having problems of his own. Some of them had to do with incoming flak, others with his worsening visibility.

Supported by enormous pontoons, the rebuilt floating dock at the north end of harbor was one of his predetermined mission objectives, and he'd ordered bombing runs at it from multiple directions, a task that was getting harder as smoke and concrete dust from the pens drifted northward to further veil it from sight. The dock was now practically invisible from any angle other than straight overhead, and in terms of risk-reward, its value as a target fell appreciably below the danger to his planes as they tried to home in through the haze and antiaircraft fire.

In LM 489, A for Apple, Pilot J. A. Sanders had executed five separate runs but was unable to identify the dock, dropping a single Tallboy in what a subsequent pass had shown was a near miss. And after nine passes at the smoke-obscured dock, Flight Officer Martin had dropped one of his Tallboys just to overshoot it by about a hundred yards. Meanwhile, he was taking bursts from Flak 38s, Flak 40s, and Flak 88 guns on the ground, with a heavy pattern from the last coming closest to his tail.

Under the circumstances, Fauquier decided to rule out continued action against the floating docks and transmit a modified command: Flight Officer Martin's force was to forget its previous orders and instead join the larger group of aircraft on the prowl for targets in the harbor.

This came as good news to Martin. After that final run on the dock, his bomb aimer, Flight Sergeant Don Day had spotted a "fat merchantman" racing into the bay to escape the strike. Verifying with Fauquier that it was all right to abandon the floating dock in pursuit, Martin turned over navigation to Day, who got a "perfect sight" on the ship as they came up on its rear. The SABs had an autorelease option that would drop the Tallboy when its target lined up in its crosshairs, and Martin's was flashing its five-second warning light when "there was an almighty crash mixed with a sound akin to hundreds of coins being thrown against the fuselage door."

The Lanc jumped in the air, and the bomb plummeted from its bay, splashing into the ocean to the portside of the ship, missing it by thirty yards without detonating. Martin and his crew would not learn how close they'd come to being blown out of the air until they landed and examined the damage to their bomb-bay doors: The Tallboy had taken the brunt of a direct hit by an 88 shell and had its arming wire detached in the process.

Not far off, meanwhile, Lancaster WDV 405—radio call sign J for Jack—was another of the floating-dock strike force to have gotten Fauquier's revised instructions. At slightly before 1300 hours, its pilot, Flight Officer Fred Watts, dropped a Tallboy between fifty and seventy-five yards to port of the German cargo ship *Olga Siemers,* virtually knocking it out of the water. As orders required, they were coming around for a fuller damage assessment when they saw a pair of Focke-Wulf interceptors appear from the northwest in pursuit of another Lanc, NF 992—call sign B for Boy—flown by Watts's close friend, Aussie flight officer Ian Stewart Ross.

This was only Watts's second mission and Ross, a veteran of fifty ops, was one of the most experienced men in the squadron, someone he looked up to. Now he was in very serious trouble. Ross had no hope of outmaneuvering the swifter, lighter enemy aircraft unless the Germans were somehow drawn off. And with no sign of the Polish escort, Lanc WDV 405 was the only bomber that was even near.

Flight Officer Watts quickly notified Fauquier that he was flying over to aid him and turned his plane toward the attackers. He had become Ross's only chance.

4.

The Focke-Wulfs were elements of Gruppes 9 and 12 of Jagdgeschwader 5 Eismeer—or Fighter Wing 5 Ice Sea—and had taken off from the Luftwaffe airfield at Herdla, a tiny island substation of the larger Bergen command about thirty miles northwest of Laksevåg. Just two days before, the dozen or so fighters in Gruppe 9 had belatedly reached Herdla as reinforcements, having been grounded for weeks at the Værnes airbase near Trondheim—their inability to take wing during that stretch resulting from the same tempestuous weather that had kept the British Lanc squadrons in their hangars at Lincolnshire.

The transfers had arrived none too soon for J5's operational needs. At about 1250 hours—ten minutes to one in the afternoon—on January 12, they hastily scrambled from their runways in answer to reports of enemy bombers flying toward Bergen. Among them was a fighter call-signed White 11, piloted by Unteroffizier Heinz Orlowski, and another White 1, with Leutnant Werner Gayko in the cockpit.

The first plane Orlowski and Gayko sighted as they buzzed over Laksevåg Harbor was Lancaster NG 257 of the 9 Squadron. Flight Officer E. C. Redfern had left Bardney at 8:48 A.M. and had just dropped his load over the Bergen U-boat pens when the two fighters closed in on him spitting machine-gun rounds. Nine Squadron's Lancs had attacked from a higher altitude than the 617s, and the fast-climbing German fighters took Redfern by surprise. His fuselage chewed up by the enemy fire, his tail aflame, Redfern was unable to maintain control of his aircraft and went into a wild, spiraling dive, crashing into the sea with everyone aboard.

Although they were the first British casualties of the bombing raid, Flight Officer Redfern and his crew would not be the last— nor even the last claimed by Orlowski's Fw 190.

Twenty-year-old Flight Lieutenant Ray Harris was in the pilot's seat of Lanc PD 198, call sign WS-W or Willing Winnie. He had no sooner dropped its Tallboy from 17,600 feet and turned back toward base when he heard his intercom crackle. As a precaution against German eavesdropping, intercom silence was standard procedure during ops. But with the "bombs away" followed by a "bombs gone," and the target zone now behind him, Harris had relaxed and lit a cigarette, as he always did after a drop was completed. Wafting back through the cabin, the smell of smoke from his unfiltered Woodbine was a sign that 'com silence could be similarly relaxed.

"Four Mustangs approaching on the starboard bow, Skipper." The voice issuing from the speaker belonged to rear gunner Will Gabriel, and Harris instantly picked up its sardonic edge. The Polish escort had been nowhere in sight when they were in the thick of their mission, taking ground fire from German AA batteries.

Harris blew streams of tobacco smoke out his nostrils. "Why

bother turning up now?" he said with mingled irritation and amusement.

But as they watched the formation close distance, the men in the Lanc grew more than a touch curious. Surely the Poles could tell that they were heading back over the sea toward England. There was no use in them tagging along now.

Mid-upper gunner Mac Williams was the first to distinguish the German markings on the aircraft. His eyes widened in dismay as he peered through his view panel. "Christ . . . they're 190s," he shouted. "Corkscrew starboard go!"

Harris heard the tension-charged words blare from the intercom and gripped the pilot's wheel, his heart thumping in his chest. The corkscrew tactic had been devised to give Lancs a shot at evading nimble pursuers like the Focke-Wulfs. Combining a series of steep dives, climbs, and hard banks, it was intended to throw off an enemy and frustrate gunners trying to align a bomber in their crosshairs. But with four German planes making a rapid approach, Harris could not have liked the odds of dodging all of them.

He would have no time to test those odds before Orlowski opened fire, hot on his tail, his cannons chopping away. A fusillade tore through the Lanc's metal skin, rupturing the hydraulics. Harris kept banking and diving over the ocean but the swarm of Fw 190s stayed on him without letup.

Harris would record fifteen attacks by the German harriers as he dipped and rolled through the sky, at last finding himself down to four thousand feet, the water a mirror-smooth blue expanse beneath him. While he'd managed to shake three of the four planes—the absence of gunfire told him they'd spent their ammo—the Fw 190 that had shot out the hydraulics showed no sign of giving up the chase.

Willing Winnie herself was a battered mess. Her turret guns used hydraulic firing mechanisms and the fluid leaks had disabled them, leaving her defenseless. Moreover, two of his crewmen had been wounded by gunfire and flying bits of metal. Harris's VHS radioman, Bill Brownlie, had seemingly taken a grazing wound to his lower back—"I think I've been shot up the arse, Skipper!" he'd shouted when it happened—and Gabriel looked even worse off at the rear of the aircraft. In severe pain, he was hemorrhaging profusely, his trousers shredded and blood soaked where shrapnel had torn into his leg.

Besides all this, Harris still had to contend with the Fw 190. Giving a quick word to his flight engineer, Maurice Mellors, he took a final corkscrew down to a thousand feet to try to lose him. It didn't work. The enemy plane tached forward and was soon pulling up alongside his port wing.

Harris prepared for another strafing . . . but he had no idea how lucky he'd gotten. Like the other German pilots, Orlowski was out of ammunition and ready to break off the attack. Staring out the cockpit window, his eyes meeting Harris's through his flight goggles, he grinned and saluted the pilot as he made his fly-past—an honorary gesture of respect for a skilled, courageous adversary he assumed was about to perish.

In no mood for the German's admiration, Harris tugged his Webley service revolver from its holder, looked back at this smiling face, and fired a shot out the canopy at him. Stunned, Orlowski peeled away from the bomber to rejoin the rest of the Focke-Wulfs in his group, and then turned back to Herdla Island.

Harris now decided on a course for RAF Carnaby, an emergency landing ground near Bridlington on England's extreme northern coast. He knew its single runway ran inland for two miles and had a width of seven hundred feet—many times that of ordinary strips. Also, its Fog Investigation and Dispersal, or FIDO, fuel pipelines on either side of the runway spouted up flames day and night, creating twin rows of fire that burned off the blinding English fog and marked a bright path for crippled bombers. Above all there would be fire trucks and ambulances ready to assist on landing.

While there was no way Willing Winnie was flying the distance home to base, Harris believed he just might be able to nurse her along to Carnaby . . . not that reaching the field guaranteed a happy outcome. The plane's undercarriage, like its turret guns, relied on the debilitated hydraulic linkages for normal operation, and it remained to be seen whether he'd be able to lower his gear. Coming down without wheels could be devastating for a plane the size of a Lancaster.

Yes, Harris thought, he'd have his hands full assuming he got that far. Meanwhile, Gabriel wasn't doing very well. He'd been assisted onto the rest bunk in the Lanc's midsection, then been bandaged up and given a morphine injection—but his profuse bleeding had not been staunched. And though Brownlie admittedly seemed to be in much better condition, he was still in evident need of medical care.

Still, one thing at a time. One thing at a time.

Reaching for the handset of his wireless, Harris radioed ahead to notify Carnaby of his dire situation, hoping for the best, while preparing for the very worst.

5.

The Germans simply called the Tallboy the *schwerste Bombe*—or heavy bomb. But if anyone inside Bruno had been familiar with the British moniker *earthquake bomb,* they would have gotten a terrifying firsthand demonstration of how it was earned.

As the air-raid sirens had started clamoring around them, the bunker's naval and infantrymen, engineers, mechanics, smiths, welders, construction workers, and other assorted personnel had taken cover in its bomb shelters and waited in nerve-racking expectation. Then three of the twelve-thousand-pounders scored direct hits on the roof, drilling craters into concrete that was between eight and nineteen feet thick.

This attack bore no resemblance to the one in October, when the hundred-pound bombs had detonated ineffectually. Now the boom of the explosions was deafeningly loud, overpowering the wail of the sirens. On a rooftop mezzanine level, storage rooms and a cafeteria were left in pulverized ruins. Tools were scattered, tables and chairs flattened. Walls shuddered in offices and workshops, stress fractures spreading across their surfaces, sagging and buckling from their supports before they finally tumbled to the floor.

The terrifying strikes shook everyone and everything inside the fortress walls. Power lines and wiring spilled from the ceiling and hung over piles of rubble like snarled, limp tentacles. Smoke and cement dust churned in the air. Throughout the immense structure, water pipes burst, lights flickered, and machinery sputtered as men went dashing toward the emergency generators to try to restore electricity to the bunker. Two technicians in one of the shops were crushed to death under a cascade of falling debris.

Twelve days earlier, U-864 had pulled into Bruno with her cranky snorkel system and damage from the grounding near Farsund. With the repairs completed in one of the dry-dock pens on the south side of the harbor, the boat had been moved to Pen No. 3— one of the smaller wet pens on the north side, where the entrance was open to the harbor. Stocked, fueled, her equipment checked and rechecked, she had been declared fit to embark on the final, extended leg of her journey when the Lancasters struck.

Now a Tallboy slammed into the submarine pen's roof, gouged a deep hole into it, and detonated with a bellowing roar, sending down a rain of crumbled cement and other material. The sides of the pen vibrated. Wreckage splashed around the U-boat as she rolled and banged against the work platforms along the enclosure's walls. On the other side of one such dividing wall in Pen No. 1, the Type VIIC submarine U-775 had been undergoing repairs. She heaved in the water tossing beneath her keel, but the ceiling overhead remained intact. Of the six submarine pens and seventh fuel storage pen, U-864's was the only one to take a direct hit.

Minutes passed. As more bombs fell over the harbor, Bruno's personnel waited edgily in the shelters where they'd taken refuge. There was nothing else they could do.

The ground kept trembling.

6.

Eastward over Bergen, Tony Iveson's plane was ablaze and threatening to fly out of control. The sky had erupted into fireworks around him, tracers ribboning past his canopy, rounds shredding the air. And the Focke-Wulfs his rear gunner had spotted were coming on fast.

He'd barely gotten a handle on the situation when one of the fighters moved ahead of the others, surging from behind M-Mike with his cannons angrily cycling out armor-piercing rounds. Iveson felt the plane shudder as they struck it.

"A yard to the right and he would have been firing shells right up the fuselage, killing us all," Iveson recalled. "As it was, he hit one engine, the port fin and rudder, and the tail plane and elevator, blasting lumps out of them."

With those lumps chewed out of it, and the cables to its trim tabs severed, the plane had become destabilized. Its tail swinging downward, its nose kicking up, M-Mike was bucking like a rebellious winged stallion.

Commanded by Lieutenant James Stuart Launders, HMS *Venturer* (P68) was the lead boat of the Royal Navy's Vampire-class fast attack submarines in World War II. In February 1944, she would become the only sub in history to sink another sub underwater.   BRITISH NATIONAL ARCHIVES

One of the few existing photos of the crew of U-864. They are assembled on the boat's deck prior sailing out on their covert mission to the Far East.   BUNDESARCHIV

Bunker Bruno after the RAF's unsuccessful air raid on Bergen in October 1944. Although surrounding structures were pulverized by the bombing, the submarine shelter, a prime British target, sustained no appreciable damage.
BUNDESARCHIV

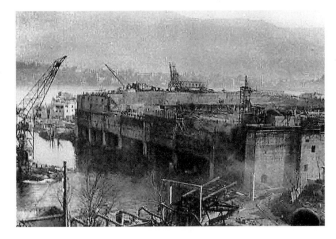

Houses of dockyard workers near the Kriegsmarine's submarine base in Laksevåg, Bergen. Most had been the homes of Norwegian families that were seized by their German occupiers.
U.S. NATIONAL ARCHIVES AND RECORDS ADMINISTRATION

A "dry" submarine pen inside Bruno. It was in one such pen that U-864 would have emergency repairs done to her engine and snorkel system.
BUNDESARCHIV

The ruins of the Holen School, where eighty innocent civilians—sixty-one of them children—perished in the October 1944 raid. Norway's greatest wartime tragedy, it would prompt the British to completely reassess their methods when they launched a second airstrike at Bruno three months later.   BUNDESARCHIV

A Lancaster bomber of the type flown by the RAF's crack 617 Dambusters during their attempt to destroy U-864 at Bergen in January 1945.

NATIONAL ARCHIVAL SERVICES OF NORWAY

Nazi and Japanese banners hung side by side at an Axis submarine base in Penang, Malaysia, symbols of their often uneasy cooperation   BRITISH NATIONAL ARCHIVES.

German and Japanese sailors on joint operations in Penang, Malaysia, where U-864 was bound with her secret cargo and passengers.
U.S. NATIONAL ARCHIVES AND RECORDS ADMINISTRATION

Germany's Messerschmitt Me 163 Komet rocket fighter. BUNDESARCHIV

Me 262 Swallow jet fighters were high-tech Wunderwaffen coveted by Tokyo. U-864 carried components and plans that would have allowed the mass production of both experimental aircraft in Japan. BUNDESARCHIV

The V-1 flying bomb, a
precursor of the cruise
missile.
BUNDESARCHIV

V-2 rocket (pictured
under Allied guard shortly
after the war ended).
American and British
intelligence feared the
Japanese would use these
rockets as delivery systems
for atomic weapons—and
U-864's "guests" included
top scientific experts who
would have been
instrumental in their
manufacture.
U.S. NATIONAL ARCHIVES AND
RECORDS ADMINISTRATION

Lerwick, in the Shetland
Islands, was a launching
spot for British espionage
against occupied Norway
during World War II.
Shown here are one of the
submarine piers where
HMS *Venturer* would have
stopped for refuel and
resupply before embarking
on her missions.
SHETLAND ARCHIVES

Fishing cutters used by the Shetland Bus to shuttle special agents and supplies to Norway. SHETLAND ARCHIVES

A 12,000 pound Tallboy "earthquake" bomb being loaded aboard an Avro Lancaster.

BRITISH NATIONAL ARCHIVES

The mansion known as Bletchley Park, where an enormous task force of British and American code breakers secretly labored night and day on Project Ultra.

The Colossus at Bletchley Park, used to break coded Axis transmissions at a rapid clip, was the world's first electronic computer.

As Iveson fought to wrestle the Lanc back to a level position, he "saw one Focke-Wulf perform an upward roll right in front of the nose," the German pilot's boldness seeming to confirm that he thought the Lanc a goner . . . an opinion for which Iveson couldn't have faulted the "cheeky bugger." Iveson was not only pitching and yawing in the air, but had gotten reports from his gunners that the port engine was in flames—dire news. If the fire spread to a fuel tank, everyone aboard would be incinerated in the consequent explosion.

His next decision, then, required no thought whatsoever: The crew had to be ready to bail to safety.

"Stand by to abandon aircraft," he barked into the intercom. There were now three crewmen in the bow with him—Flight Officer Harrison, Flight Sergeant Chance, and Sergeant Desmond "Taff" Phillips, his flight engineer. The other three crewmen had shrugged into their emergency chutes and gathered at the rear door.

Meanwhile, tongues of flame continued licking at the engine. Turning to Phillips, Iveson shouted for him to pull the copper Graviner fire extinguisher off its mounting bracket on the cabin wall and then hastily ran through their oft-practiced drills with him. Phillips's first order of business would be to feather the engine—or twist its propeller blades so they were parallel with the airflow and stopped rotating. This would reduce drag on the plane and make it easier for it to stay aloft on the remaining three Merlins. Just as critically, it would stop fuel from pumping through the engine to worsen the fire.

As Phillips turned the Graviner's nozzle on the engine, releasing a stream of methyl-bromide fire retardant, Chance had a flash of inspiration, got up, and went aft to rummage a length of rope out of a storage compartment. Dashing back to the cockpit, he coiled and knotted it around the yoke to improvise a sort of harness, "easing the strain" for Iveson as he fought to keep the column from tearing free of his grasp.

Chance's trick had worked, and worked well to stop M-Mike from rearing crazily in the air—but the men were far from out of jeopardy.

With a homeward journey of hundreds of miles still ahead, most of it over the open sea, Iveson knew they had to somehow restore the aircraft's center of gravity and give it a semblance of balanced flight. He also wanted to jettison the second Tallboy from its bay. The ground fire directed at the Lanc had been drawing an accurate fix, and as he obviously had to abandon the mission, it was best to be rid of its twelve thousand pounds of extra, explosive weight—especially with the plane running on just three of its four engines.

The fire doused, Taff Phillips again hastened into the aft section and "scrabbled around" to rig the detached trim tab cables back onto the servos, working on them until Iveson "got some control" of the plane. Banking off from Laksevåg's densely inhabited harbor area, Iveson wasted no time fusing the bomb and dropped it in the unpopulated woods outside the village.

That was when Phillips, still in the aft cabin where he'd been fiddling with the cables, noticed an odd banging sound behind him, accompanied by a cold, roaring draft of wind inside the cabin. Uncertain what to make of it, he went farther toward the rear to investigate.

It only took him an instant to grasp what had transpired.

The aft entrance hatch was on his left, directly in front of the starboard tailplane, and when he reached it he found the door wide open and "three helmets on the step." The Lanc's two gunners, Sergeant Smith and Flight Officer Tittle, had bailed along with Ted Wass, its radio operator.

Slamming the door shut, Phillips rushed forward to inform Iveson, Chance, and Harrison of his discovery.

Iveson took the news in unruffled stride. With the plane nearly out of control, and the racket of the engines drowning out the intercom, it was reasonable to assume the men had "misheard" him, taking his standby as the jump order. But whatever the circumstances, their evacuation had left him short almost half his crew and missing an engine, with "a flapping tail unit, no gunner, and no mid-upper [gun] turret."*

Iveson refused to tempt fate any longer. "I think I can get her back," he said to his remaining airmen. "Where's the nearest airfield?"

Harrison moved to his chart table. "Sumburgh," he said. "On the main Shetland Island."

Iveson nodded. The RCAF 404 Squadron flew its coastal patrol planes from the station. It had two runways, one a good eight hun-

---

* The Avro Lancaster typically had a mid-upper gun turret with two rear-pointing .303 inch (7.7mm) Browning machine guns as part of its standard arms complement. But prior to the *Tirpitz* raid, the turret was removed from the bombers of the 617 and 9 Squadrons to accommodate added fuel storage and give them greater flying range. Ironically, had the turret guns been available to Second Lieutenant Iveson's M-Mike and Flight Lieutenant Harris's Willing Winnie, both aircraft might have escaped the critical damage they sustained to their tail sections.

dred yards long. He asked the navigator for a "course to steer" and received a set of bearings. The trip was no minor challenge for the hobbled Lanc, especially in January, when winter squalls and pea-soup fog could swirl up over ocean without forewarning. But it was the best destination available.

With a wing, a prayer, and a length of rope holding his jerky control column in check, Iveson set out across 340 miles of water for the Shetlands.

7.

As he swung toward the beleaguered Lancaster flown by Flight Officer Ross, Fred Watts realized the two Fw 190s had borne in hard at Ross's Lanc, their cannons chopping out salvos of fire, staying on the attack as thick black smoke poured from the crippled bomber's number three engine—the inner engine on his port wing.

Watts did what he could to draw off the German interceptors, his front gunner, Ken Jewell, opening up on them with his machine guns. But before the Focke-Wulfs finally scrammed, Ross was swerving madly across the sky, his remaining three engines whining as he overshot the southern Norwegian coast in a desperate bid to reach water.

Watts followed close, not wanting to lose sight of his friend, and then suddenly there was blue underneath them and the mortally wounded Lanc had gone into a spiral. Just before he hit the water, the experienced Ross somehow managed to turn into the wind and pull up for a perfect ditch, smacking the surface on his belly, bouncing forward as friction with the water slowed his momentum, sheets of foam-flecked spray splashing up around the huge aircraft's wings and tailfins.

By now a second Lanc—LM 492—had joined Watts circling above the plane. Its pilot, Jimmy Castagnola, was another good friend of Ross. His first bomb, aimed at the Bruno bunker, had overshot its target, and he had then dropped his second Tallboy on an M1 minesweeper, hitting its stern square-on. Three minutes after the bomb plowed into its bowels, a huge explosion aboard turned the vessel over on its side and sent it to the bottom of the harbor.

Castagnola had been swinging off on his return home when he saw Ross's plane spinning downward into the sea and roared over to see what he could do to assist.

A Lancaster bomber had several small escape hatches on its roof for water landings, one aft of the wings, one at the midline, another at the pilot's position. Overhead, the observers in the two planes saw those hatches flap open and watched all seven crew members slide out onto the wing. To every appearance they were uninjured.

There was a self-inflating dinghy in a compartment on top of the wing, but no one aboard either Watts or Castagnola's planes saw it appear. They concluded the raft's release mechanisms had gotten jammed, leaving Ross and his crew without a means of escape as the plane took on seawater.

Castagnola dropped some Mae West life vests down to them, for what negligible good it would do; the men would freeze to death within minutes if they were forced to dive off the sinking Lanc into the bitterly cold ocean swells. Meanwhile, Watts's radioman had contacted RAF Coastal Command's air-sea rescue liaison at Sumburgh—the same base that Tony Iveson had decided to try to reach with his stricken aircraft.

But Sumburgh was hours away, and Watts was afraid that Ross's Lanc wouldn't stay afloat long enough for the ASR plane to arrive at its coordinates. He'd even begun to think it was a perverse stroke of luck that they were so near the Norwegian coast—thirty-five miles, by his estimate. The Germans would almost surely be first to arrive, and although that meant Ross and his men would spend the rest of the war in captivity, it was better than what would happen if they weren't rescued at all.

Watts now called Castagnola in LM 492 and told them to head for home—both orbiting planes were low on fuel, and there was no need for more than one to keep an eye out. In fact, the two together only stood a greater chance of drawing enemy fighters back to the scene. Unable to argue his reasoning, Castagnola left.

Afterward Watts continued to circle the floating Lanc at five thousand feet. It was past one-thirty in the afternoon, the sky bright with sunshine, the wave crests low, almost no wind. That was a positive; the calm conditions would keep the aircraft from drifting too far. But the northern winter days were brief, and the coming of darkness would complicate rescue efforts. On the wing of the downed plane, its crewmen were already huddled together for warmth. Watts feared what nightfall would bring

Two hours passed. Watts kept overflying the plane, not wanting to abandon his friends and squadron mates. But the needles of his fuel gauges were dropping fast. If he stayed on any longer, his tanks wouldn't have enough petrol left to get him home. He had never before in his life felt so helpless, and hoped to never feel that way again.

Thirty minutes later, with no other recourse open to him, he muttered a prayer for the seven on the wing below, and reluctantly turned for Scotland.*

A good while earlier, however, Sumburgh had dispatched a Vickers Warwick search-and-rescue plane to the crash site. The Warwick was fitted out to carry a wooden airborne lifeboat with a mast, sails, twin outboard motors, a wireless transmitter/receiver, and survival supplies. Weighing sixteen hundred pounds fully loaded, the stout little craft would be released from the Warwick's undersection on a cluster of parachutes.

The Warwick reached its destination at twilight and found the Lanc in the water a few miles off Bergen, very close to Watts's reported location. As Watts had surmised, the calm weather conditions had largely eliminated drift, though the sinking aircraft was slowly moving toward shore with the inbound current. The plane was now almost completely engulfed, seawater lapping at the wing Ross and his airmen had used for a platform. In their struggle to keep from being washed away, some of the men had climbed atop a section of the fuselage that was barely projecting from the surface.

Coming in low at seven hundred feet, the Warwick dropped its

---

* Watts's plane had run so dangerously low on fuel by the time it left the area that air command would not let him attempt a return to Woodhall Spa. Instead he was directed to fly to the RAF Coastal Command station in Milltown, Scotland, a straighter shot across the North Sea from Bergen. The concerns proved valid; Watts had no sooner executed his landing than his thirsty engines choked off. The Lanc's tanks had gone completely dry.

lifeboat within sixty feet of the wreckage, then hovered above the whitecaps as one of the downed airmen leaped off the plane and swam toward it, splashing closer and closer in his heavy, soaking wet flight suit, struggling not to let the weight of its saturated fabric drag him under. Finally he reached the lifeboat and reached up for the gunwale, trying to haul himself over onto its deck.

That was when the Warwick's crew heard the buzz of nearby planes, and not theirs—the bombing raid was long since over, and they would have been informed of any other Allied aircraft in the vicinity. The sound was growing louder by the second.

It all happened fast. Gazing out his window, horrified, the Warwick's pilot saw two Focke-Wulfs dive down almost level with the water in a strafing run. Seconds after he'd first heard the drone of their engines, they were chopping away at the defense-less airman who'd swum for the lifeboat, then making a pass over the sinking Lanc to pour fire at the men clinging to its fuselage for dear life. And even as they swung around for another run, a third Fw 190 came zooming over the water, straight for the rescue plane.

Sickened and dismayed, the pilot knew at once that he'd have to quit the scene. It was a wrenching decision. But in its ASR configuration, the lightly armed Warwick stood no chance against a single Fw 190, let alone three. Sticking around for a fight would accomplish nothing besides contributing to the mission's loss totals. He was responsible for the lives of his crew, and taking on the 190s would have been suicide.

The pilot pulled away, flying just above the crests to thwart enemy radar. He had done what he had to, made the only rational choice open to him. But necessary decisions often come with a cost, and the ghosts that arise from them may never be exorcised.

He would see seven such ghosts in his mind's eye for decades to come.

8.

The bombing of fortress Bruno was violent but brief, like a racing cyclone. Although the men inside the bunker could not have known it as they cautiously emerged from their shelters, the failure of the Polish escort to appear had something to do the raid's swiftness; high above Laksevåg, RAF bombardiers had had to drop their initial loads and then break out of their damage-assessing orbits to fend off the scrambled fighters of Gruppes 9 and 12.

Had all the rubble from the penetrated roof struck her, U-864 likely would have sustained irreparable damage. But the mezzanine floor added a four-foot layer of reinforced concrete to the ceiling that softened the brunt of the explosion and caught some of the tumbling debris before it would have crashed down on the submarine.

U-864 did not escape the chaos unscathed. Fragments of the partially collapsed ceiling spilled over her conning tower and battered her masts, bridge, deck, rails, and wintergarten gunnery platform. After the dust cleared, an inspection of the submarine would reveal what the Kriegsmarine's war diary called slight damage. But it was enough to require another round of repairs that would again stall her trip.

All told, the Germans must have been very grateful, however. Things could have been worse. Even with the destruction that occurred, Bruno held up well against one of the most powerful weapons in the Allied arsenal.

U-864's mission would again be delayed, but her cargo was intact, and it looked as if she'd be under way before too long.

9.

Tony Iveson reached Sumburgh at a little before three in the afternoon. But as relieved as he was to see the airfield, he feared his touchdown might be a rough go.

Like Ray Harris in Willing Winnie, he was flying with "buggered" hydraulics. When he'd tried to lower the landing wheels, the undercarriage hadn't budged. He was fairly confident he could still deploy the wheels using his emergency backup lever, but without the servos he would be unable to retract them again. If anything went wrong with his approach, and he had to climb back into the air, he would be flying with lowered gear. On four engines that wasn't a terribly big deal, but three was a different story. On three, it could throw off the Lanc's already precarious balance and turn it back into a renegade horse.

Iveson inhaled, pulled the emergency landing gear handle. The wheels went down without a problem and he started to make his pass.

That was when the Spitfire swung in front of him, cutting straight across his aerial path. The small one-man fighter only had a single propeller on its nose cone and it was out of commission. Its pilot was trying to glide in for a desperate landing.

"He had priority," Iveson recalled.

The Lanc had to circle now, the very thing that had concerned him when he deployed the wheels. Carefully, Iveson guided the plane into a slow loop over the field until he got permission to land. It "behaved beautifully," remaining level through her descent, touching down lightly on the concrete strip.

Then suddenly and unexpectedly, it went into a skid that jolted it off the runway onto the field.

The plane bumped and shimmied along. Equipment rattled, maps, pencils, rulers, and protractors flew off the navigator's table. Tossed about in his seat, Iveson kept his composure and at last brought the Lanc to a halt on the frozen sod.

When Iveson climbed out of the front emergency hatch with Harrison, Chance, and Taff Phillips, they saw that one of the tires had been blown by bullets. Everyone, Iveson remembered, "started to shake."

Their trembling must have been worse for the realization that the plane had made its return with three fewer men than had gotten aboard at Woodhall Spa.*

---

* Petty Officer Ted Wass, Sergeant A. L. Smith, and Flight Officer A. Tittle, M-Mike's radioman and gunners respectively, would all survive their parachute jumps and land safely in the snowy countryside below. Picked up by enemy soldiers, they were brought to Germany and interned at the expansive Stalag VII-A POW camp outside Moosburg in southern Bavaria. Fortunately, they remained prisoners only until April 29, when the U.S. Army's 14th Armored Division liberated the camp's estimated 130,000 prisoners. All three men would later confirm that they had in fact believed Iveson had given the affirmative jump order. Wass would remain in the supply branch of the RAF

10.

It was almost four o'clock when Ray Harris finally brought Willing Winnie over Carnaby. Looking down at the field, he saw ambulances and fire trucks gathered around the runway. He'd notified flight control that he had wounded on board, and knew the ambulances were partly there to whisk them off to triage. But, no mistake, the emergency teams were also ready to pull Harris and his crew out of a burning wreckage.

He himself had secured his safety harness and instructed the men to take their crash positions. Aside from Gabriel, who remained on the rest cot, they were seated on the cabin floor in their specified areas, braced for the worst.

As it turned out, the hydraulic lines to his undercarriage were in decent shape—better than Tony Iveson's, whose plight Harris would not have known about at the time. The Lanc's wheels went down without any need for him to pull his backup lever, and he was soon taxiing smoothly between the bright, fiery margins of the FIDO strip.

There was a hospital in Driffield about ten miles inland, and Gabriel was quickly sped over for surgery on his leg. Meanwhile, Bill Brownlie, the radioman whose lower back had been cut, felt well enough after receiving on-the-spot first-aid treatment to accompany his other five crewmates to a pub in the nearby village of Lissett.

---

after the war, where he was commissioned as a squadron leader. He died in 2009 at age seventy-nine.

Gabriel would make a full recovery from his operation, although his flying days with the RAF were over. The rest of the crew, including Brownlie, were back out on combat missions by early February.

But years later, Brownlie would become a living reminder that a war's cruelties can far outlast the roar of its guns. A small piece of shrapnel had entered his body through his wound; undetected, it would eventually migrate to his spine and cause serious infection.

In 1964, he would die as a result of complications from a minor nick.

11.

The Leigh lights skimmed across the water, tracing radiant paths toward the shoreline near Bergen. It was pitch dark out, and the rescue aircraft had flown hundreds of miles to search for the crew of NF 992.

On his return to Sumburgh earlier that night, the ASR Warwick's pilot and crew had horrified their commanders with accounts of the strafing of the downed Lanc. Luftwaffe airmen were known to be disciplined professionals. It was expected the British fliers would be treated in accordance with the Geneva Conventions* and

---

* Ratified after the end of World War II, the present version of the Geneva Conventions incorporates principles for the treatment of military prisoners and civilians during wartime conflicts set forth in the earlier Hague Accords and Geneva Conventions I–III. Article 12 of 1906's Geneva Convention II for the Amelioration of the Condition of Wounded, Sick and Shipwrecked Members of Armed Forces at Sea

rescued by German search-and-rescue teams. Because a sea rescue required time and manpower they might choose to spare for their own personnel in the wake of the attack, it was conceivable they would choose to look away from the airmen's plight. But a cold-blooded slaughter . . . it was hard to imagine such an atrocity had been committed.

Coastal Command had wasted no time sending several aircraft to investigate the scene—Warwicks, Liberators, and amphibious American-made Catalinas that could make water landings. The Luftwaffe had nothing close to the night-flying capabilities of the Royal Air Force, and the group would be relatively safe from observation.

But thus far their hunt had yielded no encouraging results. Nothing had been seen of the Lanc's crew, nothing heard from them on the wireless. The radio equipment could have been damaged when the lifeboat was dropped, but that seemed a reach. The reports from the men aboard the Warwick had understandably led to a grim outlook.

Still, it was possible some of the airman had survived the straf-

---

states: "Members of the armed forces and other persons mentioned in the following Article, who are at sea and who are wounded, sick or shipwrecked, shall be respected and protected in all circumstances, it being understood that the term 'shipwreck' means shipwreck from any cause and includes forced landings at sea by or from aircraft." It goes on to specify: "Any attempts upon their lives, or violence to their persons, shall be strictly prohibited; in particular, they shall not be murdered or exterminated." Germany was a signatory to 1929's Geneva Convention III, which included the 1906 language. The strafing of NF 992's crewmen was thus a clear violation of international humanitarian law.

ing runs. If they had made it to the boat, they could hang on awhile. Built to withstand rough sea conditions, Uffa Foxes were no flimsy pieces of work, and could offer some protection against exposure. With winds light, and currents mild, it was discouraging to find no trace of it. To look down and see only black emptiness.

After a while the group concluded their fruitless mission and returned to base. The good weather was supposed to hold up for at least another day, and a thorough attempt to find the crew would be made when the sun was up.

The next morning, two Warwicks set out early with a pair of Mosquitoes for escorts. The aircraft patrolled across wide sections of ocean in full daylight, using the crash site as the center of their expanding search box. Again nothing came of the effort. The lifeboat had vanished without a trace, and all the ASR crews could theorize as they called off their search was that it had been found by the Germans and towed to shore. But there would be no record of its discovery, or notification that any of the Lanc's crew had been taken prisoner. Ross and his men were not to be seen alive again . . . and only one was ever accounted for at all.

On March 13, the body of Flight Officer Mowbray Ellwood, NF 992's radioman, was recovered by a fisherman either near or on the rocky shore of Slyngen Island north of Iceland. He would be buried not far from there in the village of Nesna, though his remains were later transferred to Stavne churchyard in Trondheim, one of the Foreign War Graves Service's cemeteries in Norway, where many British war casualties are interred to this day.

After two months of the ocean's ravages, Ellwood was identifiable only by his tags. The official war records provide no information about his cause of death.

12.

In the days following the raid on Bergen, the Allies would receive and collate a series of reports on German losses from the Norwegian underground. The highest number of human casualties was aboard the minesweeper that Jimmy Castagnola's Lanc LM 492 hit with a Tallboy. Three crewmen were killed and another seventeen listed as missing, although all twenty were later confirmed dead. Fourteen more men were injured, four of them seriously.

The merchantman *Olga Siemers* suffered no fatalities to its crew although it was damaged beyond repair.

The only casualties for Bruno's personnel were the two technicians struck by falling debris. The Kriegsmarine's war diary for the Norwegian West Coast would confirm local accounts that the bunker took three direct hits from Tallboys. It stated that "many machine shops, all offices, end walls and dividing walls are partially destroyed." The diary also specified that "U-864 is slightly damaged by ceiling debris." No submarines were destroyed.

Norway did not suffer a single civilian loss in the bombing attack, and in that respect it might have been considered successful. But the damage to surface vessels and harbor facilities had been no more than a secondary objective. Bruno had endured. Inside the concrete stronghold, a U-boat filled with deadly cargo was preparing to leave for the Far East. The Allies knew they had to act quickly to stop it—and that they would need to find a different way. A scalpel was needed, not a hammer, even one capable of striking precise blows.

The RAF had done what it could; the next strike would not come by air.

Now it would be left up to the spies, saboteurs, and submarines of Dundee-Lerwick.

CHAPTER NINE

FAREWELL GREETINGS

1.

On Sunday, January 21, 1945, Lieutenant Sven Plass penned a letter to his father, Dr. Ludolf Plass, from his in-laws' home in Senftenberg, where he was nearing the end of his extended holiday leave with Lilly and their infant daughter, Maja. Sven's reason for writing the senior Plass was to break the news that he'd gotten a telegram from Berlin to inform him of his imminent departure for the Far East. The note, though brief, bears a certain wistful tone that suggests the message had come as no surprise to either father or son:

Dear Father,

*This morning the OKM [Naval High Command] called. Thursday
I am to report to Dönitz and then I depart. Nearly four weeks of
vacation with my little family—this will be a beautiful memory for
a long time ahead. Maja is very amusing now—she cries out with
joy. She is sometimes able to stand up in her little crib, but will usually fall and get very scared. Every day she gets more tiny hairs and
her little head is already quite blonde. Right now she is reading a
Swedish newspaper very intently with lots of rustling around. I have
enclosed the message from the OKM. It is not very pleasant, I'm
afraid. Dear father, once again I thank you for all our blessings and
all your love, and hope we will meet again in good health.*

Sven

The young officer would now rush to prepare for his journey and
say good-bye to his loved ones, knowing it would be a very long
time before they were reunited . . . two years or more, and that was
if things went well.

A few days later, Lilly accompanied Sven to the village railway
station in the cold fog and dimness before sunrise, kissed him good-
bye, and watched him step onto a long-distance passenger train
heading north to Berlin. Although she'd managed to keep her composure as they held their parting embrace, her eyes had been desolate watching the train clank from the platform. Reports of rapid
Allied advances on Germany were pouring in from two separate
fronts, the most distressful for Lilly being word that the Red Army
had massed its tanks and infantry units east of the Oder River on

the Polish border—only sixty miles from Senftenberg. Sven was going off into the unknown, yes, and she was desperately worried about his safety. But some deep part of her could also feel the unknown encroaching on the world she knew, threatening to slip, wraithlike, over the placid country hamlet where she'd come to shelter Maja from the ravages of a war that was already much too close.

Her husband gone, Lilly all at once felt terribly alone. She feared for herself, and she feared for the welfare of their child.

The rail connection from Senftenberg to Berlin was fast and direct, and Sven would have arrived there no later than midday. In the capital, he attended a series of top-secret briefings that seem to have included an appearance at the headquarters of the RHSA or Reich Main Security Office, at 76/78 Tirpitzufer, adjacent to the offices of the Naval High Command. Then, at some point, Admiral Dönitz had summoned Plass for their personal reception. While making his rounds, Plass was joined by Lieutenant Jobst Hahndorf, a former classmate at the Murvik Naval Academy and the other officer Dönitz had selected for the posting to Japan.

Informed of the difficulties that had beset U-864, Plass and Hahndorf were instructed to rendezvous with the submarine at Bergen, where her repairs had been complicated by the Allied bombing of the Bruno pens, setting her departure back almost a month. It is difficult to imagine that the canny Dönitz would have thought the raid's timing coincidental, or failed to suspect the British had strong inklings about the boat's cargo and destination. But those were not the sort of suspicions he would have shared with two young lieutenants. With the sub at long last ready to embark, the important thing was that the crew set out for Norway immediately.

Plass and Hahndorf would leave Berlin shortly after receipt of their mission orders, arriving in Bergen sometime before the end of the month using both air and rail connections. Sven reached Lilly by telephone several times while en route, in each instance asking as cautiously as he knew how about her welfare. The tidings of deep Soviet incursions into Prussia had done anything but hearten him.

Ever the proper husband and military man, Plass remained stoic about his own circumstances and would not discuss his secret destination. He told Lilly he missed her and their daughter, but she knew that. Otherwise, he would merely reassure her that all was well with him.

Besides the calls to his wife, Plass wrote at least one more letter to his father. Dated February 3, it was sent after his arrival at the Norwegian port and had been clearly meant to be his last before the voyage to Japan—something he had discussed openly with his father, Dr. Plass, both because of their close relationship and because Sven required his input for the business to be conducted between the Nazi regime, the Lurgi Metals Company, and the Japanese military.

In a few short paragraphs, Sven hinted at his knowledge of the British air raid on the submarine pens and shared his positive assessment of Wolfram and his crew. But the apprehension he felt for the safety of his family was pervasive:

Dear Father,

Tonight we will finally depart. I flew to Oslo and then we traveled along the coast. Thus we (1) saved time and (2) were spared some unpleasantness. I have a nice colleague with me. The commander and crew give a calming and highly competent impression. With them we will be in good care.

Dear father, I hope we will see each other in due time and in happier circumstances than the present ones. They do not make the separation easy but what can we do? It has to be done.

I wish you health and happiness.

Good-bye,
Your Sven

P.S. You can reach me through Heimatstab Ausland in Kiel, or in urgent matters through Korvettenkapitän V. Koenigls, OKM , Tirpitzufer Berlin, Attaché Gruppe.

You must count on a half year passing before you receive word from me.

In Senftenberg on February 4, Lilly also sat down to write a letter—this one of a series to Sven that she had no intention of putting in the mail, her husband never having told her of his destination . . . although, like many a wife, she had her own ways of finding out. But the letters were, in reality, an emotional outlet, a means of carrying on an inner dialogue to help her cope with events faraway and beyond her control. As the people of Senftenberg fled their homes in fear of a Russian invasion, loading whatever possessions they could fit into crude horse-drawn carts, Lilly had planned a trip to see Sven's cousin Annemarie, a worker at the Swedish embassy in nearby Altdöbern, with the desperate hope that her husband's partial Swedish ancestry would gain her and Maja exit visas. Frightened as the Germans were of the Anglo-Americans, they dreaded the reprisals they might suffer at the hands of the wrathful Communists.

Written in an angst-ridden, confessional tone, Lilly's unsent letters might be considered journal entries more than anything else, as she herself seemed aware:

My Beloved Sven!

After long reflection, I've now decided to write you—even if I know you will not receive my letters. It gives me a certain feeling of relief to express and write about the things that touch me so, that consume my actions and thoughts.

I believe what comes in the very near future will be frightening—of what use is keeping the faith? Germany has died before it even started to live. If we ever meet again, this period will be the most terrible and difficult in my memory. As soon as you left, the endless refugee wagons started to pass through, it seems the whole of Germany is on the move. The Red storm from the east pushes everyone ahead of it, the good and the bad—nobody wants to deliberately fall into the hands of the Reds.

Everything falls apart, it could be that the weeks we so happily spent together were our last. At Steinau/Oder the Red Army crossed the Oder with armor and infantry. The Jauer officers' school* defended Steinau like heroes. But a new front has been established.

---

* Unteroffizierschule Jauer at the Steinau-on-Oder bridgehead was an NCO academy whose cadets defended the river crossing against Soviet troops for five days before they were overcome and killed almost to a youth.

When you last reached me by phone, your anxieties for us were clear.

The breakthrough at Oder, Kustrin, and Frankfurt (100 km* away from us) . . . the front is so near now, Sven, and you are so far, and I am so alone with my fears for our child. Will the Russians succeed in destroying us? Will they come here? When one sees the endless lines of wagons moving through the streets from morning till night, one is overcome with fear.

Sven, I still wish deep in my heart for a miracle, and cling to every possible hope. I wonder if Annemarie can do something for me and Maja? I will visit her on Tuesday and explain everything. But what if she can't do anything? What shall I do then? Where can I go?

There are throngs of people everywhere—and once they arrive, the brown masses† will flood the whole country. Even if we're able to leave, there is a danger that Maja won't survive. The weather, nothing to eat—can a child of seven months endure that?

Oh my Sven, no one could ever understand how much I miss you. Dear Sven!

Just two days later, on February 6, Lilly wrote another letter-cum-journal entry. She was crestfallen. Annemarie had not found a way to secure asylum for her and Maja in Sweden. This time she admitted to having intuited that Sven was destined for Japan—

---

* Approximately sixty-two miles.

† Lilly refers to the brown uniforms worn by the Soviet infantrymen.

though there is little question that someone, probably Ludolf, had divulged this to her in confidence.

No matter that her husband was unlikely to ever read her words, Lilly was writing them as if for his eyes, and did not want to compromise whoever had shared the secret. She may also have feared that the letter would at some point find its way into the hands of a third party, and hesitated to reveal that Sven had violated his oath of silence about the mission—a breach that could potentially have exposed him to court-martial.

Lilly's sense of gloom on her return home from Altdöbern might almost be seen as a reflection of the darkening outlook among the German populace:

> *It was cold, the streets dirty, and in the meantime the embassy is not allowed to receive visitors—so Annemarie and I went walking in the park. We walked around the beautiful lake and smoked a strong cigarette, which did me good.*
>
> *Annemarie was very unhappy about being unable to help me. She will write to Moster Elsa* to see if she might have any solution— we were both quite discouraged—my throat was closed from my having choked back tears. It is terrible, Sven, to have to stand eye to eye with such a threat without knowing how to save yourself and your child. I want to live for you and for your child.*
>
> *I wish you could be here in these difficult days—oh, if only there were a hope in which I could believe. It looks bad for our Germany—*

---

* *Moster* (the German word for "maternal aunt") Elsa was the eldest sister of Sven's mother. See notes for additional information.

Berlin has been declared the front*—they are fighting in Kustrin. Is there any way to hold out against the enemy? Where are they? Where are the new weapons?† If they have them, why do they not use them? It would be a crime to tell us about them and then still let the enemy take us. What will Germany be like when you come back? Was ours a forever good-bye? You are my life—I cannot exist without my you, my heart!

Our little Maja is a tiny, brilliant ray of sunshine in these dark times. She squeals contentedly in bed and is quite full of mischief. God keep this little creature of ours safe. If only we may be reunited—I yearn so much for you, dearest—when your train disappeared into the morning mist, I was seized by such horrible fear—I could no longer keep my composure—I could have run after the train to fetch you back. But it was over.

And you go where? To the Far East, where the cherry trees blossom, that my heart tells me. And what awaits you there? Good night, my infinitely beloved Sven, there far away—sleep well, you too!

But it is doubtful that Plass had much rest that night. In Bergen, he'd been notified that U-864's stay for repairs was over. After many delays, the boat had been declared fit for her journey at last, and would get under way in the early morning.

---

* On February 1, 1945, Berlin was declared a "fortified place," or "defense zone," and surrounded by German garrisons in preparation for an attack by the Russians, who had now sent motorized forces across the frozen Oder River.

† Hitler had long touted his secret *Wunderwaffen* as game-changers to the German population, insisting that, once fully deployed, they would mean the destruction of the Reich's enemies.

2.

In the submariners' barracks near Bergen Harbor, Willi Transier, like Lilly, had settled into a pensive mood. Although official word of the U-boat's departure would have reached him through one of his NCOs, it would not have caught him by surprise. The submarine's crewmen had been called upon days earlier to perform equipment checks. Their cargo would have had to be given a once-over, and in some instances even loaded back aboard, as it would have been necessary to remove and rearrange many of the crates to make room for the repair work. As the preparations for sailing gained intensity, Willi would have dismissed whatever private thoughts he'd held about being reunited with his Edith in the foreseeable future. By the time he'd been told to ready his seabag and write any final letters he might wish to send home, he would have spent many long hours emotionally girding himself for the announcement.

But what words would he send his fiancée? His letters to her would be read by the navy censors. He could not tell her of the Japanese passengers with their odd, aloof habits. He could not tell her of the rigors at Kristiansand, the problems that brought the submarine to Farsund, or the mishap in the channel outside its harbor. He could not tell her of the air strike on Bergen only a week after the boat hobbled in for repairs. He could not even tell her he was in Bergen, and had been for over a month.

In the end, what could he tell Edith? He loved her. He hoped someday they would be together, make babies, and raise them as husband and wife. And he hoped she would often think of him, as he would think of her. But all this she already knew.

On the writing stand before Willie was a small sepia photograph—a sailor portrait that a Bergen street photographer had snapped of him. He would mark it with a simple dedication and drop it into the mail before going to bed. There would be no need to enclose a letter with it.

Turning the picture over, he reached for his pen and scratched out six words:

Farewell greetings and kisses, your Willi.

Reading them over, he was satisfied. He gave the ink a moment to dry, carefully slipped the photograph into an envelope, and closed its flap.

Willi Transier had well and truly said everything there was left to say.

3.

In the six or seven weeks since they had left Kiel, Toshio Nakai and Tadao Yamato would have had only minimal interaction with German personnel aboard their submarine transport. In their dealings, the German and Japanese seamen had established a polite professional relationship, but the Germans were intolerant of Asian customs and even refused to exchange courteous bows. Although reconciled to the Japanese insistence on individual berths, they were never quite accepting of it. They would have been bemused by Nakai and Yamato's bland diet of rice and soybean sauce, yet must have been simultaneously pleased not to share their precious meat rations. For their part, the scientists would have been just as glad to forgo the German chow that was so alien to their palates.

Between the Japanese passengers and their hosts, there would be correctness and decorum but no real familiarity. Most of the time, Nakai and Yamato would have kept quietly to themselves.

The long holdup in Bergen must have been more bearable to them than it would have been elsewhere. Like the people of Japan, Norwegians lived off the ocean's bounty, and fishermen the world over were in harmony with the rhythms of the tides. Some of what the scientists saw would have reminded them of home—the cutters setting out before dawn, the busy docks as the fleet came in from the fisheries, the local markets with their animated bartering and fresh seafood. It is likely they relished the popularity of whale meat, a Norwegian staple and a Japanese delicacy, that would have been rare at best during their multiyear assignments to Germany.

It had been a stormy January in Bergen, with turbulent gray skies and strong winds piling snow up along the city's cobbled streets and avenues. When the weather was poorest, Nakai and Yamato would have stayed cloistered in their rooms at the officers' residence, perhaps writing journal entries or reading from publications they had brought along for their journey. On calmer days, they might have gone out for walks to exercise, breathe the sharp salt air, and take in the local scenery. But this was an occupied land,

and its populace held deep hostility toward their swaggering con-
querors. The scientists would have been cautioned to stay close to
the Gestapo-policed harbor.

They must have been relieved to learn that the transport was
finally seaworthy. The fits and starts they had experienced since
Kiel would have dampened their optimism about returning to
Japan in anything close to their expected time frame. And they
would have thought it of paramount importance that they did
return as soon as possible. The picture in Europe was dismal, and
they could not have failed to wonder if the war might be over for
the Germans before they arrived in their country. But the technology they brought with them was vital to their national hopes, all
the more if they found themselves standing alone against the Americans.

Nakai and Yamato probably slept very little on the eve of their
journey, but for different reasons than U-864s crew, or the German
technicians and diplomats who were their counterparts aboard the
boat. Whatever mixed feelings those others had about putting out
to sea were not for the two Japanese expatriates to know.

At long last, they were on the brink of the moment they had
waited for.

CHAPTER TEN

FEDJE

1.

On February 2, Jimmy Launders took HMS *Venturer* out of Lerwick on her eleventh war patrol. His orders were similar to what they had been back in September when he'd attacked the freighters *Vang, Friedrichshafen,* and *Force,* namely to hunt for enemy targets of opportunity. This time, however, he was instructed to keep an eye out primarily for U-boats. His operating area would be the waters around Marstein lighthouse outside the Korsfjorden, or Cross Fjord, the southern entrance to the city of Bergen. Perched atop a wide, saucer-shaped island headland, the lighthouse overlooked a direct lane used by the Nazi submarines as they entered the base.

Returning boats were Launders's favored prey. At the end of their patrols, tired U-boat crews might be caught napping as they cruised on the surface, a lesson the young skipper's men had learned firsthand when they'd pounced on U-771. "The Germans were less watchful when they sailed into Bergen after raids than they were when they sailed out again on new missions," Ensign John Watson remembered.

On Monday, February 5, soon after her arrival in the patrol area, *Venturer* had surfaced to recharge her batteries and scan for radio traffic when a brief coded message from the flag officer of submarines* came in over the long-range receiver via Dundee. It read:

IMPORTANT SECRET

U-BOATS PROBABLY USE FOLLOWING ROUTES:

FROM 60° 47' NORTH 004° 26' EAST

COURSE 110° R/V OFF HELLISOY

1. PROBABLE THAT U-BOATS PROCEED TO

SEAWARD OF R/V.

Hellesøy, or Hellisoy, was a different lighthouse on yet another weather-beaten stone island—this one called Fedje. Over a hundred feet tall, painted in bands of red and white, it had stood on the edge of the sea at Stormark, the island's southern coast, for almost a century.

* In 1945, the FOS of the Royal Navy was Rear Admiral G. E. Creasy.

214

So much for the British sub's easier pickings. "We knew that the Germans entered Bergen from the south and exited to the north," Watson said.

Meaning the *Venturer* had now been specifically tasked with intercepting U-boats making their departures for the Arctic Circle—and points beyond. To pass from Norway's chain of coastal fjords they would circumnavigate Fedje, wend their way east of the Shetlands, and then eventually slip out into the open sea.

What Launders and his crew were not told was that HMS Ambrose had been tipped off to the imminent departure of the transport U-864. On the heels of the RAF's January bombing raid, and subsequent reports from the Bergen underground that she had escaped serious harm, Dundee-Lerwick had been handed the mission order to use whatever assets were at its disposal to track and annihilate the submarine.

The Shetland base's exact sources of intelligence about U-864 are unrecorded. But conscripted Norwegian dockworkers at Bergen could have provided fairly accurate updates on her preparations for sailing, and the strong likelihood is that resistance members eavesdropping on German radio transmissions supplemented that information with their intercepts. All of it would have reached the Admiralty via Dundee . . . and none would be shared with Launders. Other than the fact that *Venturer* was being diverted from its original patrol box to a point where it could intercept outbound boats, there was nothing extraordinary about the message, no hint that a particular submarine was being sought, no mention of its high-priority cargo. Only a general heads-up.

"Classified information of that kind never leaked from those who knew—a few military commanders and Churchill, of course," said Watson. "Crews at sea weren't given that kind of information."

They would receive most of it years afterward. But as they left the vicinity of the Korsfjorden, bearing northward for Fedje past the barrier islands along the coast, only one thing mattered:

Venturer had been given her orders and she would carry them out. Whatever it entailed, and wherever they took her.

2.

Before dawn on Wednesday, February 7, Korvettenkapitän Ralf-Reimer Wolfram pulled U-864 out of Bruno on her first war patrol, a standard antisubmarine escort ushering her from the harbor. Along with the armed trawlers, she would cruise on the surface into the Feje Fjord and then head northwest toward Fejeosen, a deepwater channel opening to the ocean south off the Stormark's steeply irregular ledges and towering old lighthouse.

Passing through the channel, Wolfram ordered his boat to submerge and left the trawlers behind in the mouth of the inlet. He was finally at sea.

Already on the hunt in those same waters, *Venturer* may well have spotted U-864's escort vessels after the German submarine left the fjord. Her crew had detected suspicious fishing boats in the area almost on their arrival the day before, and the escorts would have looked no different from any of those vessels. Possibly aided by the fact that Launders would have been careful to keep a hidden distance from the trawlers, U-864, traveling submerged on her two electric motors, stole out of the channel into the sea unnoticed.

If all had gone smoothly for the U-boat afterward, *Venturer* might never have prevented her from leaving the area to get on with her mission. But the luck her commander had so recently praised as a traveling companion was about to abandon him.

3.

The opening leg of U-864's journey was to take her north around the Shetland cluster, then back down beyond the western Scottish and Irish coasts toward Southern Europe and eventually Africa. But Wolfram knew those were dangerous waters, with the travel lanes scoured by Allied air and naval forces. The submarine had been in and out of dry dock twice during the stay in Bergen, initially due to her snorkel issues and the grounding at Farsund, and then because of damage from January's bombing. Some minor problems with the hydraulics had also materialized and been fixed.

Wolfram's responsibility as commander was to make sure the submarine was now in good running condition. He knew, moreover, that the men had been inactive for a month and needed to shape up. Before he began the trip, he would put the boat and crew through vigorous submerged paces in local waters.

Wolfram spent nearly an entire day conducting several rounds of dive and snorkel drills in the open sea west of Fedje and must have been thankful when no hitches arose with the boat's performance. The men's seamanship obviously pleased him, too, for sometime on February 8, Wolfram completed his submerged trials and, snorkeling at a shallow depth, started off on a northerwesterly course toward the upper extremity of the Shetlands.

It was soon afterward that one of his diesels began to hiccup.

4.

The root cause of U-864's engine malfunction was probably inside one of its air compressors. The compressor had a large internal piston that would push forward, or stroke, through a horizontal shaft, driven by the internal combustion of air and fuel, forcing the air in front of it to become pressurized within the cylinder. As the piston stroked, smaller vertical pistons along its path were actuated by the pressurized air to create horsepower for the boat's propulsion. The opposing pistons were set inside rack-and-pinion mechanisms that, among other things, would synchronize their movements. If those mechanisms were damaged, or the big air compressor piston was improperly installed or worn out, they would fall out of sync and the engine would misfire. The result would be loud, fitful vibrations, a progressive reduction of engine performance, and, over time, possibly even a complete breakdown.

The frustration aboard the U-boat must have been palpable. Though major onboard repairs were almost impossible at sea, it was not unknown for a submarine to conduct an entire war patrol with a failing or failed engine. U-864's journey, however, would be double or triple the duration of a usual patrol and cover many times the average distance. Not only would the engine noise draw the enemy's attention, but a breakdown in remote waters, far from any hope of assistance, would be catastrophic. The latest development was a serious complication.

Wolfram would contact U-boat Command at once to report his situation. The mission's gravity dictated that he seek recommendations from his superiors, but there was really never any doubt that he would have to abort.

The instructions from headquarters, therefore, would have been unsurprising to Wolfram. U-864 was ordered to turn back to Bergen at once, retracing her course through the Feje Fjord. With Allied air and sea patrols combing the area, she was advised not to attempt her return to base alone.

A succinct message radioed to the sub from BdU West read:

NEW ESCORT WILL BE AT HELLISOY

Wolfram's sense of defeat can only be imagined as he ordered the boat to about-face, bringing her down to periscope depth. He would make for the lighthouse at Stormark, Fedje's south coast, and rendezvous with the escort vessels there as soon as possible.

5.

At 9:32 A.M. on February 9, *Venturer* was submerged outside Feje-osen, trolling on a northerly course, when her ASDIC operator heard the faint sound of a fishing boat to the northwest, seemingly heading in her direction.

Or was it a fishing boat?

The frequent trawler sightings had continued since *Venturer*'s arrival at Hellisoy, and just a half hour earlier, ninety minutes after the submarine had dived with her batteries recharged, one had been heard and spotted in the near distance.

Watson had the watch that morning, and he was puzzled when a sweep through the periscope revealed nothing. ASDIC had two modes, active and passive. In its active setting, a pulse of A/C current was sent through a thin quartz crystal, or transducer, to create a pie-zoelectric effect—a vibration. Beamed through water at intervals, the sonic pulse bounced off solid objects toward its source and was heard as a characteristic *ping* to the listener. The speed of sound underwater varied with depth, temperature, and salinity, but a set of practical calculations allowed the distance of an object from the transmitter to be determined by the lapsed time between sending and receipt.

ASDIC in its active mode was used when the operator was searching for or targeting a particular object in the water. In its passive mode, the receiver's underwater microphone, or hydrophone—in *Venturer*'s case, a Type 129—was simply used to listen for sounds made by a vessel's propeller or engine. But a proficient ASDIC man might recognize the type of vessel he was picking up, or even possibly glean something about its behavior, from its unique hydro-phonic effect, or sound signature.

Venturer's ASDIC man was capable indeed. He'd told Watson that the ship he had heard seemed to be starting and stopping its engine as if "doing something with its fishing." It was the sort of noise one might expect from a trawler as it was letting out anchor, or laying or retrieving its nets.

What concerned Watson was that he couldn't get a visual. It was cloudy overhead, but there was no fog, and the sea was quiet. That virtually eliminated the chance that waves and wind had created bogeys on the ASDIC. In Watson's mind, then, the engine noises could not have been false readings. But when a trawler was close enough to hear, it was generally close enough to see, and the ASDIC man had assured him the vessel was nearer than the others they'd detected that morning. Watson hadn't had the slightest bit of trouble spotting them . . . so why was he unable to find this latest pickup?

Although the sound faded soon after it was registered, Watson had the man at the ASDIC console keep a close ear to things as he lowered the scope. You did not want to keep it raised for more than two or three minutes for fear of being observed. But anytime an unidentified ship was heard in those waters, it was reason to stay highly alert.

For a while, nothing more was heard on the ASDIC set. Then at a little past ten, as Watson was about to be relieved, there were more engine noises. He went over to the scope and brought it back up.

Almost at once he saw a fishing boat, heading on a southerly course. Several, in fact. He might have exhaled with relief. But at ten minutes past ten there were more sounds—these still to the northwest, and louder. As before, they disappeared quickly. Fifteen minutes later, however, they returned. In both instances the ASDIC man heard that odd engine cough. And this time, the distinct whine of propellers. Yet again there was nothing to be seen.

By now Lieutenant Chalmers, the submarine's veteran second officer, had arrived to take over the watch. Before Watson left the control room, he and the ASDIC man briefed Chalmers on the enigmatic sonic readings. Chalmers went to the periscope and gripped the knobs to focus it.

For the next quarter hour, Lieutenant Chalmers carried out a careful, methodical search. He was concentrating on the sector from which *Venturer* was picking up the ship noises. At the same time, he had to be mindful of the fishing boats to the south. They could easily be German ASWs.

Chalmers stayed at the scope, following his careful procedures; it would remain raised no more than two or three minutes at a time. Then, at ten to eleven, he spotted something to the south. A thin mast . . . probably a raised periscope. It was a good distance away. Five thousand yards, Chalmers estimated. But there was no mistaking that it belonged to a submarine. And it was staying up long enough to give him a good, long look.

The discovery raised a combination of powerful feelings in the lieutenant, his relief at finding the source of the suspicious noises— and the quarry Lerwick had obviously diverted them here to find— quickly yielding to unease. It was a reaction that did not take long to spread as Chalmers reported his discovery to Lieutenant Launders over the phone, then immediately called the crew to action stations. There were no other Allied subs in the area. The submerged vessel had to be a U-boat.

At his station in the torpedo room, Harry Plummer was struck by an unsettling realization that would be shared on some level by everyone aboard.

His boat had arrived at the scene first, true enough. But this was not at all the same situation as back in November, when *Venturer* had struck at the German submarine outside the Andfjord. That other boat had been running on the surface, where it could be clearly observed and taken out in a stealth attack. In that encounter, *Venturer*'s men had known they were hidden from the enemy, and the U-boat had never had a chance. It had been the proverbial sitting duck.

But now both vessels were underwater. There were no instructions for how to deal with this sort of thing, no precedents, no aspects of the crew's training that covered it. Submarines were meant to prey on surface vessels, not engage in dogfights with other submarines. While submerged, hunter and prey were blind to each other . . . and who was to say that *Venturer* was really the hunter? The German submarine could sink them, the same as they could sink it.

Shaky as it made them, Plummer and his shipmates could not dismiss the thought.

6.

In the conn moments after receiving Chalmers's report, Lieutenant Jimmy Launders stepped up to the periscope, announced that he had control of the submarine, and ordered a northward turn to close with the enemy. Now at his action station, Watson was back in the control room at the navigator's table.

Peering through the viewer, Launders needed only a short time to discern the U-boat's periscope at the distance his second lieutenant had given him—about five thousand yards, or three miles, off to the northeast.

It was 11:15 A.M. and *Venturer's* attack on the German sub was in full progress.

Launders knew he had to make some hurried decisions based on equally swift assessments. These would require updated readings from the ASDIC man. The vessel's noise, he informed Launders, was much louder than before—it sounded like diesel engines running, with noisy machinery—say, an air compressor—and appeared to be crossing to starboard. Speed, unknown. Range, uncertain. The three-mile estimate was certainly in the ballpark, but fluctuating water temperature gradients and atmospheric distortion made the information less than altogether reliable.

For Launders, that was crucial. His target was invisible to him. Without better speed and course reckonings, a snap attack of the type he'd launched against the Narvik submarine could easily fail. And if that happened—if his torpedoes went wide—the tables would be turned. By retracing their trajectory, the U-boat's crew could pinpoint his exact position and return fire. Only *their* salvo would be right on the money.

The snap attack was ruled out, then. It was, Launders believed, far too hasty a move. He couldn't risk his submarine, or chance letting the objective of his two-day hunt off Fedje slip away. Instead, he would track the boat—get around back of her, tail her through the water, and fire when he could gain better estimations of her course and speed.

On the sketchy information available, Launders had *Venturer* brought around behind and parallel to the U-boat at three and a half knots—no more, no less. Safety was one consideration for his order: His boat was, of course, on quiet running, and he needed to go along as slowly as possible to avoid having the sound of its engines alert the enemy to his presence. There could be no active ASDIC for the same reason; the sonar pings would be tantamount to a blaring announcement that *Venturer* was on the chase.

But stealth was just one of Launders's motives for remaining on station. He had another, and it was directly tied to his keen mathematical brain. By tracking the U-boat at a constant speed, he could observe whether she pulled ahead, or dropped astern, of his boat. That would allow him to calculate the enemy's speed relative to his own and in so doing draw more accurate target bearings.

At 11:22, Launders looked through his viewer again and was stunned to see that his quarry's periscope was still up. In fact, he could see what he was convinced were both the attack and surveillance scopes, one showing eight feet above the water's surface, the other about three.

Part of Launders recoiled. The German submarine's captain allowing a single periscope to remain raised for such a long interval revealed an utter absence of discipline. And then bringing up a second? Advantageous as it was to him, Launders could not help but reflect that it was a demonstration of suicidal recklessness by his opponent.

But that was something for his combat report if he was fortunate enough to survive the encounter and get to write it. Right now Launders was simply grateful that his sighting of the German boat's periscopes had given him some new information to mull over. Most obviously it confirmed that she was at periscope depth.

Judging by what he saw, Launders had gained on her quite a bit . . . pulled, he guessed, to a range of within twenty-five hundred feet. But the position of the scopes gave the appearance that *Venturer* was very broad on her bow, meaning the U-boat had suddenly nosed west; if he was correct in assuming she was headed for Fejeosen to the east, then she would have to alter her course to starboard.

Which made him wonder why her nose was pointing in the wrong direction.

Launders, casting his thoughts about for an answer, did not need to wait very long before it came to him.

7.

Aboard U-864, Wolfram's own apprehensions had steadily mounted as he drew closer to Fejeosen. He had known the inlet was a favored interdiction point for the Allies. If one of their submarines or ASW aircraft was nearby, it would be in the very area he'd reentered— and that had been enough of a concern to make him risk several sweeps with his periscope. The greatest threat to a submerged boat was from patrol planes, and Wolfram would have tilted the mirror of the scope to look up above the horizon. It is possible that by concentrating on the sky in this way, he missed spotting *Venturer*'s periscope above the water—though both Chalmers and Launders had been stingy with its use.

Despite Wolfram's anxiety, however, he'd had no choice but to backtrack.

His best bet had been to order his helmsman to head on toward the inlet at slow speed. That would reduce strain on his engine, mute its racket, and give the promised escort a chance to make the rendezvous at Hellisoy lighthouse. Once there, he would not simply wait for the boats to arrive with his engine throwing off noise in every direction. Nothing would be a more telltale sign of his presence. Whether or not the escorts came to meet him, Wolfram would proceed on a steady course into the Fejeosen, keeping his radio mast elevated to pick up any signals they might send out.*

At about 11:20 A.M., Wolfram's nervousness increased exponentially—turned into something that might better be described as alarm. His Balcongerat sound detection apparatus was superior to the older arrays it had replaced, but U-864 was snorkeling, and the pounding of her erratic diesel engine was enough to shake one's guts. So loud was it, in fact, that her hydrophone oper-

---

* It was the mast that Commander Launders must have spotted and confused with one of the submarine's periscopes. In his postaction report, he would call Wolfram's use of the attack and surveillance periscopes "indecent" and "suicidal." But Wolfram was only weeks removed from intensive drills at the Horten offshore training grounds and had himself been conducting refreshers hours before the start of his engine problems. With his escort expected and BdU West likely to send out additional instructions, he would have been monitoring the airwaves for their transmissions as he made his return to Bergen. As will be explained later in this narrative, Wolfram made another critical mistake in his use of the scope, but it was a single scope. Using two at the same time would have been a pointless violation of tactical principles that defies explanation.

ator had been unable to hear anything that wasn't at close range. Yet as *Venturer* swung south on her starboard side and pulled to within 2,500 yards—halving the distance between the two submarines at the time of her original ASDIC detection—the German boat was first observed to zigzag.

Wolfram had become intensely concerned about an enemy submarine shadowing U-864 in the nearby water. The U-boat's hydrophones had finally gotten a whiff of *Venturer* and prompted him to set her into an evasive pattern, a zigzag course he had repeatedly practiced in his drills at the Horten training school. He could not know where the other boat was located, not without keeping his periscope raised longer than his training required—a risk he was willing to take.

He who sees first has won. The motto was drilled into the heads of all U-boat commanders, laid out in the handbook issued to them at submarine school. Wolfram had already let it guide him while scanning for his escort and watching the sky for enemy aircraft, and his situation had now become even more urgent—as well as more dangerous.

But Wolfram's nerves had gotten the better of him. He had misapplied the rule, and in doing so violated another key tactical principle laid out in the training manuals—one that took precedence over any other. If a submarine was spotted, it would be deprived of almost every chance of success. In choosing between attempting to locate his stalker or remaining hidden without knowing its exact position, the latter practice was to be followed, though it went contrary to human instinct.

The natural urge was to see the enemy, and Wolfram gave in to it, a mistake that would prove as costly as any could be. It was an action a more seasoned U-boat commander would not have taken, fearing detection by sight or aircraft-mounted radar. But the veteran commanders were gone along with the happy times. Wolfram's tour aboard the U-108 had been brief, and even his recorded sinking of a British merchant vessel during its single combat operation had been untrue—a harmless fudge, in his mind, that had been a common practice among young commanders seeking to bolster their résumés.

Wolfram must have hoped his zigzagging course would offset the prolonged use of his scope. He had practiced the drill repeatedly at the Horten training school, a way to make himself a difficult moving target. In the meantime, he would keep a sharp lookout for the enemy. If Wolfram acquired him, he would reverse their roles. Become the cat to the mouse—and pounce*.

It was no sure bet his gamble would succeed. But whatever ensued, one thing was indisputable: U-864's long, tedious days of offshore maneuvers in Oslo Fjord were about to be put to good use.

8.

At nine minutes before noon, *Venturer* had pulled within approximately two thousand yards of the U-boat when Launders again saw her moving with her periscope up.

---

* Launders's postaction report includes a hand-drawn track chart that shows Wolfram's zigzagging to have begun as *Venturer* came up close at 2,500 yards—when she would have been most vulnerable to detection by the Balcongerat hydrophones. Prior to that, the sketch makes it clear that U-864 was on a straight course.

Watson, who was with Launders at the navigator's table, could tell that the lieutenant's mind was working. He knew his commander had the ability to absorb information very quickly, process it, and then use it to make his decisions. And from the thoughts Launders had been sharing with him, it was obvious he was now preoccupied with the "problems of attacking."

Those problems concerned his realization that the German sub was on a zigzagging course. Launders had gotten a solid inkling of this when he'd seen its bow angled in his direction half an hour before. The subsequent ASDIC reports, and his latest periscope sighting, had confirmed his hunch. The next thing for him was to "work out what the zigzag was. Which were the short legs, and which were the long legs."

As it turned out, the plot Launders derived from the combined data showed the legs were roughly equal. The U-boat was on a mean bearing of about 120 degrees, with fifteen-degree alterations at ten-minute intervals.

That would ultimately bring her to Fejeosen, where Launders had surmised she was heading, though more slowly than if she were traveling in a straight line. Doubtless, he thought, the German commander was trying to make his boat a more difficult target than she would be on a fixed course. At the same time, however, her regular deviations had allowed *Venturer* to gain on her even though they were traveling at roughly the same speed—three and a half knots.

In *Venturer*'s control room, Launders's mental computations had inspired the usual admiration and confidence among the men . . . but there was also a growing, and occasionally acute, feeling of trepidation. They had now shadowed the U-boat for almost two and a half hours—and for the last half hour had stayed close to her rear on their parallel course. Whenever the U-boat turned away, stomachs tightened in the conn. As Watson later remembered, that would be the angle for firing her aft torpedoes at them as she took flight.

During the next twenty minutes, their tension swelled inside the conn like a balloon. "We were hoping that she would surface," Watson recalled. "And then, when she surfaced, we would be able to torpedo her straightaway. We'd get much more accurate information about her from the direct angle. But there was no sign of her doing that."

This fact left Launders with no real choice. The German sub was two miles west of Fedje, sailing south toward the Hellisoy lighthouse. If he waited any longer, she would jag east toward the Fejeosen, and from there it would be too easy to lose her.

He would have to do what had never been done and fire blind, trusting in his calculations. But from everything he'd observed of her engine noise, motion, and periscope positions, the German submarine was a large one—a cargo type. She would have six torpedo tubes to *Venturer*'s four. And his Mark VIII torpedoes were very loud as they shot through the water.

"We were certain he would turn away as soon as they were fired," Watson recalled.

Away, that was, from whatever bearing the U-boat's commander had ordered when the torpedoes were detected. He would turn sharply away in the opposite direction and go deep. It was the textbook evasive profile, and they had no reason to expect that the enemy would do anything different now.

For Launders, that meant one more sweaty estimate. If he could correctly predict when the submarine would zag to port, and triangulate his torpedoes' paths so they intersected with her evasive crash dive to starboard—if he could accurately make that calculation, she would move directly into the path of his torpedoes.

9.

12:10 P.M. Aboard *Venturer,* the men could feel the stress of the situation weighing on them like sandbags.

Lieutenant Jimmy Launders took a last look through the scope, and saw the U-boat altering it course to the starboard leg of the zig—turning in his direction.

Glancing at at his stopwatch, Launders began his two-minute countdown. The spread of torpedoes he'd had the men ready was known to British submariners as a "hosepipe salvo." In theory, all four would be fired at the same point on the heading of the target at intervals of 17.5 seconds. As the target passed through that point, it would be hit in four different spots.

But that tactic had been devised for surface vessels. Anticipating that the submarine would angle and dive, he'd worked out a modified firing solution and adjusted the running depths to thirty and thirty-six feet. The first torpedo was to be aimed at the bow, and then the other three at half-lengths midships and aft. His goal was to target four slightly different points to account for the U-boat's submerged depth and attempt at evasion.

At 12:12, Launders gave his firing commands to Plummer in the torpedo room. His voice, as always, quiet and calm. "Fire . . . fire . . . fire . . . fire . . ."

Four times, Plummer pressed the red button.

10.

With the torpedoes shearing through the water at forty-five knots, Wolfram had scant minutes to react—between two and four, depending on which torpedo struck the submarine.

It is probable that his hydrophone operator heard the first of the torpedoes rush past as it barely missed the boat. If the first torpedo had struck U-864, she would not have had time to dive. But dive she did, taking the evasive maneuver Launders had anticipated. Hard to starboard and down, hydroplanes angled upward like the ailerons of a plane.

After the first torpedo, the second and third shot past at sixteen- to seventeen-second intervals, detonating against the stony under-sea base of Fedje Island. Aboard *Venturer* the crewmen could hear the explosions rumble through the sea with their unaided ears.

On U-864, Sven Plass had no chance to think of Lilly or his daughter. Nor was Willi Transier able to spend a final moment saying a silent good-bye to his Edith. Rolf von Chlingensperg, the scientists Yamato and Nakai, Schomerus, Hahndorf, the modeler Franz Türk—their lives were snuffed out almost instantly as the fourth torpedo struck the boat broadside, blowing a massive hole just aft of the command center.

About two miles distant, standing on one of Fedje's western cliffs, twelve-year-old Kristoffer Karlsen had strayed from his grandmother while collecting peat for the kitchen and hearth. But no sooner had he ascended from the bog, wanting to look out at the sea, than he became mesmerized by the sight and sounds of destruction across the water. There was a roar, a tall spout of spray, and then the smoke and silence. The memory would stay with him as long as he lived.

For the men of *Venturer,* there was only the loud, sharp clap of the underwater explosion—and then the unholy crackling as the U-boat came apart. The inrush of water into the blast hole was so rapid that her flooded midsection had immediately become far heavier than the bow and stern, creating stresses that snapped the boat in three almost at the moment of impact. Listening over a mile away, Harry Plummer compared what he heard to someone crushing a matchbox in his fist. He had heard similar noises after torpedoing U-771 months ago, but these came much more quickly.

U-771 had needed time to sink. The submarine *Venturer* had hit now was already underwater.

The middle of the boat dropped straight to the seafloor between 460 and 490 feet below its surface, the canisters of mercury in its ruptured keel scattering across the silt in a wide debris field. Her bow and stern sections drifted down more slowly, the bow landing on a muddy slope in an upright position, the aft likewise burying itself at a steep angle. Both sections were relatively intact and must have had sealed bulkheads, the hatches closed to leave them airtight. Wolfram would have kept the hatches to the aft section closed to drown out the clamor of the diesels while he was snorkeling.

Inside *Venturer,* there had been a burst of relief and exhilaration.

As the crewmen registered the hit they had felt the oppressive weight lifted off their backs. Their submarine was a powerful weapon and its job was to attack and escape. It had performed beautifully for them.

But after a minute, the men's euphoria went flat. Their whoops of congratulatory delight quieted. A minute, Harry Plummer remembered, and the mood aboard *Venturer* changed radically, became somber and almost reverent throughout the boat's compartments—evocative of the moments following their sinking of U-771 much earlier.

Venturer's crew had sunk yet another submarine. More submariners had been killed. Never mind that this time, unlike the last, the British crew had not had the cards stacked in their favor. They had been as blind as their target. A single miss, and they would have been killed themselves.

"No matter where they came from, we took our hats off to them," Plummer would reflect. "Poor bastards."

11.

Half an hour passed before *Venturer* glided up to inspect the area where the U-boat had gone down.

Launders had observed it from a guarded, stationary distance for several minutes after he'd heard the torpedo explosions, followed by the noise of the boat breaking up. There were several nearby fishing trawlers, and he'd waited to see if any took an interest. When none did, he had turned a course for the enemy submarine's estimated position in the water.

As he'd drawn closer to the spot, a peek through his eyepiece had revealed seagulls gathering to starboard. That had been at 12:40 P.M. Six minutes later, *Venturer* approached at periscope depth and entered the oil patch outside the Fejeosen inlet.

The farther the submarine went into the spreading oil patch, the thicker its surface became. Soon the wavelets around the scope looked yellowish brown as they lifted against the afternoon light. Floating in the slick were many pieces of wood and numerous dead fish. Launders saw none of the seagulls alight. They wheeled and dipped in the air currents overhead but kept well clear of the oil.

Scanning the oil slick through his periscope, Launders noticed something floating with "fair buoyancy." A long cylinder slightly larger than a torpedo, it appeared to be made of steel and had several brackets on its length. One end had a door with butterfly nuts, the other appeared to be welded.

Launders's first guess was that the container might be an empty upper-deck torpedo stowage that had torn free from the explosion. That seemed to confirm what he and his ASDIC man had deduced earlier from the sound of the boat's propellers. The screws had made 170 revolutions per knot for a travel speed of between three and three and a half knots—a low number of revs. That had indicated a large, heavy vessel, probably a supply U-boat. It would have come from the extra torpedo up top.

Later, when he wrote out his full war patrol report, Launders would have second thoughts about what the canister might have been. The big IX D2 supply boats had carried a kind of glider known as an autogyro—a Focke Fa 330 Sandpiper with rotary wings and a seat for a single crewman. The autogyro would be stored in two canisters, assembled on the deck of the submarine, and deployed from a steel cable spooling out from a winch. A crewman aboard the flying platform would be towed along by the surfaced U-boat as he monitored the surrounding waters from his soaring vantage. If he spotted a threat, he would use a telephone to alert the submarine's commander.

Launders wasn't entirely positive his guess was correct. The canister might indeed have housed a spare torpedo or something else. The one thing he knew was that the U-boat had never gotten a chance to surface or launch her autogyro into the air. She had not gotten a chance to do anything after *Venturer* ran into her but try to elude him as she made for home. He wondered where she'd been coming from, if she was returning from a deployment. Probably it had been the last day of her patrol. That last day was when a tired submarine commander could get a bit down on his guard. For his German counterpart it had been a fatal mistake.

After inspecting the site for about twenty minutes, Launders decided it was time to withdraw. The submarine had been heading into Bergen. It would have radioed in. He didn't want to push his luck and run into the search vessels that were bound to appear when it failed to reach base as expected.

Turning southwest, he began his return passage to the Korsfjorden, where he'd been patrolling before the message from Dundee-Lerwick had diverted him toward Fedje. En route, he had the men reload the torpedo tubes while working on the track chart for his pursuit of the U-boat. The war was over for the men on the German submarine. But not for him. One of his duties as a commander was to record his actions after the fact, when he was of a relaxed mind, and the coppery taste of adrenaline had faded from the tongue.

At little after six o'clock that night, *Venturer* was back near the Marstein. The sun had set and the ocean and sky blended together in darkness. Still submerged, Launders raised his periscope and saw a searchlight move over the water, making regular sweeps of the surface. Looking northward, he saw the lights of fishing vessels off near Fedje. There were a great many boats spreading out to the south of the Hellisoy.

After an hour and a half, Launders surfaced to recharge the batteries and check for messages. He was over five miles out from shore, a cautious distance. The fishing boats remained in view. It was a large fleet. They moved slowly over the water, their lights twinkling in the dark. He did not know if they were ASW vessels or rescue vessels or had simply come out to trawl for their catches. But it was an odd time for that in the middle of the winter.

The next several hours were uneventful. The fishing boats stayed out but did not wander too far out from shore. A few minutes after 11 P.M., hovering about on the surface, *Venturer* received a message from Dundee. An aircraft would be flying by on a mission, but he was not to be concerned.

It was a friendly on patrol of the waters around Fedje Island.

12.

On February 9, 1945, the day Sven Plass perished at sea, his wife Lilly wrote another unsent letter to him from her parents' home in Senftenberg. In the Crimean resort city of Yalta on the Black Sea, meanwhile, Franklin Roosevelt, Winston Churchill, and Joseph Stalin had convened to discuss the partitioning of Europe among their respective nations after the war ended. Germany's surrender now seemed a foregone conclusion, and with the Red Army pushing across its eastern borders, the Western powers, leery of Stalin's intentions, wanted to come to an armistice agreement that ensured that his forces would not roll through the entire continent, seizing control for the Communist dictator.

Lilly's fears, though very personal, in many ways echoed theirs as expressed in her letter:

> *Escape plans are the main topic these days. The more horse carts roll by, the more we try to get used to the idea that we also have to leave. Aunt Hilde (who has made a stop here) and I are talking about how we could manage to go to Liebenstein. It would be impossible by train—we would not be able to take anything with us and we would expose ourselves to the danger of air attacks. Even with Aunt Hilde's wagon it would be difficult, as there is hardly any food left for the horses. It gets harder and harder as the danger gets closer.*

Unlike Lilly Plass's earlier letters, that one would end abruptly, without any closing endearments or postscripts to her absent husband. The front was relentlessly moving toward her and Maja, and her mind was on fleeing as she wrote.

One week later to the day, February 16, Lilly prepared Maja's bottles, bundled her crying daughter in blankets, and fled the village on her aunt's wooden horse cart, joining the caravan of desperate evacuees heading west away from the advancing Russians.

As was the case for millions of her fellow Germans in those last days of the Nazi Third Reich, Lilly's struggles had only begun.

13.

In April 1944, Grand Admiral Karl Dönitz sent a second transport submarine to the Far East roughly on the same course as U-864. The Type XB U-234 carried many *Wunderwaffen* among its estimated 240 tons of cargo, as well as a dozen supernumerary passengers, including two Japanese naval engineers.

On May 10, two days after the chief of staff of the German High Command, General Alfred Jodl, unconditionally surrendered to the Allies, and one day after the governments of Great Britain and the United States formally declared the war to be won, U-234 surfaced and received Dönitz's final order to his beloved U-boat force, praising their valor and ordering them to hoist their flags in surrender.

It would take until May 17 for the U-boat's captain to finally obey that order and capitulate to a pair of U.S. destroyers south of the Grand Banks. A short while before the American boarding party arrived, the Japanese engineers retired to their quarters and committed suicide, impaling themselves on their swords.

When the submarine was searched by the Americans, a half ton of uranium oxide was found aboard with the rest of the freight. There is no record of the uranium's final disposition, and its presence on the boat would remain classified U.S. government information until the 1990s.

14.

On July 27, 1945, almost three months after the end of World War II, Lieutenant Jimmy Launders had a bar added to the Distinguished Service Order he'd received for the sinking of U-771. The reason was his successful attack on the Fedje U-boat, as it had come to be known. Presenting the decoration in London was King George VI, who praised Launders as a "fearless and skillful commander." Several of his crewmen were also given awards for their exemplary conduct during the encounter. The methods Launders improvised to track and target U-864 have become the blueprint for modern-day sub-to-sub surveillance techniques.

Action 9 February 1945 of the HMS *Venturer* remains the only publicly acknowledged instance in history of one submarine sinking another while both were submerged.

AFTERWORD

May 15, 2005

Maja Grisotti could feel anticipation tighten her throat as she stood inside the wheelhouse of the *August Brinkmann,* a white fishing cutter owned by the retired Fedje skipper Otto Gullaksen. Although she would have preferred to stand out on the deck during the trip out of Austrheim, on the western edge of Norway's mainland, the rainy weather had kept her inside.

In Bergen, it often rained.

Maja had come a long distance—all the way from Germany via Copenhagen. During the Danish passenger flight, she had passed through a violent storm that shook the plane in the air. Lightning had forked through the clouds and struck its fuselage, causing the cabin lights to flicker.

It is my father knocking, she had thought.

On this, the Northern European celebration of the Pentecost, the sixty-year-old Maja had reserved her holiday leave for a visit to her father's final resting place. She had never known Sven Plass. He had died when she was less than a year old, and her mother Lilly had not gotten an official announcement of his loss from the German Red Cross until January 1948, three years afterward. By then, the war was over. Also by that time, Maja was no longer living with her mother. In postwar Germany, with food and housing scarce, Lilly had sent three-year-old Maja to live with relatives in Sweden. Lilly had been able to obtain an exit visa only for the child because of Sven's half-Swedish ancestry. She herself was German, and had not been granted one. But at least she had gotten it for her daughter. In the cheerless, frantic weeks before she had fled Senftenberg, such a mercy had been impossible.

That was in 1947. Maja and Lilly had boarded a plane together in Hamburg, and Maja remembered her mother explaining that she had to go back outside and get her purse. Young though she'd been, a terrible dread had come over her. And then the plane had sped up on the runway and taken off. Maja was three and alone on an airplane.

In Sweden, Old Moster Elsa, Sven's aunt, had taken her in and eventually adopted her. Maja had grown up Swedish. So soon after the war, anti-German sentiments were high, and Moster Elsa had often warned her about mentioning her national background to anyone. "You must not say you were born in Germany," she would remind her.

It would not be hard for Maja to keep her secret. Her early recollections were vague. She had no memory of her mother's hurried departure from Senftenberg as the Allied planes flew overhead and dropped their bombs. Years later, as an adult, she would receive the letters Lilly had written to Sven. The unsent confessionals. From them she would learn some details of the evacuation.

Aunt Hilde was from Breslau, Poland. Fleeing ahead of the Russians in a heavily laden cart, she had picked up Lilly and Maja and joined a refugee column. In the dead of winter and in deep snows, the journey had been arduous.

As her mother had left town, the main road out had been closed with barricades, and all the wagons were forced onto a small side road. The *Volkssturm,* or German national militia, had been posted at checkpoints everywhere. Most were fanatical Nazis, members of the Hitler Youth. Coarse and obsessed with keeping order, they had shown little sympathy for the refugees.

Eventually Lilly had gotten through to the Elbe bridge. But the crossing had been dangerous with the weight of all the horse carts upon it, and the horses had been anxious and hard to control. Before they reached the other side, the basket containing Maja's bottles had fallen off their wagon. Two of the bottles broke, and the others leaked out. Horrified, Lilly had not known how she would manage to feed the infant.

That night they had reached a small village. No one there would take them in, but someone had told them there was a farmhouse outside town where they could shelter. It was February, and bitterly cold, and they had slept in the hay of a barn with dozens of other refugees. But there were things crawling in the hay. Rodents and insects. Everyone had been bitten as they tried to sleep, and Maja had screamed and cried from hunger until sunrise.

There were many more stories in the letters. Lilly's traversing of the mountains between Leipzig and Halle on the sixth day was the most frightening experience. The air strikes had been at their most frequent, and the refugees had been able to see the planes directly above them. The bombs had shaken the steeply wooded hills, and their strafing blown the limbs and branches off the treetops.

The horses had been a serious problem on the high mountain passes. Aunt Hilde had gotten them in Breslau, Poland, where the land was as flat as a board, and the climbs had panicked them. Leaving one village, they had slid back on the roads twisting uphill, and Lilly had been terrified her baby would fall off and get trampled under hoof and wheel.

After eight days, mother and daughter had reached the village of Erfurt in central Germany. There the horses gave out, exhausted. Lilly and Maja found refuge in an estate owned by the church. A local family known to Sven's parents had assisted them.

Finally Sven's father Ludolf had arrived to pick the two of them up. He had come in his car and driven them to the family home in Schönberg, Lilly crying tears of joy in the seat beside him. Many others had showed up at Ludolf's door looking for safe haven—relatives, people whose homes had been bombed, even garrisoned soldiers whose units had been scattered. He had not turned them away.

In the coming months, as the Allies crossed the Rhine at Oppenheim and Germany capitulated, Lilly had lived there with Sven's family, waiting out the end of the war and hoping to receive word from her husband. But she never did, and her hope shrank more and more with time, until at last she'd accepted the thought that he would not be coming back.

Two years later, Maja was put aboard the plane to Sweden.

It was only as an adult, after Ludolf's death, that her aunt Grauhan had given her the photos, letters, and drawings from Sven's travels that came to everything that was left of her father and mother . . . only then that Maja had heard about U-864.

And now, after six decades, she was here on a boat off the Norwegian island of Fedje, rain pocking the water's surface, wavelets lapping at the little vessel's keel in the harsh northern currents.

She had heard many things about the submarine. It carried some sort of weaponry that was central to Hitler's final machinations, a secret cargo he'd sent to Japan in an effort to change the outcome of the war. It also had liquid mercury aboard, sixty-five tons, contained in almost two thousand rusting canisters. When studies showed that some of the mercury had seeped out into the surrounding water, the people of Fedje had campaigned to have the submarine raised,* saying the mercury would destroy the fisheries from which they drew their livelihoods. They spoke of a disease that could result from mercury poisoning, Minamata, that would cause brain damage, coma, even death. There were assertions that the contamination could destroy the fishing industry of Bergen, with local environmentalists comparing the possible devastation to Chernobyl in the extent of its consequences. There were even suggestions of a more destructive freight aboard—uranium that had been meant for Japanese nuclear weapons. But of that, she had heard, there was no evidence.

* See Notes.

"Here it is."

Maja looked up at Gullaksen. He had stopped the boat and opened the window of the wheelhouse. Though his years of laying nets were over, he occasionally brought tourists out to Fedje. Scientists, historians, and politicians with an interest in the wreck as well.

The Fedje submarine was an object of controversy for the local population. In 2003, the same year Maja was finally given her grandfather Ludolf's letter to read along with other family documents, the Norwegian coast guard had located the sunken boat using a remotely operated underwater craft. Their expedition had been launched after the German engineer, Wolfgang Lauenstein, had discovered old war records about the boat's freight of toxic mercury and persuaded the Norwegians to take it seriously as an environmental threat.

Norway's government had since spent tens of millions of dollars to research the possibility of bringing the boat to the surface or entombing it in concrete to contain the mercury. Decisions to do one or the other had been made and rescinded. Some believed the submarine's rotted hull would break apart if they tried to hoist it from the bottom, scattering the noxious mercury irrevocably into the sea. Others thought encasing it in cement was futile, that sooner or later the mercury would leak out into the seabed anyway.

Everyone seemed afraid of something, and no one agreed on anything, and as a result nothing was ever done.

For Maja, it was equally complicated in some ways—yet her heart's concerns were simple enough. Although solutions were for the experts, she understood the environmental concerns of the Norwegians. But the boat was more than mercury. It was the mass grave of her father and seventy-two others. Whatever was done, it was her hope that the task could be carried out with respect.

And meanwhile, she had come to pay her own respects. In her purse was a small wreath she had brought from home, made with flowers from her garden. She had fashioned it with love for a father she had never known, whose face she recognized only from yellowing scrapbooks.

Moving to the window of the wheelhouse, she tossed the wreath into the ocean and watched it float away, raindrops battering the delicate petals. Beside her, the old captain had taken the cap off his head. Maja noticed through her blurred, wet eyes that he was crying.

And then he was back at the wheel, and they were motoring for Austrheim through the rain and mist. From the dock, Maja still had quite a taxi ride to the inn where she was staying in Norway, though she knew she would have a great deal to occupy her mind along the way.

Her story was just one, she reflected. Imagine how many others there were about the things that happened in an old war whose last battle had been fought, and final casualty counted, more than sixty long years ago.

ACKNOWLEDGMENTS

Some special words of appreciation are due to those who stepped up to help make this book possible.

Thanks to Maja Grisotti, daughter of Lieutenant Sven Plass and his wife, Lilly, for her generosity in sharing her personal documents and reflections. They not only gave the narrative a human dimension but led to a fuller understanding of Germany's plans for sharing technological secrets with Japan late in the war.

Thanks also to Christian Klambauer, whose painstaking research into U-864's mission was a tremendous asset.

Gerty Agoston, Christopher Morris, Halvor H. Halvorsen, Christiane Engel and Ivonne Sebesi tirelessly lent their time and effort to difficult translations of German and Norwegian articles, letters and archival documents. A grateful bow of the head to you all.

Dr. Axel Niestle and Platon Alexiades gave their insights into U-boat losses and Allied submarine activities in the European theater. These provided and pointed the way toward many indispensable primary research sources.

Jannicke Moldoen and Reidun Moldoen detailed the concerns of *Hev U-864*, a political action group of Fedje residents who have been campaigning for removal of the wreck from their local waters.

Captain Jerry Mason, USN (Ret.), who with his wife, Charla, administrates the excellent website Uboatarchive.net, graciously provided several photographs from his extensive collection.

The book would not have been the same without the fine journalistic work of Eystein Rossum and Jon Tufto of the Norwegian newspaper *Bergens Tidende,* who were kind enough to share vital contact information with me.

David Berne created the superb map of U-864's intended and ultimate routes, putting his masterful digital imaging and drawing skills to work on very short notice. He may be reached at djberne@gmail.com.

My editor, Tom Colgan, had the confidence to give this project life based on an idea given to him over lunch. A nod to his assistant, Amanda Ng, for getting things done.

I'm grateful to my longtime friend and agent John Talbot for his years of support.

And, of course, I'm indebted to my wife, Suzanne Preisler, for all the usual reasons.

NOTES

In writing *Code Name Caesar,* a great effort was made to use primary source research materials whenever possible, and perhaps a third to a half of the references consulted were of that nature. A few of them were drawn on throughout the book and bear mentioning up front.

Kristian Klambauer, a relative of one of the crewmen who perished aboard U-864, was generous enough to forward the thick stack of notes he compiled during his long and extensive personal research into the submarine's history. As Mr. Klambauer (or Klammi, as he prefers) wrote the papers entirely in German, they were translated pro bono and with only occasional complaint by my friend and neighbor Gerty Agoston, who spent a quarter century as a journalist with the German-American newsweekly *Staats-Zeitung,* and was also a cultural correspondent for the German Press Agency.

Klammi has, besides, sought out photographic copies of most surviving records of U-864, as well as many for HMS *Venturer* that relate to their fateful encounter, obtaining them from private collections, museums, crewmen's families, and the government archives of three different nations. The documents and much more information about U-864, including source links and photos of interest, can be viewed at his website, www.klammi.de/html/u864.html.

A significant amount of information for this book came from an exhaustive series of Norwegian and English technical documents that the global risk-management firm Det Norske Veritas (hereafter referred to as DNV) conducted of U-864's wreck site in 2007. The study, which utilized information from dives to the submerged wreck site by Remote Operated Vehicle and other research, was commissioned by the Norwegian Coastal Administration to investigate different alternatives to salvage the wreck and remove the mercury from the seabed.

The letters of Dr. Ludolf Plass, Lieutenant Sven Plass, and Lilly Plass were provided by Maja Grisotti, Lieutenant Plass's daughter. Ms. Grisotti also helped translate and put the letters in their proper context, both in terms of her family background and the historical time line of events discussed in the book. These letters not only brought the sweeping and violent global events that surrounded U-864's mission into very human focus, but shed a valuable historical light on some of the reasons Germany undertook to send the submarine to the Far East.

INTRODUCTION

1.

Several sources were used to reconstruct Kristoffer Karlsen's eyewitness sighting of U-864's destruction from atop a bluff on Fedje Island. Of great help were the newspaper articles "Nazi U-Boat Imperils Norwegians Decades After the War" by Alan Cowell and Walter Gibbs (*New York Times,* January 8, 2007); "Let the Fallen Germans Rest in Peace at Sea" (*Bergens Tidende,* December 20, 2003, uncredited, translated by author); "I Hope the Submarine Raising Gives Fedje a Boost" by Bear Asle North (*Bergens Tidende,* February 2, 2009, translated by author). The DNV report was valuable to the technical accuracy of this section, and the BBC documentary *Timewatch: The Hunt for U-864* also proved very useful.

Excellent background information on traditional methods of gathering peat for home fuel came from the online article "Heat with Peat Moss" by Sarah Matthess (www.countrysidemag.com).

The location of U-864's wreckage 2.3 miles from Fedje raises questions about one particular aspect of Karlsen's account of the sinking in the *Timewatch* documentary. While his vantage, and the prevailing weather conditions, would have allowed him to hear the detonation of the torpedo that struck the submarine, and observe the resultant waterspout and smoke, Karlsen would have been too far away to see the boat slowly sinking underwater, as he asserts. Recollection can be mutable, and as a twelve-year-old boy, he may well have spotted one of the undetonated torpedoes as they approached Fedje underwater, and gotten confused, though it is also possible his youthful imagination filled in certain blanks. But that suspect detail has been omitted in this narrative.

2.-3.

Wolfgang Lauenstein's online article "U-864 and Willi Transier—a Tragic Fate" (www.rheingoenheim-info.de, translated by author) provides details of his meeting with Karstein Kongestol, the fisherman who discovered U-864's sunken wreckage, and Lauenstein's search for clues about the submarine, Willi Transier, and Edith Wetzler. The German-language piece "Hunt for Caesar" by Marc von Brasse, Clemens Höges, and Karl Vandenhole (Spiegel Online, www.spiegel.de, translated by author) added greatly to my knowledge, as did "Norway Tackles Toxic War Grave" (www.news.bbc.uk). The BBC's *Timewatch: The Hunt for U-864* was again instructive.

The background information on Fedje's fishing community came from www .nordhordlandsbilder.no and other sources too varied to enumerate.

PROLOGUE

Many different sources were used to reconstruct the departure of U-864 from Kiel and its surrounding circumstances.

A partial record of U-864's workup for her first combat patrol exists in the *"Kriegstagebücher (KTB) and Stehnder Kriegsbefehl des Führers/Defehlshaber der Underseeboote U-864,"* or "War Diaries and War Standing Orders of the Commander in Chief, Submarines for U-864." These include "U864/KTB 12/09/1943 to 01/05/1945," which are in the custody of the Operational Archives Branch of the U.S. Naval Historical Center, Washington, D.C.

The "high priority" or classified files U864/CIV-Cefasche (12/30/1944 to 02/12/ 1945) reside in the Bundesarchiv-Militärarchiv (German Federal/Military Archive) at Freiburg, Germany.

A wealth of Information about Kiel Harbor and the 33rd U-boat Flotilla was extracted from the declassified "Report on the Interrogation of Survivors from U-162 Sunk on September 3, 1942," Navy Department, Office of the Chief of Naval Operations, Washington, D.C.

Some biographical data about Tadao Yamato and Toshio Nakai is from the article "U-Boat's Mercury Posing Threat: Japanese Pair Aboard Wreck off Norway" (*Japan Times,* June 6, 2007).

Rolf von Chlingensperg's Nazi-sponsored adventures on the slopes of Nanga Parbat are documented in the book *Fallen Giants: A History of Himalayan Mountaineering from the Age of Empire to the Age of Extremes* (Connecticut:

Yale University Press, 2007). Added information came from *Testing the Limits: Aviation Medicine and the Origins of Manned Space Flight* by Maura Phillips Mackowski (Texas: A&M University Press, 2006).

The feature-length Nazi propaganda film *U-Boat Westward!* mentioned in the Prologue and Chapter Four may be watched in its entirety on Google videos (www.video.google.com). More information about it can be found at the Internet Movie Database (www.imdb.com).

The DNV report "Salvage of U864—Supplementary Studies—the Midship Section" included diagrams of the keel hold that were very useful. Again, much is owed to "DNV: Supplementary Studies—Study No. 7: Cargo."

The book *Reluctant Allies: German-Japanese Relations in World War II* by Hans-Joachim Krug, Yoichi Nirama, Berthhold J. Sander-Nagashima, and Axel Niestle (Annapolis: Naval Institute Press, 2001) was immensely helpful in fleshing out my knowledge of the preparations U-864 made for her departure. Dr. Niestle, a leading international expert on U-boats, was gracious enough to recommend his work, send copies of documents, and point toward other invaluable sources in a brief but vital series of e-mails we exchanged in 2010. Indispensable reference information came from Clay Blair's two-volume history of the U-boat campaign: *Hitler's U-Boat War: The Hunters, 1939–1942* (New York: Modern Library, 2000) and *Hitler's U-Boat War: The Hunted, 1942–1945* (New York: Modern Library, 2000). The booklet *A U-Boat Far from Home* by Deitrich M. W. Wille (UK: Chatham Dockyard Historical Society, 1999) is an illuminating firsthand account of the 1944 journey of the Type IX D2 Class U-181, U-864's sister submarine, from France to Penang and Singapore.

Peter Cremer's *U-Boat Commander* (Annapolis: Naval Institute Press, 1985); Gordon Williamson and Ian Palmer's *Kriegsmarine U-Boats 1939–45*, Vol 2 (UK: Osprey, 2002); David Mason's *U-Boat: The Secret Menace* (New York: Ballantine, 1968); and *Hitler's U-Boat Bases* by Jak Malmann Showell (Gloucestershire, UK: Sutton, 2007) were all solid references on German submarines, their crews, and their home ports.

U-864's secret cargo is largely known to the world from a series of numbered ULTRA intercepts that Dr. Neistle extracted from the British war archives and then compiled for the DNV report. The list is presented below essentially as it appears in the study, with the archival serial number of each intercept alongside it on the left. The plans for Caproni submarines named in intercept 04044 refer to midget submarines similar to those recently found to have been used in the Japanese attack on Pearl Harbor. The Campini plane in 12714 (manufactured by Caproni) was an experimental Italian jet aircraft comparable to the Me 262. Intercepts 12702 and 14025 refer to plans for the Campini's engine. Intercept 12662 (plans for the Rheinmetall MG 151) refers to an autocannon favored by the Luftwaffe for various fighter aircraft.

It is of great historical significance that the intercepted transmissions are from February 28, 1945, weeks after U-864 was sunk by HMS *Venturer*, and also that their processing and decoding by the Allies did not occur until March (per the codebreaker's final notation). Despite popular accounts, then, it couldn't have been ULTRA decrypts that revealed the German sub's secret cargo to the British prior to their January 12 air raid on Bergen or *Venturer*'s diversion to Fedje. This leaves close-up intel as Dundee-Lerwick's only possible source for that knowledge.

From: Chief Inspector in Germany #024 1000/28 February 1945
To: Chief, Bureau of Military Preparations

The following was aboard the German submarine (temporarily called CAESAR) which departed for Japan last year. {handwritten note on page margin: U-864}

12719:	Plans for ME-163	
	ME 1 of 20 to 20 of 20	20 packages
	Plans for ME-262	
	MF 1 of 34 to 33 of 34	33 packages
	Supplement to plans for ME-262	
	ME-A 1 to 9	9 packages
	Supplement to plans for ME-163	
	ME A 1-A to 3-A:	3 packages

Parts for ME-163 and 262   1 box

Junkers plans and parts

JU-1 to 6:   6 boxes

Plans for BMW

BMW-4 1 to 4   3 rolls, 1 box

Plans for Walter

WA 1 to 2:   2 drums, 1 box

Informative data for technicians aboard:

EC 1 to 19

ES 21 to 23

ES 24 AB to 35

ES 36 AB to 37 AB

ES 38 to 56

ES 58 to 62

CASPAR 63

Total: 60 packages

02200 Plans for MB 511:   1 set, 1 drum

04044 (3{second number ?})

Caproni Company

1 set of plans for submarines 2 boxes

02201 Bolinder Company

1 set of radio graphs: 1 box

02364C Zeiss Company

1 set of plans for fire control equipment: 18 packages

Documents on non-magnetic values: 3 packages

02634B Plans for Kreisel-Geräte Company equipment: 3 packages, 1 box

Same as above, 5 packages and 2 packages of related books and magazines.

12662 Rheinmetall

Plans for MG 151: 2 boxes

12701 Plans for fuel pump: 1 box

1 set of Zankoening measuring device: 3 boxes

12714 Plans for Campini plane: 3 tubes

12702   Plans for Isota Company's gas turbine: 4 tubes

14025   Plans for Isota Company's supercharger: 2 tubes

12699   Plans for Galileo Company's air camera 8 tubes

12847   Plans for Siemens Company's radar, 1 package

German (Naval Technical Bureau secret?) #058

      Plans for Freya and Bisma and explanatory material; 2 packages

German (Naval Technical Bureau secret) #243

      Plans for manufacturing the same type of switchboards: 7 packages

02216   Mercury: 1857 flasks

      (Part of it includes that handled by officials in Italy; we shall report the details later.)

(CZ/{illegible}A#8124-{illegible}I)

GI-A COMMENT: This is probably the manifest of one of the 2 German U/B's believed to have left Europe in August 1944, and to have reached the Far East.

(SU {illegible}.151300/ Q March 1945)

CHAPTER ONE

The article "From Hour to Hour" by Bear Bjornset gives an excellent overview of Operation Weserübung. It may be found in its original Norwegian at http://www.aftenposten.no.

Richard D. Hooker Jr. and Christopher Coglianese discuss the invasion from a strategic and tactical perspective in their lengthy article "Operation Weserübung and the Origins of Joint Warfare," *Joint Force Quarterly,* Summer 1993.

For a running account of the German attack on Narvik from an official British naval perspective, see the declassified "The War Diary of Vice Admiral Commanding, Battle Cruiser Squadron." Its transcription is available online at www.naval-history.net.

German objectives and justifications for the invasion of Norway are laid out in detail by Admiral Dönitz in his lengthy paper "The Conduct of the War at Sea," which Dönitz had originally dictated in German to Colonel General

Alfred Jodl shortly after the war. In January 1946, it was translated and published as a restricted document by the U.S. Navy's Office of Naval Intelligence (ONI) with appendices based on Dönitz's interrogation prior to his trial at Nuremberg. It is now declassified and in the public domain.

More information on the subject came from *Memoirs: Ten Years and Twenty Days* by Grand Admiral Karl Dönitz (New York: Da Capo 1997).

A library of archival video footage available at http://wn.com/weserübung was a tremendous resource for an author trying to get a visual feel for Norway at the time of the invasion.

My description of Bunker Bruno and account of its construction was aided by a variety of sources. A good basic reference is *German U-Boat Bunkers: Yesterday and Today* by Karl-Heinz and Michael Schmeelke (Atglen, PA: Schiffer, 1999). *U-Boat Bases and Bunkers* by Gordon Williamson and Ian Palmer (Oxford, UK: Osprey, 2003) has some very fine photographic material.

Many superb photos of Bergen Harbor circa 1942 are available online at www.uboatarchive.net/POWInternmentHunkirchenPhotos.htm. The website www.marineholmen.com also offers some useful visual and historical detail about the harbor. Good information about U-boat base Bergen also may be found at www.uboat.net.

Eystein Rossum, a reporter for the Bergen news daily *Bergens Tidende,* did some of the most thorough and conscientious journalistic work to be found anywhere on U-864 and was generous enough to share many of his contacts with me. His feature story "The Fedje Submarine" (translated from the Norwegian by Halvor Halverson) was a tremendous asset both for this and other sections of the book.

CHAPTER TWO

1

A great deal of information about the Royal Navy Submarine Service can be found at http://www.rnsubs.co.uk, the official website of the Submariners

Association, Barrow-in-Furness Branch. The organization's listing of HMS *Venturer*'s early operational highlights jump-started my research into her early patrols. A brief history of the career of HMS *Vulcan* is also available on the site.

My knowledge of HMS Ambrose's role during the war owes much to a superb article by Mark C. Jones, "Experiment at Dundee: The Royal Navy's 9th Submarine Flotilla and Multinational Naval Cooperation During World War II," *Journal of Military History,* October 2008.

Distributed by the Press and Information Branch of Forsvarsnett (the Norwegian armed forces) and written in English, the booklet *The Norwegian Navy in the Second World War* is another source of information about the close relationship between Norway's naval-forces-in-exile and the Royal Navy, outlining the joint wartime operations they launched from Dundee and elsewhere.

I gained many insights into *Venturer*'s activities throughout 1944 from the declassified document ADM 1-30052, "Recommendations for Honors and Awards: Services off Norwegian Coast, Including Sinking of Enemy U-X-Boat, 10 Awards." It is preserved in the British Archives, London.

There are to this day no declassified records documenting the relationship that Dundee-Lerwick's submarines had with the Royal Norwegian Naval Special Unit (or Shetland Bus), MI6, and the Special Operations Executive. My account of that relationship therefore required some historical detective work, and in giving it I relied on my ability to piece together and interpret available facts, along with a dash of common sense. The transport and resupply missions that *Venturer* and other 9th Flotilla submarines conducted along the Norwegian coast are a matter of record; all that was really necessary was to deduce the most probable chain of command by which their orders originated and came down to an operational level. Whatever steps I took to connect the dots were conservative. It would take a strenuously obdurate thought process to imagine the small island of Lerwick playing home to MI6, the SOE (at one point in time), the Shetland Bus, and a submarine provisioning and refuel depot by anything but design. The British intelligence services, moreover, oversaw the training and support of Norwegian spies, saboteurs, and ship watchers; any Royal Navy submarines used to aid the resistance would have been on loan to those groups. Their covert missions along the Norwegian coast would have required a very high degree of integration, which is to say the sharing of resources and information.

The Shetland Bus: A World War II Epic of Escape, Survival, and Adventure by David Howarth (Connecticut: Lyons Press, 2001) is the definitive book on the RNNSU's formation and actions throughout the war. I strongly recommend it to readers interested in the subject.

A comprehensive online resource for those who wish to learn more about the Shetland Bus is www.shetlandbus.com. Additional information on Dundee and HMS Ambrose can be found on the Internet at www.dundee-at-war .net/ambrose.htm and www.frigateunicorn.org. Melanie Reid's article "Memorial to Dundee's Lost Submariners" (UK *Sunday Times,* September 18, 2009) is an account of modern efforts to commemorate the largely forgotten base and its men.

Precisely because his career was with the naval intelligence community, and his long contribution to the Allied war effort was made under conditions of highest secrecy, Edward Thomas is an obscure figure in the history of the conflict. What makes this ironic is that Thomas later wrote of his work with a revealing detail and candor that is still unequaled in national intelligence annals—and that this official history was carried out by a team of scholars and former intelligence operatives with the full approval of the British government. In the five-volume *British Intelligence in the Second World War,* edited by F. H. Hinsley (New York: Cambridge University Press, 1990), Thomas clearly delineates the ways that intelligence about the Germans was gathered and disseminated in the Northern European theater of operations. The picture he presents of coast watchers and local spies as the true sources of intelligence on a fast-moving operational level—specifically in Norway— with ULTRA and MAGIC used primarily as background by a handful of far-off upper-echelon planners, was key to my solving the mystery of how the British were able to track and target U-864 in the limited time available to them.

2

The dedicated historical researcher can dig a bounty of obscure information about Allied and Axis shipping convoys from the websites http://www .warsailors.com and http://www.naval-history.net. Much of what I learned about the merchant ships SS *Vang,* SS *Friedrichshafen,* and DS *Force* sprang off information obtained on those sites. The website of the Wurttemberg State Library in Stuttgart, http://www.wlb-stuttgart.de, provided some key facts about the *Friedrichshafen*'s history up to the time she ran into *Venturer.*

The World's Merchant Fleets 1939: The Particulars and Wartime Fates of 6,000 Ships by Roger Jordan (Annapolis: Naval Institute Press, 2006) was critical to my understanding of the events in this chapter and aided my ability to put them into context. *Chronology of the War at Sea, 1939–1945: The Naval History of World War Two* by Jürgen Rohwer and Gerhard Hummelchen (Annapolis: Naval Institute Press 1992) was of near-equal value as far as reconstructing an accurate time line. The same can be said for its related volume, *Allied Submarine Attacks of World War Two: European Theater of Operations 1939– 1945* by Jürgen Rohwer, J. S. Kay, and I. N. Venkov (Annapolis: Naval Institute Press, 1997).

The open-air Hanstholm Museum in Denmark has one of the best-preserved German World War II coastal batteries in Northern Europe. Among the viewable artifacts that can be seen at the museum's information center are horned mines of the sort that seeded the Skagerrak when *Venturer* and HMS *Taku* attempted to slip through a field of them during their joint patrol. Images may be found at http://www.museumscenterhanstholm.dk.

The website www.atlantikwall-research-norway.de is a source of highly detailed information about MKB Egersund.

Dönitz's essay "The Conduct of the War at Sea" was again invaluable to my understanding of German naval activities in Norway.

The article "The Distribution of Swedish Foreign Trade via Swedish Ports and Frontier Railways" by Sven Erik Nordin (*Geografiska Annaler,* 1937) satisfied many of my particular curiosities about Norway's geographic value as a conduit for iron ore to the Third Reich.

There is scant information to be found in World War II histories about Egersund's importance as a transcontinental telegraph hub for the British Empire. The opportunity to pore through the *Journal of the Telegraph,* Vol 3 (New York: James D. Reid, 1869), a copy of which resides at the Princeton University Library in New Jersey, was essential to my knowledge. *The Manual of Submarine Telegraph Companies* by Joseph Wagstaff Blundell (London: published by the author, 1872) provided complementary data. It is in the public domain and downloadable through www.books.google.com.

CHAPTER THREE

1–2

The Holen School tragedy that resulted from the RAF's botched October 4, 1944, air strike on Bergen Harbor is among the least internationally known tragedies of World War II, perhaps in part because of Norway's relative isolation. Due to the scarcity of literature about the incident, I relied primarily on non-English source materials for my research.

Among the few references written in English was the article "No. 6 Bomber Group" by Flying Officer H. A. Halliday (*Roundel,* April 1963), and it would serve as a springboard for my research. It is also to Flight Officer Halliday that I owe my knowledge of the attentive and compassionate Mrs. Mudd at Tholthorpe.

The official website of the No. 6 Group is www.6grouprcaf.com.

The daily operations log of the "Campaign Diary of the Royal Air Force Bomber Command, October 1944" is the official record of the air units involved in the strike.

Another useful article that can be found at www.dambusters.org.uk was "Bergen—A Personal Account of the Bergen Raid" by Kurt Monsen.

Despite its minor inaccuracies, the article "Norway: The Bombing of Bergen 1944/45" by Anna Duus is an excellent eyewitness account by a survivor of the October raid.

Trygve Freyvald Guldbrandsen's harrowing experiences inside the Holen School during the raid are drawn from his personal account, cowritten with Ragnar Askeland, titled: "Four Hours Trapped in Ruins" (*VI Menn*, December 12, 2008, translated by author). In his editorial "Holen School, Again" in the November 15, 2006, edition of *Bergens Tidende,* Mr. Guldbrandsen, like Ms. Duus, raises the possibility that civilian targets were struck by design. Implicit in any such conjecture is the thought that British planners may have been motivated by suspicions that those targets held a dual military purpose or because they wished to disrupt and destroy local infrastructure. But while I discuss British air marshal Arthur Harris's carpet-bombing strategies elsewhere in the book, the pains taken to avoid civilian losses in the subsequent January 12 attack strongly support my narrative's conclusion that October's widespread destruction was unwanted and accidental.

"The Day Laksevåg Never Forgot" by Oivind Ask (*Bergens Tidende,* October 4, 2004, translated by author) gives a poignant overview of the destruction that fell on Laksevåg on the day of the attack

Bjorn Davidson's article "Bombers over Laksevåg" (translated by author) was written in 2004 to commemorate the sixtieth anniversary of the Holen School tragedy. It is available in Norwegian on the website of the Norwegian Association of the Deafblind (NADB) www.home.online.no, and may also be viewed as part of a comprehensive online exhibition dedicated to the event on the website of the National Archives of Norway, www.arkivverket .no. NAN has also made available a number of war damage and economic assistance reports prepared by postwar committees in Laksevåg, including a May 29, 1948, report from the Main Committee for Donation Distribution, a September 1947 accounting report of donations from local churches, and an exhaustive searchable casualty database.

The Laksevåg Historical Society stores in its electronic files digital copies of many contemporaneous records of the air strike, including original fire department and sheriff's documents.

The University of Bergen's communications department quarterly journal, *Hubro,* features an enlightening article about the long-term traumatic after-effects of the October raid.

CHAPTER FOUR

1

The excerpts from the "Tripartite Pact Between Germany, Italy and Japan," the "Secret Supplementary Protocols to the Tripartite Pact," and "The Fuhrer's Directive No. 24 on Cooperation with Japan" are from Appendices A–C (pp. 245–257) of *Reluctant Allies.*

Some books that filled the gaps in my knowledge of the German, Japanese, and Italian submarine forces and allowed me to better understand their wartime relationship are: *U-Boats: The Illustrated History of the Raiders of the Deep* by David Miller (Virginia: Potomac Books, 2002); *Hitler's Grey Wolves: U-Boats in the Indian Ocean* by Lawrence Paterson (UK: Greenhill, 2006); *The Penang Submarines* by Dennis Gunton (Georgetown, Malaysia: City Council of Georgetown, 1970); *The Japanese Submarine Force and World War II* by Carl Boyd and Akihiko Yoshida (Annapolis: Naval Institute Press, 1995); and *Yanagi: The Secret Underwater Trade Between Germany and Japan* by Marc Felton (UK: Pen and Sword, 2005); *Germany's Last Mission to Japan: The Failed Voyage of U-234* by Joseph Scalia (Annapolis: Naval Institute Press, 2000); and of course *Reluctant Allies.*

Found at www.uboataces.com, the online article "U-Boats in the Far East" also offers a broad and painstakingly researched examination of German submarine operations in the Pacific.

My preparation of a time line for this chapter was facilitated by the I-30 Tabular Record of Movement by Bob Hackett and Sander Kingsepp. Compiled from Japanese and American sources, it may be viewed at www.combined fleet.com.

The arrival of I-30 at Lorient was the sort of staged event in which the Nazi Party excelled and would become a model for state propaganda machines of later eras. My grasp of the principles and techniques used to sell political ideologies and military claims to the public during World War II was aided by the book *Wartime: Understanding and Behavior in the Second World War* by Paul Fussell (New York: Oxford University Press, 1989).

The book *World War II German Women's Auxiliary Services* by Gordon Williamson (UK: Osprey, 2003) helped texture my depiction of Commander Shinobu Endo's reception.

Purnell's History of the Second World War: German Secret Weapons: Blueprint for Mars by Brian Ford (UK: McDonald and Company, 1969) improved and enhanced my knowledge of Hitler's covert weapons program.

An excellent article on the Me 163's chief developer titled "Alexander Lippisch: From Germany to Iowa" by John A. Goodlove (January 2010) can be found at http://alexanderlippisch.blogspot.com.

A visit to the National Museum of the United States Air Force at Wright-Patterson Air Force Base outside Dayton, Ohio, allowed me to get close-up looks at the Messerschmitt 163B Komet and 262A Schwalbe, along with other Axis and Allied aircraft, aircraft engines, and weapons of their era in its breathtaking galleries.

Shortly after the end of World War II, the United States Air Force formed its T-2 Technical Intelligence Branch for the evaluation and cataloging of German documents relating to *Wunderwaffen* aircraft and rocketry. In July 1946, T-2's first lieutenant F. D. Van Wart prepared a then-classified "ME-262 A-1 Pilot's Handbook" from information culled from the captured papers. Complete with design specifications, flying instructions, and diagrams, it was a very useful primary resource for my book—and is in all likelihood very similar to at least one of the manuals that were carried aboard U-864.

All the newspaper passages cited in this chapter are from microfilms or digital scans of the original texts.

Heller's *U-Boat Commander* and Hille's *A U-Boat Far from Home* both provided detailed descriptions of the type of food provisioned aboard a German submarine. More information was found at http://uboat.net/men/foodstuffs.htm.

My information about recruitment for the German submarine service comes
from Williamson's *Kriegsmarine U-Boats 1939–1945.*

Three of the best published references on the Enigma code and Allied ULTRA
and MAGIC code-breaking efforts are *Codebreakers' Victory: How the Allied
Cryptographers Won World War II* by Hervie Haufler (New York: New American Library, 2003); *Seizing the Enigma: The Race to Break the German U-Boat
Codes 1939–1943* by David Kahn (New York: Barnes and Noble, 2001); and,
for its irreplaceable firsthand accounts from British cryptographers, *Codebreakers: The Inside Story of Bletchley Park,* edited by F. H. Hensley and Alan
Stripp (UK: Oxford University Press, 2001). Another excellent general work
on cryptography is *The Code Book: The Science of Secrecy from Ancient Egypt
to Quantum Cryptography* by Simon Singh (New York: Doubleday, 1999).

2

U-864's KTBs list the time and place at which she was retrofitted for her snorkel
apparatus, as well as the location where offshore snorkel and torpedo trials
were conducted.

I owe a great deal to the DNV study for information about the IX D2's keel hold
and the type of containers used for the transportation of mercury aboard U-864.

AG Vulcan Stettin was one of Germany's leading shipbuilding and locomotive companies from its founding in the middle of the nineteenth century until the end
of World War II; between sixty U-boats were constructed at its Hamburg yard.
Yet there is scant historical literature about the firm in book form, and virtually
nothing available in the English language. One of the few published texts I
found was the German volume *Lokomotivebau be der Stettiner Maschinenbau
AG Vulcan* by Dieter Crusenick (Germany: Neddermeyer; Auflage, 2006).

The Stettin Mini-Guide, edited by Walkowski Wydawnictwo and translated by
Jarowslaw Kuociuba (Poland: Wydawnictwo/Szczecin City Hall, 2010) contained an excellent history of the city as well as several clear and detailed
street maps.

"Information from Abroad: Notes on Naval Intelligence" was issued as a classified document by the USN's Office of Naval Intelligence (Washington,

D.C.) in 1899. Now in the public domain, it was a bounteous primary source of information on the evolution of German naval maneuvers at Danzig and added to my knowledge of AG Vulcan Stettin.

Very useful to my research of German submarine workup maneuvers at Danzig and elsewhere were a pair of declassified British Royal Navy documents: "Report on Interrogation of Survivors from U-357, a 500-Ton U-Boat, Sunk at 2140 B.S.T. on 26th December, 1942" and "Report on Interrogation of Survivors from U-517, a 740-Ton U-Boat, Sunk at 1017 on 21st November 1942. By Aircraft from HMS *Victorious*."

The page of the 4th Flotilla's guest book signed by Korvettenkapitän Wolfram and his officers can be viewed at Klammi's website. The translation and interpretation of Wolfram's inscription are mine, as is the blame for any errors in same.

CHAPTER FIVE

1

A trio of published references gave firm and balanced footing to my research into Gruppe Mitte, U-771, and Operation Hangman: Hinsley et al.'s *British Intelligence in the Second World War*, Vol 3, Part 2; *History of United States Naval Operations in World War II*, Vol 10: *The Atlantic Battle Won May 1943–May 1945* by Samuel Eliot Morison (Illinois: University of Illinois Press, 2002); and *Hunter Hunted: Submarine Versus Submarine Encounters from World War I to the Present* by Robert C. Stern (Annapolis: Naval Institute Press, 2007).

For this section I once again consulted Rohwer and Hummelchen's *Chronology of the War at Sea: The Naval History of World War Two 1939–1945* in building my narrative time line, specifically for the June 26, 1944, confrontation between Flight Leader G. W. T. Parker's RAF antisubmarine patrol plane, Liberator III FL916, and the German submarines U-316 and U-771. The book's capsule account of Gruppe Mitte's stalking of Allied supply convoy JW 61 was also a great help to me.

The convoy cruising order and other historical information for JW 61 can be viewed at http://www.warsailors.com/convoys/jw61.html.

"The Operational Record Book of the RAF Coastal Command's Number 86 Squadron" was a primary source for my account of the June 26 incident. In reconstructing the details of the sortie, I used the online article "Leigh Light" by J. Rickard, which can be viewed at www.historyofwar.org/articles /weapons_leigh_light.

"FdU/BdU's War Log, 16–30 June 1944" was a primary source for the movements of Gruppe Mitte, U-316, and U-771 during the period covered by the document.

Information about Flight No. HR123 of the RAF's Number 333 Squadron—the plane that was lost at sea in the August 2, 1944, attack on U-771 and U-1163—is available online at www.aviation-safety.net.

Stern makes no mention of U-1163 in his account of the Stavanger incident but records clearly show that she departed with U-771. I differ with him as to the extent of the damage U-771 suffered from the strafing by Allied Mosquitoes; he calls it "major," but from the available information, I would describe it as something less than that.

The two Norwegian airmen who perished aboard the Mosquito that ditched into the sea were Axel Reider Eikemo (pilot) and Klaus Harr (copilot).

A brief organizational history of the RAF 333 (Norwegian) Squadron can be found at www.rafweb.org.

An operational record for U-771 can be found at http://www.ubootwaffe.net.

The Wolfpack operations of U-1163 and specific information about the August 2 attack from the 333's Operational Record Book is available at http://uboat.net.

2

My account of the HMS *Venturer*'s attack on U-771 is mainly drawn from the declassified primary sources "HMS *Venturer*, Attack Form, HMS *Venturer*, Section G, Commanding Officer J. S. Launders, Royal Navy, 9th S/N Flotilla, 11 November, 1944," and ADM 1-30052, "Recommendations for Honors and Awards: Services off Norwegian Coast, Including Sinking of Enemy U-Boat,

10 Awards." A photograph of the relevant sections of the attack form were kindly provided to me by World War II submarine expert Dr. Platon Alexiades.

Lieutenant Commander Andy Chalmers died in 2005 at age eighty-four. His obituary in the *Daily Telegraph* (November 24, 2005) has some details of the encounter as well as the rest of Chalmers's distinguished naval career, which lasted until his retirement in 1970. It may be read online at www.telegraph.co.uk/news/obituaries/1503758/Lt-Andy-Chalmers.html.

Stern's *Hunter Hunted* again served as a trustworthy reference.

The book *Iron Men and Tin Fish: The Race to Build a Better Torpedo During World War II* by Anthony Newpower (Connecticut: Greenwood Publishing, 2006) was useful to my reconstruction of *Venturer*'s torpedo launch at U-771.

In reconstructing *Venturer*'s "special operation" in the Andfjord, as her rendezvous with members of the Norwegian resistance is termed in Hangman's still partially classified official records, submarine and naval history students will have noticed my unambiguous portrayal of Hangman as a Shetland Bus, or Royal Norwegian Naval Special Unit, operation, an assertion that others may contest. Per my notes to Chapter Two, the resupply of coast watchers and resistance fighters was not standard Royal Navy activity and would only have been undertaken at the behest of Lerwick's intelligence chiefs. Indeed, its logistics required their input and participation.

CHAPTER SIX

1

My biographical information about Sven Plass comes mostly from a January 18, 1955, letter written by his father, Dr. Ludolf Plass, provided to me by Sven's daughter, Maja Grisotti, and translated from its original German by Christopher Morris and Christiane Engel.

The connection the letter reveals between the senior Plass and AG Lurgi, where he held a high executive position, answers a long-standing question about Sven Plass's early selection for U-864's mission to Imperial Japan among those with an interest in the subject. Lurgi's synthetic fuel research and services were vital to the Japanese, who faced a growing shortage of petroleum products for their military-industrial machine. My conclusion that Sven Plass was chosen as a liaison between Lurgi and the Japanese government, perhaps to negotiate licenses for the processing of synthfuels, is the result of a thorough analysis of Lurgi's unique technologies and dealings with Japan.

Dr. Axel Niestle's scans of the U.S National Archives and Records Administration's (NARA) SRGL-series document 222, pages 1–2, gives the names of the nine German officers chosen for special assignment to Japan. These are taken from intercepted messages to and from the office of the German naval attaché in Tokyo. The original messages were destroyed before the war's end by order of the OKW.

Of key importance to my research was the highly classified CIOS report, "Metallgesellschaft-Lurgi Frankfurt am Main Germany, Reported by Captain C. C. Chaffee, U.S. Army Ordnance, Lieutenant Colonel Oliver F. Thompson, Ministry of Fuel and Power, Major J. G. King, Ministry of Fuel and Power, Mr. Harold V. Atwell, U.S. Petroleum, Adm. Irvin H. Jones, U. S. Bureau of Mines on behalf of British Ministry of Fuel and Power and the U.S. Technical Industrial Intelligence Committee, September 14, 1945," Combined Intelligence Objectives Subcommittee, G-2 [U.S. Army Intelligence] SHAEF [Supreme Headquarters Allied Expeditionary Force] on behalf of British Ministry Fuel and Power and U.S. Technical Industrial Intelligence Committee, APO [Army Post Office] 413.

For general information about Lurgi, which exists to this day as a licensor of fuel and chemical processing technologies, I suggest scanning their website, www.lurgi.com.

A highly technical discussion of Lurgi's petrochemical innovations and their significance to the Japanese can be read in the textbook *Industrial Organic Chemistry,* fourth edition, by Klaus Weissermel and Hans-Jurgen Arpe (Germany: Wiley, 2003).

My representation of Lilly Plass's knowledge—or lack of knowledge—about her husband's mission comes from Sven's letters to her, and the unsent letters she wrote her husband following his departure from Senftenberg.

Reluctant Allies explains and documents Grand Admiral Dönitz's reduction of plans for the German-Japanese arms and technology transport program toward the end of the war.

2

U.S. and British interrogators were able to extract a large amount of information about U-boat test, training, and patrol activities from captured German submariners during the war. Their reports were essential primary sources for my description of the diving and snorkel trials at Horten. Whereas it would be cumbersome to list every report used in my research of the maneuvers, a couple bear noting here.

One is the declassified "Navy Department, Office of the Chief of Naval Operations, Washington, Report of the Interrogation of German Agents, Gimpel and Collepaugh, Landed on the Coast of Maine from U-1230, January 13 1945"; also useful was the British Naval Intelligence Division's June 1944 summary report "U-413, U-1209, U-877 and U-1199, Interrogation of Survivors." All quoted passages in the narrative are from these reports.

Mason's *U-Boat: The Secret Menace* and Cremer's *U-Boat Commander* helped flesh out information from the official reports.

3

My reconstruction of U-864's grounding outside Farsund is based primarily on the data provided by the U-boat's KTBs and informed by Ken Sewell's first-hand experiences aboard a submarine.

Additional information is from *Hunter Hunted* and the BBC's *Timewatch: The Hunt for U-864,* although I differ significantly with the documentary's highly speculative dramatization of actions taken to inspect the submarine's cargo aboard the submarine while it was grounded underwater. If such actions were undertaken at all, they would have occurred much later, after the boat pulled into Farsund—or perhaps even at Bergen.

My layman's understanding of the glacial processes that form the unique underwater topography of fjords was amplified by the textbooks *World Geomorphology* by E. M. Bridges (UK: Cambridge University Press, 1990) and *An Introduction to Coastal Processes and Geomorphology* by G. Masselink and M. Hughes (UK: Hodder Arnold, 2003).

An excellent online summary of glacial processes for the nonexpert reader can be found at www.physicalgeography.net.

CHAPTER SEVEN

1

The story of Bletchley Park and the breaking of the ENIGMA and MAGIC codes are well documented in historical literature, and virtually all of my information is derived from printed or online materials.

Haufler's *Codebreakers' Victories* and Kahn's *Seizing the Enigma* were again fundamental to my line of study.

I am also very indebted to *Battle of Wits: The Complete Story of Codebreaking in World War II* by Stephen Budiansky (New York: Simon & Schuster, 2000). The story of the Polish bombe's development is presented here in excellent narrative fashion.

Some of my information about Bletchley Park, and the Colossus computer in particular, is from the article "Churchill's ULTRA Secret of the Century" by Jerome M. O'Connor (*British Heritage Magazine*, September 2000).

For anyone wishing to explore the subject of the Allied code-breaking effort on the Internet, I would advise starting at the official website of the Bletchley Park National Codes Center (www.bletchleypark.org.uk).

An informative essay on the Polish contribution to cracking ENIGMA titled "Enigma-German Machine Cipher Broken by Polish Cryptologists" by Brandi Dawn Brown can be found at http://math.ucsd.edu/~crypto/students/enigma.html.

Pastscape (www.pastscape.org.uk) is a comprehensive search engine with nearly
four hundred thousand records held in the national historic environ-
ment database of the English Heritage National Monuments Record. It
has superb descriptions and photos of the huts and outbuildings at Bletchley.

The March 2011 photographic essay "Bletchley Park Huts" by Roland Jeffery,
project manager for the restoration of Bletchley Park, was an excellent
resource and is viewable at www.c20society.org.uk.

A time line and some fascinating details about the birth of British and U.S.
intelligence cooperation can be found at the official website of the British
Codes and Ciphers Heritage Trust: www.codesandciphers.org.uk.

Our Secret War (http://www.our-secret-war.org) is the website for a documentary project whose ongoing mission is to preserve, via videotaped interviews,
an oral history of Britain's covert activities during the Second World War. I
used it extensively for my research into the Y-Service and WRENS and recommend it to anyone interested in the stories of the men and women who
served with unlauded dedication in the British intelligence sections.

Blood and Water: Sabotaging Hitler's Bomb by Dan Kurzman (New York: Henry
Holt, 1997) is a definitive—and thrilling—account of the clandestine efforts
of the Allied secret service and Norwegian underground to destroy the
Norsk Hydro plant and cripple Germany's nuclear weapons program.

All communications on supply and personnel transfer excerpted in this segment
are from primary sources, specifically the NARA SRNA-series of ULTRA
and MAGIC intercepts, which covers the signals sent to and from the Japanese naval attaché in Berlin from 1944 to 1945. A profound debt is owned to
Dr. Niestle for pointing me toward these documents.

The Edward Thomas quotes are again from British Intelligence in the Second
World War.

2

Lancaster Bomber by D. B. Tubbs (New York: Ballantine, 1972) is an excellent,
if hard to find, historical reference on the evolution and use of the Lanc by
the RAF.

Visit the website www.thedambusters.org.uk/index.html for a varied multi-media experience dedicated to the 617 Dambusters.

For information about the Upkeep "bouncing bomb," photographs and videos of the weapon as it was deployed by the Avro Lancaster bomber, and other relevant graphics, see http://www.1001crash.com/index-page-bomb-lg-2 -numpage-1.html.

A map of Woodhall Spa and other information about the air station is viewable at www.raf.mod.uk/bombercommand.

As one may assume from its title, *The Guide to World War II Hangars 02-Type T2 Hangar* (UK: Defense Works Services, British Ministry of Defense, 1995) was a terrific resource for my description of the hangars at Woodhall Spa as they would have appeared almost seven decades ago.

The primary source for the New Year's meeting that Group 5 CO Air Chief Marshal Hugh Alex Constantine called at Coningsby is the AIR27/2128 "Operations Record Book of the No. 617 Squadron," which resides in the British National Archives at Kew, outside London. The weather conditions I describe are documented in the operations record book and in German and Norwegian records for the same period.

A short biography of Sir Hugh may be found at www.elshamwolds.50g.com/ constantine.html.

As discussed in my introduction, there have until now been two main schools of thought about the preparation and timing of the RAF's January air strike on Bergen as it relates to U-864. The one held by many academicians who are acknowledged experts on the U-boat war is that the Allies were unaware of the submarine's arrival at Bruno, and that its presence at the base was coincidental to RAF Bomber Command's directive to launch its strike on what had, in any case, become a vital strategic target. The other view—we can call it the popular one, because it is most commonly suggested in tele-vised documentaries and newspaper and magazine stories—is that the Allies had learned of U-864's sailing and cargo list (or partial cargo list) from ULTRA intercepts, and that the air raid's principal objective was to destroy the submarine while it was in its pen for repairs, and make sure the scientists and technology aboard never reached Japan.

When I began work on this book, I was unsure which of those scenarios would prove accurate and was fully prepared to offer one, the other, or both alternative scenarios as possibilities. Midway through my research and writing, however, I realized that neither was acceptable from a logical or factual perspective—and that only a third set of circumstances made sense.

The documentary *Timewatch: Hunt for U-864,* produced for Germany's Spiegel TV (and later distributed to international markets) was in large measure a well-researched effort that raised popular awareness of U-864 and its encounter with HMS *Venturer* as the only documented underwater sinking of one submarine by another in naval history, and also exposed the environmental threat its wreckage presents to modern-day Norwegians. But *Timewatch* unfortunately distorted two key aspects of the story, and that has led to misconceptions that have been picked up by newspapers and magazines around the world. One was the representation of U-864's mission as a singular, last-ditch attempt by Hitler to win the war—a kind of doomsday run—rather than an operation that belonged to an ongoing, and long-standing, technology and personnel exchange program between Germany and Japan.

I make plain in this book that U-864 was one of several submarines to undertake the transoceanic journey to the Far East. The Tripartite Pact and the Führer's Directive No. 24 on Cooperation with Japan were executed in 1940–1941, long before the Japanese attack on Pearl Harbor drew America into the war. It is these documents that define the parameters of the German-Japanese collaboration, and lay out Hitler's belief that providing Japan with cutting-edge weapons technology would shift the "center of gravity" of U.S. interests toward the Pacific . . . and away from the European theater.

Hence U-864 was not, as *Timewatch* suggests, sent out on an isolated mission to change the course of the war with her cargo manifest and passenger list of German and Japanese experts. If that conceit makes for dramatic television, it is also untrue. Her mission was, rather, to resume the existing transfer program after a significant delay and escalate the cooperative technological exchange between Germany and Japan to a new, unprecedented phase. This would have engendered Japanese mass production of Hitler's secret weapons and aircraft, and led to agreements for other applications of advanced German technology—very likely including the development of synthetic rocket fuels and perhaps even delivery systems for nuclear weapons. U-864 was intended to be the first of several German submarines used in the program's escalation, and that makes her mission truly unique and dramatic. There is no need for embellishments, intentional or otherwise.

The more egregious error made by the *Timewatch* documentarians was to explicitly state that Dundee-Lerwick used ULTRA intelligence to dispatch *Venturer* to sink U-864, while implicitly suggesting those same ULTRA intercepts may have alerted the Bomber RAF Command to her presence at Bunker Bruno a month earlier. That again requires an implausible stretch of historical fact.

As Edward Thomas wrote, the information provided by Project ULTRA was rarely used for ground-level actions. Thousands of intercepts were plucked out of the air by British Y-stations daily. These had to be relayed to Bletchley Park, deciphered, translated, transcribed, and sorted before they were provided to military leaders. Early in the war, the number of messages to be solved was overwhelming for Bletchley, creating a problematic lag between interception of a coded message and its distribution to military field commanders.

By late 1944, the Colossus computer had greatly sped up the processing of signals intelligence and its communication to the front lines. In addition, special channels had been created for a more rapid flow of information. But it was still primarily forwarded to strategic commands in summary fashion, and then used for "big picture" analysis and planning. Moreover, weather was also a factor in the interception of radio signals. Storms and atmospheric conditions interrupted, scattered, and weakened the transmissions. That made it difficult to collect and retransmit them to Bletchley's code breakers quickly enough for the intel to be processed and turned around in time for its operational use in ever-changing battlefield situations.

U-864 put into Farsund on December 29, 1944, and docked out early on January 1, 1945, when it was sent to Bergen for unexpected repairs. January 1 was the same day that Air Chief Marshal Constantine summoned his group commanders to Coningsby to plan the bombing of Laksevåg.

While ULTRA and MAGIC archives bear out that the Allies knew the Germans were sending arms and matériel to Japan—and that they probably had at least one cargo-laden submarine under way—it stretches credulity to think information about U-864's arrival at Farsund and dispatch to Bergen could have been gathered and forwarded to Bletchley, then processed and communicated to RAF Bomber Command in time to launch a mission to intercept it by New Year's Day. Yet somehow, the Allies were able to do just that. The timing of the strike on Bergen was no coincidence. In my view, it would be unthinkable that a massive raid involving the RAF Bomber Command's two crack Lanc units would be ordered during a period of severe winter weather without urgent cause.

So how then did the planners at Dundee-Lerwick find out?

The only way to account for their knowledge was through direct intelligence from the Norwegian underground. Indeed, it would have been a massive failure of Dundee-Lerwick's long, dedicated efforts to build and assist the resistance movement if its coast watchers and dockyard spies in Farsund had somehow missed, or neglected to expeditiously inform the base of, the arrival and departure of a hobbled U-boat carrying a pair of Japanese passengers, and loaded with provisions and fuel for a six-month journey, crates of extra freight, and a keel hold full of mercury that would have required inspection for loss of structural integrity before she set sail for Bergen.

Based on the evidence, it is even more certain that *Venturer*'s diversion to Hellisoy and interception of U-864 resulted from information gathered on the ground and not from ULTRA intelligence—but I will save that portion of the discussion for my notes on the chapter that describes those climactic events.

CHAPTER EIGHT

1

Much of my information on the conveniences afforded submariners—
particularly members of the U-boat officer cadre—at Bergen during the
German occupation comes from Rossum's article "The Fedje Submarine,"
though any errors of fact or description are mine alone.

The book *Black Flag: The Surrender of Germany's U-boat Forces* by Lawrence
Paterson (Minnesota: MBI Publishing, 2009) was also a great reference aid.

The guestbook pages signed by Korvettenkapitän Wolfram and his companions
at the Bergen officers' club may be viewed at www.klammi.de/html/U864
-7_2_2.html. Gerty Agoston assisted me in translating their penned inscrip-
tions, the most difficult of which to convert to English was Rolf von
Chlingensperg's poem. Rather than attempt a literal translation, a sacrifice
of rhyme and meter, and interpretation of German colloquialisms, was
necessary to capture its meaning and attempts at internal puns. Again, any
flaws or shortcomings in the results belong to me.

2

War is chaotic. In nearly all battle situations, accounts of a single event vary
from different perspectives, and even official records may be fragmentary
and contain discrepancies. My account of the January 12 raid on Bunker
Bruno and the submarine harbor at Bergen was pulled together from a large
number of sources. The "Operations Record Book of the No. 617 Squadron," and "The Royal Air Force Bomber Command Campaign Diary, January 1945" were major primary sources from the British side. The FdU/BdU's
"War Log of January 1-15 1945" is among the only official German records of
the strike to survive the war. In addition, I used excerpts from the logbooks
of various flights and letters written by participants in the raid to friends and
family.

After collecting and examining the available records and recollections and eliminating obvious inaccuracies, I have presented what I believe is the only full, consistent historical narrative of the air strike.

Tony Iveson gave his personal recollections in the article titled "My Lancaster Adventure" for the Royal Air Force Battle of Britain Memorial Flight veterans' website, www.raf.mod.uk/bbmf/history/vetviewpoint.cfm.

Pilot Officer Ted Wass died in 2009. His obituary in the *Sunday Times* (London) from April 3 of that year gives some of M-Mike's story from his perspective.

My information about Flight Officer Ian Stewart Ross and his crew aboard NF 992 comes from multiple sources. There has never been official confirmation from the British or Germans that Ross and his airmen were killed in a Luftwaffe strafing while defenselessly trying to escape their downed, sinking plane, but my examination of the evidence and eyewitness accounts point to it as a tragic, inarguable fact—and an atrocity committed in flagrant violation of the Geneva accords.

The Air Crew Remembrance Society is dedicated to helping the families of British airmen declared fallen or missing in the 1939–1945 air war to preserve their memories, photographs, and documents. Compiled from official records and documents, its account of NF 992's loss, along with related images, may be viewed at www.aircrewremembrancesociety.com.

More about NF 992 and its crew is at www.edbridgetown.com/in_the_past/bill_walters_story/final_mission.shtml.

The attack of the Focke-Wulf interceptors from Gruppes 9 and 12 of Jagdgeschwader 5 Eismeer is partly described from a Luftwaffe perspective at www.white1foundation.org/white1_history2.html.

Historical information about the German air base can be found at its official site: www.jagdgeschwader5.de.

Significant details of Willing Winnie's (PD 198) story come from the online article "A Belated Casualty," which may be read at www.freewebs.com/rafh/index.html.

For some of the recollections shared by Fred Watts, Jimmy Castagnola and Phil Martin, and Mervyn McKay go to www.ww2aircraft.net.

"Missing with No Known Grave" by Flight Lieutenant Alan Storr (Ret.) is an exhaustive record of RAF losses compiled, as Lieutenant Storr writes, to "assist those who are still seeking information about the circumstances in which their loved husband, father, son brother or family member went missing and has no known grave." It is derived from the collections of the Australian War Memorial and the National Archives of Australia and contains what information is officially recorded about NF 992.

A transcription of Flying Officer Mowbray Ellwood's death notice may be viewed at www.specialforcesroh.com.

The article "617 Squadron: The Later War Operations" by Colin Burgess originally appeared in the Qantas Airlines crew magazine in 1986. It contains an excellent account of the January 12 air strike on Bergen derived from official records and interviews with participants in the actions it chronicles. The few factual inaccuracies I have judged it to contain about the operation are due, I believe, to vagaries of recollection forty years after the event.

Thanks to www.flightglobal.com, I was able to read scans of a 1939 *Times* (London) ad and Graviner print advertisement for the fire extinguishers used aboard the Lancs.

CHAPTER NINE

1

This section is drawn almost entirely from the Plass family letters given to me by Maja Grisotti. They were translated into English by Ms. Grisotti, Gerty Agoston, Christopher Morris, and myself.

The book *Boy Soldier: A German Teenager at the Nazi Twilight* by Gerhardt B. Thamm (North Carolina: McFarland and Company, 2000) provided background about Lilly's reference to the defense of the Steinau-on-Oder bridgehead against Soviet troops by a group of German cadets.

2–3

As the German-Jewish philosopher Ernst Cassirer wrote in his classic *Essay on Man,* "In his quest for truth the historian is bound by the same strict rules as the scientist. He has to utilize all the methods of empirical investigation. He has to collect all the available evidence and to compare and criticize all his sources. Nevertheless the last and decisive act is always an act of the productive imagination."

My information about Willi Transier's last mailing to Edith comes from the *Timewatch* documentary. In re-creating Transier's reflective moments as he inscribed his photograph on the eve of his embarkation to the Far East, and in envisioning how the Japanese scientists Nakai and Yamato spent their monthlong stay in Bergen, I have followed the principles laid out by Cassirer and used available evidence, educated guesswork, and a conservative dose of imagination to attempt what he termed the "true historical synthesis."

It is for others to decide how successful I have been in these segments.

CHAPTER TEN

1

My narrative of the fateful encounter between HMS *Venturer* and U-864 is based almost entirely on primary declassified source material.

The most critical document is the post-action report, "HMS *Venturer,* Report of Eleventh War Patrol, Section G, Commanding Officer Lieutenant J. S. Launders, Royal Navy, Third/SM Flotilla, 9 February, 1944," which includes a hand-drawn track chart of *Venturer*'s pursuit of the German U-boats. Of almost equal importance are excerpts from the British "Admiralty Confidential Books (CB) February, 1945 Monthly Anti-Submarine Report."

The transcoded ULTRA intercepts of Axis signals intelligence regarding U-864's cargo lists, her communications to and from BdU, and loss, are culled from Appendix A to the DNV's "Salvage of U864—Supplementary Studies—

Study No. 7: Cargo Report," compiled by Dr. Niestle. Additional trans-coded intercepts are from the *Timewatch* documentary, as is the radio communiqué from Dundee diverting *Venturer* to Hellisoy.

Ensign John Watson (Ret.), *Venturer*'s navigator, has confirmed the authenticity of Dundee's coded message in interviews for newspapers and magazines, including "The Man Who Sank the Submarine at Fedje," by Terje Valestrand (*Bergens Tidende,* December 27, 2009). The interview first appeared in a Norwegian article that Valestrand kindly provided for my research, and was translated by Halvor H. Halvorsen.

Here again, my review of the evidence substantiates that it was Norway's coast watchers and underground spy network—not Bletchley Park's ULTRA cryptographers, as has been commonly accepted—that supplied Dundee-Lerwick with critical, highly specific intelligence about U-864 in the month or so before she was sunk, and that allowed them to know where and when *Venturer* would have the best chance of intercepting her.

According to her logbooks, *Venturer* was diverted to Hellisoy on February 5, two days prior to U-864's exit from Bergen Harbor. By this stage of the war, the routine of test dives and weapons trials U-boats underwent following repairs had been shortened due to the Laksevåg shipyard's facilities being crowded over capacity and also to get the submarines back at sea as quickly as possible. The British were well aware of these truncated procedures—and had spies at Bergen giving them a steady flow of detailed, up-to-date information about arrivals and departures.

Combing the ocean for a single submarine is easier said than done, and U-864 might have still slipped past *Venturer* were it not for the skill and diligence of Lieutenant Chalmers and his ASDIC operator. The popular media has reported that British intelligence picked up information that U-864 was in trouble—and it did via the intercepted communications between Wolfram and Bergen when he developed engine problems. But that information would not have been processed until it was far too late for Lieutenant Jimmy Launders or anyone else to do anything about it. When Wolfram was ordered to return to Bergen on February 8, the intel that *Venturer* had received from the Norwegian underground put her in an optimal position to pounce on her quarry at the entrance to Fejeosen.

None of this is to diminish the importance of ULTRA intelligence in general in preventing U-864 from carrying out her mission. ULTRA decrypts made the Allies aware of the German-Japanese submarine blockade-running program and technology exchange to begin with. But it is important for history to acknowledge, finally, the tremendous success of an intelligence network that the British had nurtured since 1940, and that thousands of brave Norwegian men and women risked, and in a great many instances sacrificed, their lives to maintain in defiance of their German occupiers. It was their eyes and ears that tracked U-864 up the coast of Norway and out of Bergen. *Venturer* could not have stopped her from reaching the Far East without them.

2-14

In setting Wolfram's actions in their proper context, I used a declassified copy of the German "Submarine Commander's Handbook, U.Kdt Hdb," 1943 edition. A digital version of it may be viewed at the official website of the Historic Naval Ships Association: www.hnsa.org.

Jimmy Launders insisted in the narrative section of his post-action report (Section G of the attack form cited earlier in the notes to this chapter) that U-864 "was apparently proceeding on diesels. [By the noise] or running some noisy machine like an air compressor—there was definitely no 'Schnorkel' in use."

This statement is unanimously rejected by U-boat experts who contributed to the DNV report. If U-864 was running on her electrical motors, she would have been too silent for detection by HMS *Venturer*'s hydrophones. Only if operating on diesel power would she have made the sort of sounds *Venturer* detected—as Launders himself notes. But while she was operating on diesels underwater, the snorkel would have had to be in use.

Launders's error probably arose from his unfamiliarity with the snorkel's operation. His harsher assessment of Wolfram's periscope usage also was just partly on the mark—but also understandable in view of what he could not have known about U-864's particular circumstances.

In Launders's mind, the U-boat was returning to Bergen from operations at sea. He neither knew she was hobbling back to base after experiencing engine problems, nor had any idea that the German submarine commander was scanning for radio communications for a prearranged escort.

Lieutenant Launders made a third and final misstatement in his report, writing that he did not believe U-864 was aware of *Venturer*'s presence. Yet his own track chart indicates his quarry did not begin her evasive zigzag maneuvers until precisely when he'd approached to within striking distance, an indication that Wolfram was highly concerned that he was being stalked. John Watson explicitly agrees with this in his interviews, and common sense supports that assessment.

In my judgment, it is possible Launders succumbed to a rare moment of hubris in thinking he'd been able to get as close as he had undetected. But that is conjecture. Whatever the reason, he was mistaken.

AFTERWORD

My account of Maja Grisotti's solemn and emotional trip to Bergen comes partly from my e-mail correspondence with her, but its detail owes a great deal to Rossum's "The Fedje Submarine."

Jerome Preisler is the *New York* Times bestselling author of more than thirty books of fiction and nonfiction, including the long-running Tom Clancy's Power Plays series. His narrative history (with Kenneth Sewell), *All Hands Down: The True Story of the Soviet Attack on the USS Scorpion* (Simon and Schuster, 2008) brought to life the personal stories of the men who were lost aboard *Scorpion* when the submarine sank to the bottom of the Atlantic Ocean. As a baseball writer, Jerome has been a regular contributor to the New York Yankees' YESNetwork.com since 2004. Focused largely on stirring human interest stories, his column is one of the website's most popular features. For the past three seasons he has spearheaded the website's acclaimed coverage of the New York Yankees' HOPE Week.

Jerome has also written numerous movie and television tie-ins. Among the latter are *Nevada Rose* (Pocket Books, 2008), and the recent *Skin Deep* (Pocket Books, 2010) for the bestselling CSI franchise.

Jerome lives in New York City with his wife and cats. He may be contacted at jpreisler@nyc.rr.com.

Kenneth R. Sewell is a former nuclear engineering technician and a U.S. Navy veteran who spent five years aboard the USS *Parche*, a fast attack submarine that was the Navy's most decorated ship. *Parche* conducted a number of covert operations, some of which were revealed in the book *Blind Man's Bluff: The Untold Story of American Submarine Espionage*.

Since leaving the Navy, Mr. Sewell has held both Department of Defense and Department of Energy security clearances and has worked on a number of classified programs, including assignments in the Middle East in support of American intelligence efforts. More recent projects include a supporting role in the filming of the full-length feature film *Phantom*, staring David Duchovny, Ed Harris, and William Fichtner. *Phantom* is based in part on the events described in Mr. Sewell's book *Red Star Rogue*, a *New York Times* bestseller.